HIROSHIMA
IN HISTORY

HIROSHIMA IN HISTORY

THE MYTHS OF REVISIONISM

EDITED WITH AN INTRODUCTION BY ROBERT JAMES MADDOX

UNIVERSITY OF MISSOURI PRESS
COLUMBIA AND LONDON

Library of Congress Cataloging-in-Publication Data

Hiroshima in history : the myths of revisionism / edited with an introduction by Robert James Maddox.
      p. cm.
   Summary: "Analysis of Truman's decision to use nuclear arms
against Japan through essays written by military and diplomatic historians"—Provided by publisher.
   Includes index.
   ISBN 978-0-8262-1962-6 (pbk: alk. paper)
   1. Hiroshima-shi (Japan)—History—Bombardment, 1945.
2. World War, 1939–1945—Historiography.   I. Maddox, Robert James.
   D767.25.H6H6335 2007
   940.5492521954—dc22

                                                        2006100945

∞™ This paper meets the requirements of the
American National Standard for Permanence of Paper
for Printed Library Materials, Z39.48, 1984.

Text designer: Foleydesign
Cover designer: Susan Ferber
Typesetter: The Composing Room of Michigan, Inc.
Printer and binder: The Maple-Vail Book Manufacturing Group
Typefaces: Palatino and Trixie

For acknowledgments and permissions, see p. 215.

Contents

HIROSHIMA
IN HISTORY

Introduction

T HE USE OF ATOMIC BOMBS AGAINST JAPAN at the end of World War II remains one of the most controversial issues in American history. Those who defend the decision claim that it ended a bloody war that would have become far bloodier had the planned invasion of the Japanese home islands proved necessary. Although the primary consideration was saving American lives, according to this view, millions of Japanese also were spared the catastrophic effects of an invasion coupled with round-the-clock conventional bombing, naval bombardment, and blockade. Those who have become known as "Hiroshima revisionists" contend that this version of events is nothing more than a postwar myth concocted by Harry S. Truman and his advisers to make more palatable what was basically a political rather than a military decision. The "real" reason for using the weapons was not to defeat an already-defeated Japan, but to make the Soviet Union more "manageable" by demonstrating the enormous power now in American possession. Never before has such a monstrous charge—that tens of thousands of people were callously incinerated for no better reason than to gain diplomatic advantage—been supported by such flimsy evidence. The essays contained in this volume show just how insubstantial Hiroshima revisionism really is.

The core of revisionist indictment is that Japan had been willing to surrender as early as the spring of 1945 provided only that its sacred emperor be retained as head of the Japanese polity. Truman and Secretary of State James F. Byrnes knew this through intercepted Japanese messages but refused to act upon it because they *wanted the war to continue* until the atomic bombs were ready for use. They deliberately forestalled a Japanese surrender by insisting on peace terms they knew would be unacceptable. Thus, not only were they willing to sacrifice countless Japanese in pursuit of their goal, but were equally callous about wasting the lives of Allied servicemen and prisoners of war by unnecessarily prolonging the conflict for months.

The fatal weakness of this thesis is that revisionists have been unable to produce even a shred of contemporary evidence that the Japanese *government* was prepared to surrender before the atomic bombs were dropped. Their efforts to compensate for this lack have been imaginative to say the least. One device is to point to numerous "peace feelers" received by the Office of Strategic Services (OSS) from various Japanese businessmen and minor officials in neutral countries as evidence of Tokyo's intent. The truth is that none of these individuals were able to demonstrate that they represented anyone in a position of power. This led Americans to conclude either that the overtures were the result of well-meaning individuals acting alone or that they were being orchestrated by Tokyo to take advantage of Allied war weariness.

Another revisionist effort to provide evidence for the "early surrender" thesis where none exists is to cite messages from Tokyo to the Japanese ambassadors in Moscow requesting that the emperor be permitted to send a personal envoy to negotiate with the Soviets "in an attempt to restore peace with all possible speed." Revisionists have professed to see this initiative as evidence of Japan's willingness to surrender. Even the most cursory reading of the messages reveals nothing of the kind. It was, instead, an attempt by what scholar Robert P. Newman has called the Japanese "civilian elite" (under the watchful eye of the military) to cut a deal that would have permitted Japan to retain its political system and prewar empire intact in return for various territorial and other concessions to the Soviets.

No one has made greater use of such devices than Gar Alperovitz, whose work is analyzed in the first essay in this volume. His *Atomic Diplomacy: Hiroshima and Potsdam* created a sensation when it was first published in 1965, and grew more popular as disillusionment with the Vietnam War created an atmosphere of distrust toward all American foreign policies, past or present. Alperovitz published a revised and enlarged version of *Atomic Diplomacy* in 1985, and in 1995 he produced a massive new volume, *The Decision to Use the Atomic Bomb and the Architecture of an American Myth*. Over the decades he has energetically promoted his cause through countless journal articles, op-ed pieces, and television appearances. Although most revisionists have shied away from some of his more fanciful constructions, all have appropriated one or another aspect of his work. "Gar Alperovitz: Godfather of Hiroshima Revisionism" provides an examination of the unscholarly methods he has employed to support his themes.

There can be no doubt that Japan was a defeated nation by the summer of 1945. Allied advances across the Pacific had brought them to Japan's doorstep, naval blockade had progressively cut off the flow of essential supplies such as oil, and conventional bombing had reduced most of its cities to rubble. Although a peace faction within the Japanese government wished to end the war—provided certain conditions were met—hardliners were prepared to fight on regardless of consequences. They professed to welcome an invasion of the Japanese home islands they knew was planned, claiming that it would be thrown back into the sea or at least would inflict such heavy casualties that the United States would accept peace terms favorable to Japan. Distinguished Japanese historian Sadao Asada's "The Shock of the Atomic Bomb and Japan's Decision to Surrender— A Reconsideration," an essay based largely on Japanese sources, reveals how difficult it was for the peace faction to prevail even *after* both bombs had been dropped and the Soviet Union had declared war on Japan. That such an outcome would have been possible before these cataclysmic events is impossible to credit. Asada also refutes two other revisionist fallacies: that retention of the emperor was the sole obstacle to Japan's surrender and that Soviet entry into the Pacific War rather than the bombs caused the Japanese to give in.

The United States had no direct pipeline into the Japanese government to provide information about the day-to-day political situation. What it did have was an enormous quantity of decrypted Japanese military and naval messages, all of which confirmed Japan's determination to fight to the death against all odds. As Edward J. Drea shows, in a chapter from his *In the Service of the Emperor: Essays on the Japanese Imperial Army,* intelligence gleaned from these sources revealed a massive Japanese buildup on Kyushu (site of the first planned invasion) during the summer of 1945. Standard military doctrine called for numerical superiority of three or four to one on the part of attacking forces. The Japanese were pouring so many troops into Kyushu that it was likely they would equal or outnumber the invaders. This was, as General Douglas MacArthur's intelligence chief glumly put it, "hardly a recipe for success." Kamikazes flying at close range against crowded troop transports and supply ships promised to greatly increase the butcher's bill.

Truman in his memoirs claimed that the invasion would have cost an estimated five hundred thousand American lives. Some revisionists charge that he grossly exaggerated the number of estimated casualties in order to forestall scrutiny of his real reasons for using the bombs. They most often cite Barton Bernstein's 1986 article, "A Postwar Myth: 500,000 Lives Saved." Bernstein relied on a mid-June 1945 staff study that predicted a total of 193,500 dead, wounded, and missing in action. This "low" figure, Bernstein contended, raised "troubling questions" about Truman's motives. What Bernstein neglected to inform his readers was that the 193,500 figure pertained only to ground-force *battle* casualties. It made no mention of non-battle casualties, air force or naval losses, nor any predictions of the costs that would be inflicted by kamikazes and other air attacks against the invasion fleet. In any event, as Drea's essay makes clear, the estimate was rendered irrelevant by the Japanese buildup on Kyushu during the summer. Finally, Bernstein also failed to mention that the staff figure never was shown to Truman. It was removed at the next higher level on the ground that casualties "are not subject to accurate estimate."

Dennis Giangreco's "A Score of Bloody Okinawas and Iwo Jimas" demolishes the "low" casualty thesis. He demonstrates that figures as high or higher than Truman's claim were commonplace at the upper levels of government, and at least some were shown directly to Truman. In particular, Giangreco points to a memorandum that former president Herbert Hoover sent to Truman at the latter's request estimating that invading Japan could cost as many as "500,000 to 1,000,000 lives." Truman forwarded the memorandum to key advisers for their comments, and he called a meeting with the Joint Chiefs of Staff, the secretary of war, and the secretary of the navy to discuss "the losses in killed and wounded that will result from an invasion of Japan proper." The title of a shorter Giangreco (and Kathryn Moore) essay, "Half a Million Purple Hearts," tells it all. The number of these medals struck in anticipation of the invasion by itself mocks the "low" casualty thesis.

Some revisionists have set great store by the United States Strategic Bombing Survey (USSBS) of 1946. This was a postwar study based largely on interviews with surviving Japanese officials, one part of which stated that the Japanese would have surrendered by November 1, 1945, "even if the atomic bombs had not been dropped, even if Russia had not entered the war, and even if no invasion had been planned or contemplated." Criticizing Truman on the basis of information that was unavailable to him before the bombs were dropped is intellectually untenable, of course, but there is more. As Gian Peri Gentile in "Advocacy or Assessment? The United States Strategic Bombing Survey of Germany and Japan" and Robert P. Newman in "Hiroshima and the Trashing of Henry Stimson" show, the USSBS was "cooked" by Vice Chairman Paul Nitze to fit predictions he had made earlier that conventional bombing alone would have caused the Japanese to surrender before November 1. The actual content of the interviews provides little support for such a notion. Newman also offers a reassessment of Secretary of War Henry L. Stimson's role in events leading to use of the bombs and his influential 1947 article defending the action.

In 1995, the fiftieth anniversary of the end of World War II, the National Air and Space Museum (NASM) planned an exhibit around the display of *Enola Gay*, the aircraft that dropped an atomic bomb on Hiroshima. A firestorm of another kind erupted when it became clear that the exhibit, with only a few qualifications, hewed to the revisionist line. World War II veteran groups in particular were incensed at what they regarded as a corruption of history. The then director of NASM later dismissed their complaints, accusing them of seeking a "largely fictitious, comforting story" that was belied by "trustworthy documents now at hand in the nation's archives." Robert P. Newman, in pages from his *"Enola Gay" and the Court of History*, reveals that the exhibit was stacked from the start. Rather than consult prominent scholars in the field, NASM relied on an unqualified, in-house staff that had ideological axes to grind. As Newman's chapter subtitle indicates, the result was characterized by "Anonymity, Hypocrisy, Ignorance." The exhibit ultimately was cancelled and the NASM director fired.

The appearance in 2005 of Tsuyoshi Hasegawa's *Racing the Enemy: Stalin, Truman, and the Surrender of Japan* provided a tremendous boost to the revisionist cause. There are several "races" in Hasegawa's book, but the one that has received greatest attention is Truman's alleged determination to use atomic bombs to bring about Japan's surrender before the hitherto neutral Soviets could enter the war. Although disagreeing with some revisionist contentions, such as that Japan would have surrendered if only retention of the emperor were guaranteed, he provided support for the central thesis that Truman and Secretary of State James F. Brynes sought to *deter* Japanese surrender until such time as the bombs could be used. Their goals were to gain a general diplomatic advantage over the Soviets by demonstrating the enormous power in American hands and specifically to forestall Soviet expansion in the Far East. Hailed by reviewers as a "landmark book," "brilliant and definitive," *Racing the Enemy* already has received several prestigious awards and promises to garner even more. A close reading of the work reveals, however, many grave discrepancies between the text and the sources upon which it is based. Michael Kort's "*Racing the Enemy:* A Critical Look" exposes some of Hasegawa's fictions, particularly with regard to Truman's alleged "race" against the Soviets.

The essays in the present volume reveal that Hiroshima revisionists have constructed a ramshackle structure founded on sand. If the historical record supports their theses, one must ask, why are they compelled to resort to dubious procedures such as scissoring documents to change their meaning or relying on discredited sources such as the USSBS? A related issue is why do their works continue to receive so much favorable attention in academic circles? The answer to both questions appears to be that political agendas have trumped commitments to scholarship. Someone may yet discover evidence that validates the revisionist position. That no one has been able to do so during the more than sixty years since Hiroshima makes this prospect appear dim.

Gar Alperovitz
Godfather of Hiroshima Revisionism

A NY HISTORY OF HIROSHIMA REVISIONISM must acknowledge Gar Alperovitz as its most influential champion. Although earlier writers such as William Appleman Williams and D. F. Fleming had echoed British scientist P. M. S. Blackett's charge that atomic bombs were used primarily to make the Soviet Union "more manageable" rather than to defeat an already-defeated Japan, they had provided little in the way of documentary evidence. Alperovitz's 1965 book, *Atomic Diplomacy: Hiroshima and Potsdam, The Use of the Atomic Bomb and the American Confrontation with Soviet Power,* caused a sensation. Here was an entire volume devoted to the subject, weighed down with academic paraphernalia (some chapters had more than two hundred footnotes), which appeared to be the model of academic research. One admirer called it, "A daring and elaborate work of historical reconstruction," and another wrote that *Atomic Diplomacy* "made it difficult for conscientious scholars any longer to avoid the challenge of revisionist historians."[1] The truth is that the book was a travesty of scholarship. In it and in his subsequent writing, Alperovitz had employed the crudest devices to make the evidence appear to support his theses.

The most salient feature of Alperovitz's work has been his unscholarly use of ellipses. Whereas most writers employ these to spare the reader extraneous phrases, Alperovitz uses them as tactical weapons to render documents more suitable for his purposes. Soon after the surrender of Germany in May 1945, for instance, President Truman agreed to a curtailment of Lend-Lease supplies for the So-

---

1. Alperovitz's book was published by Simon and Schuster, New York, in 1965. The first quotation is from Ronald Steel, *New York Review of Books* 5, no. 8 (November 25, 1965), and the second in Christopher Lasch's introduction to Alperovitz's *Cold War Essays* (Garden City, N.Y.: Doubleday, 1970), 12.

viet Union to those that could be used in the war against Japan (the Soviets were neutral at the time, but had pledged to enter the Pacific War after Germany's defeat). Alperovitz in *Atomic Diplomacy* professed to see this as an example of Truman's wish to use economic coercion against the Soviets at a time when an atomic device had yet to be tested. Unable to find any evidence to support the allegation, he created some. In his discussion of alleged debates over using the curtailment as leverage against the Soviets, Alperovitz had the then ambassador to the Soviet Union, W. Averell Harriman, arguing that the United States "should retain current control of . . . credits in order to be in a position to protect American vital interests in the formulative period immediately following the war."[2] A look at the source for this claim, Secretary of the Navy James Forrestal's diary, reveals that Harriman's statement referred to *postwar dollar credits* and had nothing at all to do with Lend Lease.[3] Alperovitz's omission of the word *these* ("these credits") helped to make his misuse of Harriman's words more plausible.

Another example of Alperovitz's use of ellipses to alter the meaning of documents can be found in his discussion of how Truman assessed the significance of Hiroshima and Nagasaki. "Truman has characterized the result: 'Our dropping of the atomic bomb on Japan . . . forced Russia to reconsider her position in the Far East.'"[4] Alperovitz's version of Truman's statement appears to validate his contention about the *real* reason for dropping the bombs. This time he omitted the word *had* which, if left in, might have suggested what Truman actually was referring to: Russia's decision to enter the war against Japan as soon as it did rather than its behavior toward the United States after the war ended. The entire quotation reads,

> Without warning, while Russian-Chinese negotiations were still far from agreement, Truman (or, more accurately, his ghostwriters) had written, Molotov had sent for Ambassador Harriman on August 8 and announced to him that the Soviet Union would consider itself at war with Japan as of August 9. This move did not surprise us. Our drop-

2. Alperovitz, *Atomic Diplomacy*, 35.
3. Walter Millis and E. S. Duffield, eds., *The Forrestal Diaries* (New York: Viking, 1951), 41.
4. Alperovitz, *Atomic Diplomacy*, 191.

ping of the atomic bomb on Japan had forced Russia to reconsider her position in the Far East.[5]

It is difficult to imagine any reason for replacing a three-letter word with three periods other than to alter the meaning of Truman's comment.

Perhaps Alperovitz's most audacious use of an ellipsis (though there are many contenders) occurred in his effort to show how disappointed Truman was when he learned that, owing to technical difficulties, the atomic bomb could not be "laid on Japan" until after the Potsdam Conference, which was scheduled to begin in mid-July 1945. "Thus, Truman's twice-postponed meeting still would occur a few weeks too early for the atomic bomb to strengthen his diplomatic hand." Referring to the president's state of mind at the time, Alperovitz wrote that "Truman made no attempt to hide his feelings: 'I am getting ready to go see Stalin and Churchill, and it is a chore . . . . Wish I didn't have to go, but I do, and it can't be stopped now.'"[6] Again, the ellipsis produced a glaring distortion, this time replacing "I have to take my tuxedo, tails . . . preacher coat, high hat, low hat and hard hat as well as sundry other things," with Truman's own ellipses in the handwritten letter and another sentence in the same vein.[7] Thus, what Alperovitz presented as the words of President Truman, global strategist, turns out to be merely the dutiful son and brother complaining to "Mamma and Mary" about the formalities he would have to endure.

At times Alperovitz dispensed with ellipses and simply lopped off those parts of sentences that were inconvenient. A case in point is the way he depicted Truman's overall view toward the Soviets. "The President's attitude," he wrote, "is best summed up in the statement he made eight days after Roosevelt's death. He 'intended to be firm with the Russians and make no concessions.'"[8] The latter part of the sentence, which Alperovitz omitted, reads, "from American principles or traditions in order to win their favor."[9] This is a far cry from saying he would make "no concessions" and, in the same paragraph,

5. Harry S. Truman, *Memoirs by Harry S. Truman: Year of Decisions* (Garden City, N.Y.: Doubleday, 1955), 425.

6. Alperovitz, *Atomic Diplomacy,* 145,

7. Truman, *Year of Decisions,* 331.

8. Alperovitz, *Atomic Diplomacy,* 231.

9. Truman, *Year of Decisions,* 71.

he attached to the need for establishing relations "on a give-and-take basis." Similar examples clot the pages of *Atomic Diplomacy.*

Another device Alperovitz frequently employed was to cite statements in support of his themes, which, in context, refer to other subjects. The opening paragraph of his first chapter is typical:

> Only eleven days had passed since the death of Franklin Delano Roosevelt. The new President of the United States prepared for his first meeting with a representative of the Soviet Union. Rehearsing his views on the subject of the negotiation—a reorganization of the Polish government—Truman declared that if the Russians did not care to cooperate, "they could go to hell."[10]

The quotation, from notes of the conversation, is cited correctly, but applied to the wrong issue. In context Truman was referring to the possibility that the Russians might boycott the founding conference of the United Nations if they did not get *their* way on Poland. "He intended to go on with the plans for San Francisco," according to the notes, "and if the Russians did not care to join us they could go to hell."[11] Alperovitz's version helped to establish Truman's belligerency on the Polish question, but it is a distortion.

Time sequences fared as badly in *Atomic Diplomacy* as did subject matter. At the conclusion of a paragraph dealing with the imaginary debate over the Lend-Lease curtailment of May 1945, Alperovitz cited General John R. Deane, the chief of the United States Military Mission in Moscow, to show what American leaders believed the policy would accomplish: "This would increase America's economic leverage and would 'make the Soviet authorities come to us,' as Deane had phrased it."[12] In fact, Deane's words appeared in a letter he wrote to General George C. Marshall *in December 1944,* months before the alleged debate took place, and while Truman was still a senator from Missouri. What Deane really said is of interest, too: "We should stop pushing ourselves on them and make the Soviet authorities come to us. We should be friendly and co-operative when they do so."[13] This scarcely amounts to a recipe for coercion.

Some passages in *Atomic Diplomacy* managed to get both the tim-

10. Alperovitz, *Atomic Diplomacy,* 19.
11. Millis and Duffield, eds., *Forrestal Diaries,* 50.
12. Alperovitz, *Atomic Diplomacy,* 36.
13. John R. Deane, *The Strange Alliance: The Story of Our Efforts at Wartime Cooperation with Russia* (New York: Viking, 1947), 86.

ing and the subject matter wrong. Consider Alperovitz's analysis of what American leaders thought possession of atomic weapons would enable them to extract from the Russians. In the framework of discussion held after the successful atomic test of July 16, 1945, he cited as Secretary of State Byrnes's "new advice" to Truman that "the bomb might well put us in a position to dictate our own terms . . . ."[14] The words attributed to Byrnes actually were what Truman recalled him as having said when they discussed the bomb in April, not in July. This time the versatile ellipsis replaced "at the end of the war," which, if left in, suggested what Byrnes actually was talking about when read in context: terms with *Japan* at the end of the war, rather than terms with the Soviets after the war had ended.[15] Accusations that Truman had used the bomb to cow the Soviets already had been made by the time his *memoirs* appeared. The idea that he would have permitted confirmation of this charge to appear under his own name is far-fetched to say the least.

In 1985 Alperovitz published an expanded and updated version of *Atomic Diplomacy.*[16] In a new introduction and in several appendices, he tried to show that the evidence that had become available since the first edition of his book served to support his themes and to undermine his critics. Connoisseurs of the methods he had employed in the earlier version were not disappointed. Alperovitz showed himself to be at least as ingenious in his use of sources as he had been twenty years earlier. A few examples should suffice to catch the sense of his approach.

Within the context of Truman's attitude toward the Soviets, Alperovitz had him telling an associate on the way to the Potsdam Conference that "If [the atomic bomb] explodes, as I think it will, I'll certainly have a hammer on those boys."[17] This quotation first appeared in a book about Truman written by former White House staff member Jonathan Daniels. Daniels, who had heard the story secondhand, stated specifically that Truman had been referring to Japan but speculated that he *may* have had the Soviets in mind as well. Alperovitz's conversion of Daniels's speculation into a statement of fact would not get by in an undergraduate seminar.[18]

---

14. Alperovitz, *Atomic Diplomacy*, 229.
15. Truman, *Year of Decisions*, 87.
16. This version was published in New York by Elizabeth Sifton Books.
17. Alperovitz, *Atomic Diplomacy* (1985 edition), 6.
18. Jonathan Daniels, *Man of Independence* (Philadelphia: Lippincott, 1950), 131.

To show that the United States had no reason to drop the atomic bombs when it did, Alperovitz wrote, "Note carefully, first, that the invasion of Japan, which was estimated to cost between five hundred thousand and a million lives, was not scheduled until the spring of 1946, *roughly eight months after the Potsdam Conference and the bombing of Hiroshima on August 6.*"[19] (his emphasis) How could he have made such a statement? By the simple device of referring to the invasion of Kyushu, scheduled for November 1, 1945, as an "initial preliminary landing."[20] To describe an operation larger than that involved in the invasion of France in June 1944 as though it might entail no more than sending a few landing parties ashore is striking in its effrontery. As several of the essays included in this volume show, the "initial preliminary landing" was expected to be a bloodbath.

Alperovitz's account is misleading in another way. By emphasizing the number of months between Hiroshima and the scheduled invasion (or even the "initial preliminary landing"), he seeks to show that there was no real reason for dropping the bombs in early August other than to impress the Soviets. Truman could have simply sat back and awaited the inevitable Japanese surrender. One would never guess from Alperovitz's prose that bitter fighting was still going on in the Philippines and on the Asian mainland, air crews were being lost, and as many as 140,000 Allied prisoners of war were living and dying under barbaric conditions every day the war continued. Truman was commander in chief of American armed forces, and his duty was to protect the lives of those under his charge. The view from the White House in August 1945 was quite different from that of a writer's book-lined study decades later.

Finally, Alperovitz's 1985 introduction repeated and elaborated on a fallacy he had put forward in the first edition, and which he would continue to flog from that time until now. He claimed that the Japanese had been trying to surrender since the spring of 1945 and would have done so if only they had been assured they could retain their sacred emperor. Truman and his advisers knew this through intercepted Japanese messages, according to Alperovitz, but refused to extend such an assurance because they wanted the war to continue

19. Alperovitz, *Atomic Diplomacy* (1985 edition), 11.
20. Ibid., 11.

until they could drop the bombs on Japan to awe the Soviets. No serious scholar believes such nonsense. The truth is that some Japanese civilian officials, with the approval of the emperor but under the watchful eyes of the military hardliners, were trying to enlist the Soviet Union to act as a go-between in brokering a negotiated peace that would have preserved intact the prewar Japanese political system (not just the emperor) and empire. No American official could have accepted such a settlement, which the more realistic Japanese well knew. As Japan's ambassador to the Soviet Union put it in mid-July, Tokyo's overtures consisted of "pretty little phrases devoid of all connection with reality."[21]

Alperovitz showed his usual ingenuity in constructing his fictional scenario. He larded his own prose with phrases such as "when evidence of Japanese willingness to surrender came in" and "the highly unusual decision of the Emperor himself to become personally involved in the surrender process."[22] These phrases enabled him to cite messages that refer to "peace" or "ending the war" as though they referred to surrender rather than the negotiated peace or armistice some Japanese officials sought. This sort of thing gives casuistry a bad name.

Over the years, especially since the second edition of *Atomic Diplomacy* appeared, Alperovitz has proven himself a tireless crusader for his cause. He has advanced his themes in countless articles, op-ed pieces, interviews, and book reviews. Indeed as recently as 2005, he published at least four reviews *of the same book,* Tsuyoshi Hasegawa's *Racing the Enemy: Stalin, Truman, and the Surrender of Japan.*[23] At times he has alleged that a cover-up is still going on that is only gradually being exposed by his own tireless efforts to bare the "secrets that have been kept from the American people." In 1992 he and Kai Bird triumphantly announced the discovery of a "recently declassified" document that had been "written in 1946 but withheld from the American public for roughly four decades."[24] The document in

21. Ambassador Naotaki Sato to Prime Minister Shigenori Togo, July 12, 1945, James F. Byrnes Papers, Clemson University.

22. Alperovitz, *Atomic Diplomacy* (1985 edition), 9, 13.

23. His reviews appeared in *The Progressive Media Project,* July 27, 2003; *Common Dreams.org,* August 3, 2005; History News Network, August 3, 2005; *Winona Daily News,* August 5, 2005.

24. Gar Alperovitz and Kai Bird, "Was Hiroshima Needed to End the War?" *Christian Science Monitor,* August 6, 1992, 19.

question had been routinely declassified in 1975 and was well known to scholars in the field. A year later he was at it again. This time he declared that "Every new fragment of secret information suggests that the Hiroshima decision was totally unnecessary."[25] The "new fragment of secret information" he alluded to also had been declassified in the 1970s and also was well known to other historians.

In 1995, the fiftieth anniversary of Hiroshima, Alperovitz published a new book: *The Decision to Use the Atomic Bomb and the Architecture of an American Myth.*[26] This is a huge volume of 843 pages, written with the help of no fewer than seven assistants, and rests on a truly impressive amount of research. Unfortunately, Alperovitz's handling of his sources is, if anything, even more outlandish than that found in *Atomic Diplomacy.* To spare the reader another laundry list of his transgressions, the remainder of this essay will focus on one of his most prominent themes: that nearly all the top officials of the army and navy at the time opposed use of the bombs as militarily unnecessary, and that two of them personally confronted Truman with their objections.

Before getting to specific cases, it must be pointed out that although on the surface the opinions of admirals and generals should carry a great deal of weight—war, after all, is their business—this is not true with regard to the subject at hand. That Japan was a "defeated nation" by the summer of 1945 was a fact known by anyone who read the daily newspapers. The real question was when and if Japan would *surrender,* which was a political rather than a military decision. Unless an officer had some secret source within the highest echelon of the Japanese government (and none have yet been revealed), he would have had no more accurate knowledge of when Japan would have surrendered than anyone else. Germany, after all, had been a "defeated nation" at least by the autumn of 1944, yet the war continued until Soviet armies smashed into the heart of Berlin.

The first of Alperovitz's star attractions is Admiral William D. Leahy, whom Truman inherited from Roosevelt as White House chief of staff and who sat as both presidents' representative on the

25. Gar Alperovitz, "U.S. Spied on Its World War II Allies," *New York Times,* August 11, 1993.

26. Gar Alperovitz, *The Decision to Use the Atomic Bomb and the Architecture of an American Myth* (New York: Alfred A. Knopf, 1995).

Joint Chiefs of Staff. In a book published in 1950, Leahy wrote that dropping the bombs was "barbarous" and was of "no material assistance in our war against Japan." The Japanese were "already defeated" and "ready to surrender," he wrote, because of conventional bombing and naval blockade. "I was not taught to make war in that fashion," he declared, "and wars cannot be won by destroying women and children."[27] How he thought women and children would have fared had the air force gone on bombing Japan "back into the stone age" and the naval blockade progressively denying them food and medicine, he did not reveal.

Leahy never claimed that he had conveyed such sentiments to Truman before the bombs were dropped, and not a shred of evidence has yet appeared that he did. Alperovitz tried to make up for this discrepancy by braiding together snippets from Leahy's condemnation of the bomb with a quotation from an earlier page in which he wrote that he had "acquainted Truman with my own ideas about the best course to pursue in defeating Japan as fully as I had done with President Roosevelt."[28] This passage clearly refers to the period immediately following Roosevelt's death, hence his use of the word *acquainted.* Leahy wrote that he had expressed his preference for bombing and blockade over invasion without even suggesting any mention of the bomb, which had yet to be tested.[29] In any event the admiral at no time *before* Hiroshima contended that the siege would compel Japan to surrender before the scheduled invasion (Alperovitz's "initial preliminary landing"), only that it would do so eventually and that it was worth the wait.

Leahy's indignation about the bombs came later and may have had something to do with fear that they would reduce his beloved navy to a marginal role. During the months before their use he had confidently predicted "as a munitions expert" that they would not work, and even after the successful test at Alamogordo he scoffingly referred to them as "a professor's dream." Four days before Hiroshima he made a bet with the King of England that they would not explode and, as Truman told aides after the first bomb was dropped,

27. William D. Leahy, *I Was There: The Personal Story of the Chief of Staff to Presidents Roosevelt and Truman Based on His Notes and Diaries Made at the Time* (New York: Whittlesey House, 1950), 441.
28. Alperovitz, *The Decision to Use the Atomic Bomb,* 325.
29. Leahy, *I Was There,* 385.

"the admiral said up to the last that it wouldn't go off." Years later Averell Harriman stated at a roundtable discussion, "I remember that great genius, Admiral Leahy, saying that he would guarantee that the bomb wouldn't go off." To which former Assistant Secretary of War John J. McCloy responded, "Yeah, I remember that."[30] Neither Alperovitz nor anyone else had been able to cite evidence that Leahy expressed to anyone before Hiroshima the revulsion he later professed.

Alperovitz's claim that General Dwight D. Eisenhower, the supreme commander of Allied Expeditionary Forces in Europe, also personally confronted Truman with objections about the bomb rests on equally spurious grounds. In his *Crusade in Europe,* published in 1948, Eisenhower recalled that when Stimson first informed him about the bomb, he said he hoped "we would never have to use such a thing against any enemy" because he did not want the United States to be the first to "use something so horrible and destructive as this weapon was described to be." He added that "My views were merely personal and immediate reactions, they were *not based on any analysis of the subject.*"[31] (my emphasis)

Eisenhower's recollection of his conversation with Stimson grew more vivid with the passage of time. In his *Mandate for Change* (1963) he now remembered telling a "deeply perturbed" Stimson that "dropping the bomb was completely unnecessary" without mentioning his earlier caveat that his views "were not based on any analysis of the subject."[32] That year he provided an interviewer with an even more colorful account. "We'd had a nice evening together at headquarters in Germany," he recalled. Then, after dinner, "Stimson got this cable saying that the bomb had been perfected and was ready to be dropped. The cable was in code . . . 'The lamb is born' or some damn thing like that."

Eisenhower said he listened quietly as Stimson outlined the plans

30. The Leahy quotations are from *I Was There,* 385; his bet with the king is in ibid., 431; Truman quotation from Eben A. Ayers diary entry, August 8, 1945, Robert H. Ferrell, ed., *Truman in the White House: The Diary of Eben A. Ayers* (Columbia: University of Missouri Press, 1991), 61; The Harriman-McCloy exchange is from the transcript of "Off the Record Discussion of the Origin of the Cold War," May 31, 1967, Mark Chadwin Files, box 869, W. Averell Harriman Papers, Library of Congress.

31. Dwight D. Eisenhower, *Crusade in Europe* (Garden City, N.Y.: Doubleday, 1948), 443.

32. Dwight D. Eisenhower, *Mandate for Change* (Garden City, N.Y.: Doubleday, 1963), 312–13.

for using the bombs, but when asked his opinion he said he was "against it" because "the Japanese were ready to surrender and it wasn't necessary to hit them with that awful thing" and because he "hated to see our country be the first to use such a weapon. Well . . . the old gentleman got furious."[33] In this version, he had gone from merely expressing dismay to delivering such a scathing denunciation on moral and military grounds as to outrage Stimson.

Although Stimson was no longer alive to confirm or deny Eisenhower's later account, parts of his story are demonstrably false and the rest of dubious authenticity. The first coded cable about the atomic test arrived at Potsdam on the evening of July 16, the second on the morning of the eighteenth. Stimson did not talk to Eisenhower until the twentieth at a flag-raising ceremony in Berlin. General Omar Bradley also was present, and Stimson noted in his diary simply that "I had a pleasant chat with both of them after the show was over."[34] Eisenhower's claim that he was with Stimson when the first message about the bomb arrived, therefore, is without foundation.

Stimson next met with Eisenhower at the latter's headquarters in Frankfurt on July 27, eleven days after the first coded cable reached Potsdam. Stimson did not mention any discussion about the bomb in his diary, but an aide's notes about the Potsdam trip stated that during lunch in Eisenhower's quarters, he and the secretary "talked informally about civil affairs and General Groves' project [the bomb]."[35] As Stimson and Eisenhower met only twice during the Potsdam Conference and only one of the meetings took place at the general's headquarters, this had to have been the session during which Eisenhower recalled having voiced his objections. There is no record of any message from Stimson to Truman referring to the general's sentiments, nor could the secretary have conveyed them personally because he left for the United States later that day. Eisenhower and others breakfasted with Truman on July 30, but neither the general nor anyone else has suggested there was any confrontation at that time.[36]

33. "Ike on Ike," *Newsweek*, November 11, 1963, 108.

34. Henry L. Stimson diary entry, July 20, 1945, Henry Lewis Stimson Papers, Yale University Library.

35. Colonel W. H. Kyle, "Notes on the Trip of the Secretary of War," July 6 to July 28, reel 128, Stimson Papers.

36. "Log of the President's Trip to the Berlin Conference, 6 July to 7 August 1945," Harry S. Truman Presidential Museum and Library, Independence, Mo.

General Bradley's autobiography, published in 1983, confirmed Eisenhower's recollection about his meeting with Stimson and offered a dramatic new twist to the story. This volume not only had Bradley in the room when Eisenhower confronted Stimson, but also had him present when the supreme commander openly berated Truman about the bomb at lunch before the flag-raising ceremony on the twentieth.[37] Alperovitz uncritically accepted this version of events in his 1985 edition of *Atomic Diplomacy*. "We now know," he wrote, "that when Truman said he was going to use the atomic weapon Eisenhower challenged him directly." Alperovitz also had the president telling Eisenhower after the luncheon that he would try to get the general anything he wanted, including "the presidency in 1948."[38] That Truman would have said this to a man who had just accused him in the presence of others of pursuing a policy that was both immoral and militarily unnecessary is, not to put too fine a point on it, preposterous.

A closer look at this version of events reveals several puzzlements. Why, in view of Eisenhower's willingness to freely discuss his alleged confrontation with Stimson, did he never even suggest that he conveyed his misgivings to Truman personally? And why, if he already had made his objections known in Stimson's presence on the twentieth, did he pretend that he first learned about the bomb at his headquarters on the twenty-seventh? Barton J. Bernstein shed light on the subject in a 1987 article. Quite simply it is that Bradley's collaborator on his autobiography, who wrote the relevant section after the general's death, made up the Eisenhower-Truman confrontation in Berlin out of whole cloth and for good measure had Bradley present at Eisenhower's session with Stimson, which is also false.

Bernstein went on to point out that although no contemporary evidence has yet been found to confirm or deny Eisenhower's recollection about his protest to Stimson, it would have been entirely uncharacteristic of the tactful general to have openly defied a policy endorsed by Truman, Stimson, and Marshall. There is some indication that if Eisenhower did not actually endorse use of the bomb at the time, he at least led others to think he did. A few days after Ja-

37. Omar Bradley and Clay Blair, *A General's Life: An Autobiography by General of the Army Omar Bradley* (New York: Simon and Schuster, 1983), 445, 707.
38. Alperovitz, *Atomic Diplomacy* (1985 edition), 14, 16.

pan surrendered, Bradley triumphantly wrote to the supreme commander: "It certainly didn't take long for the Japs to make up their
minds after we started hitting them with atomic bombs." That
Bradley would have written his friend and superior in such a vein
had he personally witnessed Eisenhower denounce use of the bombs
as immoral and unnecessary must be doubted. If nothing else, the
letter shows that Bradley, at least, certainly did not oppose use of the
weapons.[39]

In his 1995 book Alperovitz chose not to respond to Bernstein's
devastating critique of the Bradley autobiography. He merely repeated the fiction that Eisenhower had confronted Truman directly
at the Berlin flag-raising ceremony and noted in passing that "some
were later to question Eisenhower's memory." He mentioned without comment Bernstein's article (and one by the present author) in a
footnote.[40] As was the case with Leahy, Alperovitz's attempt to
"prove" his allegation cannot withstand analysis.

Neither of the top commanders in the Pacific *at the time* expressed
any opposition to using atomic bombs. Admiral Chester W. Nimitz,
commander in chief, Pacific Ocean Area, learned of the planned operation months earlier because the special bombing group would operate from within his jurisdiction. According to the courier who delivered the letter stating that the first bomb was expected to be ready
in August, Nimitz read it and commented, "This sounds fine but this
is only February. Can't we get one sooner?" Alperovitz made much
of Nimitz's stated reservations after the war, but he failed to inform
his readers that the admiral was one of those who had urged *dropping a third bomb, this one on Tokyo.*[41]

General Douglas MacArthur, commander in chief, Pacific Ocean
Area, never wavered in his insistence that an invasion would be necessary to defeat Japan. In mid-June 1945 he informed General Marshall that "I most earnestly recommend no change in Olympic
[planned invasion of Kyushu]." At about that time he told the head

39. Barton J. Bernstein, "Ike and Hiroshima: Did He Oppose It?" *Journal of Strategic Studies* 10 (September 1987): 377–89.
40. Alperovitz, *The Decision to Use the Atomic Bomb,* 356, 358, 723.
41. Nimitz quotation is from Fletcher Knebel and Charles W. Bailey II, *No High
Ground* (New York: Harper, 1960), 90; his support for dropping a third bomb is in
Commanding General 313th Bomb Wing to General Nathan Twining, August 9, 1945,
and Twining to Nimitz and General Carl A. Spaatz confirming their discussions,
same date, both in box 24, Spaatz Papers, Library of Congress.

of the army air force that although conventional bombing would help win the war, "in the final analysis, the doughboys would have to march into Tokyo."[42] He continued to urge that preparations for the invasion go forward even after the first bomb was dropped. Alperovitz cited several of MacArthur's postwar statements to the effect that Japan would have surrendered earlier if only an assurance about the emperor had been extended. He was unable to produce any evidence that the general had expressed this opinion to anyone before the bombs were used.

The air force generals merit special attention because they alone during the summer of 1945 had predicted that bombing would force Japan to capitulate before the scheduled invasion. During a meeting of the Combined Chiefs of Staff at the Potsdam Conference, army air forces chief Henry H. Arnold reported that bombing commander Curtis LeMay estimated that Japan would "become a nation without cities" by the first of October and "will have tremendous difficulty in holding her people together for continued resistance to our terms of unconditional surrender." Such an optimistic view tended to be discounted by others because the airmen earlier had promised that strategic bombing would drive Germany to its knees, a promise that turned out to be a pipe dream. As General Marshall told Truman in mid-June, air power had been unable to defeat Germany and would not be "sufficient to put the Japanese out of the war."[43]

Alperovitz's handling of Arnold's views is typical. He cherry-picked those of the general's comments that supported his theme and omitted mention of those that did not. In his memoirs, for instance, Arnold stated that "the abrupt surrender of Japan came more or less as a surprise, for we had figured that we would probably have to drop about four atomic bombs or increase the destructiveness of our B-29 missions by adding the heavy bombers from Europe."[44] It should be pointed out that the heavy bombers of the types used in

42. MacArthur's June 18, 1945, message to Marshall is in JCS 1388/1, "Details of the Campaign against Japan," 3, Xerox 1567, George C. Marshall Library, Lexington, Va.; his "doughboy" statement is in Henry H. Arnold, *Global Mission* (New York: Harper and Brothers, 1949), 569.

43. Arnold report to Combined Chiefs of Staff, OPD, "Military Use of the Atomic Bomb," George A. Lincoln Papers, United States Military Academy Library; Marshall comment to Truman is from "Details of the Campaign against Japan," extracted from June 18 meeting at the White House, 4, Xerox 1564, Marshall Library.

44. Arnold, *Global Mission*, 598.

Europe (B-17s and B-24s) did not have the range to operate from B-29 bases in the Marianas, and existing plans were first to deploy them from airfields on Okinawa and then from Kyushu after the initial operation had secured the southern portion of the island.

What the general said at the time the bombs were dropped is even more devastating to Alperovitz's claim. Two days after Hiroshima, Arnold delightedly informed General Carl A. Spaatz, the commander of the United States Strategic Air Forces in the Pacific, that "atomic bombing story received largest and heaviest smash play of the entire war with three deck banner headlines evening and morning papers." Shortly after Japan surrendered Arnold confided to Spaatz that while he was "naturally feeling very good," it was, "shall I say, unfortunate that we were never able to launch the full power of our bombing attack with the B-29s" to convince "doubting Thomases" how devastating conventional air attack could be.[45] Arnold obviously thought at the time that atomic bombs had ended the war, thereby denying the air force its opportunity to continue obliterating Japanese cities.

Alperovitz's account of Spaatz's attitude toward the bombs was even more misleading. Repeatedly citing Spaatz's postwar remarks, Alperovitz again failed to inform his readers what the general actually had said at the time. First of all, two days after Hiroshima, Spaatz and LeMay told reporters that because of the bombs "an invasion will not be necessary" and that conventional armies would become obsolete. They, along with Nimitz and General Nathan Twining, the commander of the Twentieth Air Force, urged that Tokyo be the next target for an atomic bomb.[46] The following day Spaatz informed Arnold that "the psychological effect on the government officials still remaining in Tokyo is more important at this time than destruction." Arnold replied that the recommendation was "being considered at a high level." Spaatz also requested that a "hardstand" with hydraulic lift for loading atomic bombs onto aircraft be installed at Okinawa "ready for use not later than 13 September," a cu-

45. Arnold to Spaatz, August 8, 1945, cited in Knebel and Bailey, *No High Ground*, 221; Arnold to Spaatz, August 19, 1945, box 21, Spaatz Papers.
46. Spaatz and LeMay press statement of August 8, 1945, in Marshall to Spaatz, same date, warning that "However good your intentions, you can do incalculable harm," box 85, folder 25, Papers of George C. Marshall, George C. Marshall Library, Lexington, Va.; recommendation by Spaatz, LeMay, Twining, and Nimitz to drop the third bomb is in box 24, Spaatz Papers.

rious request from an individual who allegedly thought that Japan might have surrendered at any moment even without the bombs. As late as August 13 Spaatz pleaded that "every effort be made to expedite delivery of [the third] atomic bomb."[47]

Finally, there is Curtis LeMay, the cigar-chewing air general whose revolutionary use of B-29s flying at low altitudes helped make the torching of Japanese cities more effective. At a press conference held on September 20, 1945, LeMay stated without equivocation that "the atomic bombs had nothing to do with the end of the war at all." Although Alperovitz cited numerous statements LeMay had made over the years, this one clearly is his favorite because he has repeated it endlessly (three times in three pages of *The Decision to Use the Atomic Bomb* alone) over the years.[48] One would never guess from Alperovitz's text that LeMay earlier had declared that because of the bombs "an invasion will not be necessary" or that he had advocated dropping a third.

The reason for the quick turnabout by air force officers seems fairly clear. Initially they were enthused about the weapon because it was their branch of service that had delivered it, hence Arnold's boast about the "three deck banner headlines." But they soon thought better of it. If a small number of planes armed with atomic bombs could devastate an enemy's industrial and population centers, what need would there be for the seventy-group independent service the airmen dreamed of creating in the postwar period? This frightening prospect led them for a brief period immediately after the war to downplay the impact of the atomic bombs by claiming that conventional air attacks already had brought Japan to the verge of surrender. Alperovitz's presentation of the airmen's views was perfectly consistent with his treatment of other officers. He relied mainly on postwar expressions of distaste for the bomb to make it falsely appear that such opposition was widespread in the armed forces at the time they were used.

It has been a source of both amusement and dismay to witness the cries of righteous indignation within the historical profession over instances of plagiarism that have been revealed during the past few

47. Spaatz to General Lauris Norstad (Arnold's chief of staff), August 10, 1945; and Arnold's reply is in Norstad to Spaatz, same date; Spaatz to Arnold, August 13, 1945, all in box 24, Spaatz Papers.
48. Alperovitz, *The Decision to Use the Atomic Bomb*, 334–36.

years. Pilfering another person's words is indefensible, of course, but is comparatively small potatoes because the authors involved were not trying to mislead their readers as to what actually happened. Altering the sources to provide support for prefabricated interpretations is a far greater offense, yet efforts to expose the unprofessional practices of Hiroshima revisionists have tended to be disparaged as mere nit-picking or "footnote checking." In a glowing *New York Times* review of the 1985 version of *Atomic Diplomacy*, for instance, Yale historian Gaddis Smith wrote that despite a few "relatively minor" errors "the preponderance of new evidence since 1965 [date of the first edition] tends to sustain the original argument."[49]

More than thirty years ago, at the end of a book critical of what was then called "New Left" revisionism (which included a chapter on *Atomic Diplomacy*), I asked whether it was possible to sustain such views without doing violence to the historical record.[50] That Alperovitz, after more than three decades of prodigious research, still has to resort to the same techniques he used in *Atomic Diplomacy* provides a telling answer.

49. Gaddis Smith, *New York Times Book Review*, August 18, 1985.
50. Robert James Maddox, *The New Left and the Origins of the Cold War* (Princeton: Princeton University Press, 1973), 164.

SADAO ASADA

The Shock of the Atomic Bomb and Japan's Decision to Surrender—A Reconsideration

O N THE MORNING OF AUGUST 6, 1945, the B-29 Super-fortress *Enola Gay* released a single bomb that substantially destroyed the city of Hiroshima. Its power was vividly, though inaccurately, described in the flash report transmitted from the nearby Kure Naval Station to the navy minister:

> (1) Today 3 B-29s flew over Hiroshima at a high altitude at about 0825 and dropped several bombs. . . . A terrific explosion accompanied by flame and smoke occurred at an altitude of 500 to 600 metres. The concussion was beyond imagination and demolished practically every house in the city. (2) Present estimate of damage. About 80% of the city was wiped out, destroyed, or burnt. . . . Casualties have been estimated at 100,000 persons.[1]

Later that same day Lieutenant General Miyazaki Shuichi, the head of the Operations Division of the Army General Staff, wrote in his diary that "it may be the so-called atomic bomb."[2] His conjecture was confirmed shortly after 1:00 a.m. on August 7 when the Domei

I am grateful to the following friends and colleagues for their valuable suggestions: Barton J. Bernstein, Milton L. Bierman, Roger Buckley, Robert Butow, Wayne S. Cole, Roger Dingman, Edward J. Drea, Robert H. Ferrell, Richard B. Frank, Hatano Sumio, Waldo H. Heinrichs, Hosoya Chihiro, Akira Iriye, Osamu Ishii, Michael Schaller, Ronald H. Spector, J. Samuel Walker, D. C. Wyatt, and Russell Weigley.

Throughout this essay I have adopted the normal Japanese practice of giving family names first (with the exception of works that have appeared in English).

1. Edward J. Drea, "Previews of Hell," *Military History Quarterly* 7, no. 3 (Spring 1995): 79.

2. Diary of Lieutenant General Miyazaki Shuichi (hereafter cited as Miyazaki diary), August 6, 1945, Library, Military History Department, National Institute for Defense Studies, Defense Agency, Tokyo.

News Agency received President Truman's statement by shortwave broadcast. In it the president announced that the atomic bomb dropped on Hiroshima was more powerful than twenty thousand tons of TNT, and he warned that if Japan failed to accept immediately the terms of the Potsdam Declaration of July 26, 1945, it "may expect a rain of ruin from the air, the like of which has never been seen on this earth."[3]

This essay reexamines how the shock of the atomic bombs galvanized the "peace party"—Emperor Hirohito himself, Lord Keeper of the Privy Seal Kido Koichi, Foreign Minister Togo Shigenori, Navy Minister Yonai Mitsumasa, and (with some reservations) Prime Minister Suzuki Kantaro—to take actions that led to the termination of the Pacific War.[4] Their efforts met implacable opposition from the military chiefs—Army Minister Anami Korechika, Chief of the Army General Staff Umezu Yoshijiro, and Chief of the Naval General Staff Toyoda Soemu—who refused to admit defeat and clamored for a decisive homeland battle against invading American forces. It was these military leaders, especially Anami, who constituted the most volatile forces arrayed against Japan's surrender.

In both the United States and Japan, it is often argued that Japan was virtually a defeated nation in August 1945 and thus the atomic bombings were not necessary. This argument confuses "defeat" with "surrender": defeat is a military fait accompli, whereas surrender is the formal acceptance of defeat by the nation's leaders, an act of decision making. After the loss of Saipan in early July 1944 brought Japan within range of B-29 bombers, its defeat had become certain, and Japan's leaders knew this. But because its governmental machinery was, to a large extent, controlled by the military and hampered by a cumber-

3. U.S. Department of State, *Foreign Relations of the United States: The Conference of Berlin (The Potsdam Conference), 1945* (2 vols., Washington, D.C.: U.S. Government Printing Office, 1960), 2:1376–77.

4. The gist of this paper was presented at the meeting of the Society for Historians of American Foreign Relations held in Annapolis, Md., in June 1995 and the meeting of the Japan Association of International Relations held in Hiroshima in October 1995. A summary was published in the liberal-progressive monthly journal *Sekai*, no. 616 (1995): 232–42. An early Japanese version was presented at the International Conference on the Close of the Pacific War, held in Ito, Japan, in August 1995 and was later published as Asada Sadao, "Gembaku toka no shogeki to kofuku no kettei" [The Shock of the Atomic Bomb and Japan's Decision to Surrender] in Hosoya Chihiro et al., eds., *Taiheiyo senso no shuketsu* [The Close of the Pacific War] (Tokyo: Kashiwa Shobo, 1997), 195–221.

some system that required unanimity of views for any decision, Japanese leaders had failed to translate defeat into surrender.[5] In the end it was the atomic bomb, closely followed by the Soviet Union's entry into the war, that compelled Japan to surrender. This article, focusing microscopically on August 6 through 14, 1945, reconstructs the Japanese decision-making process in the aftermath of Hiroshima.

Historians and the Sources

There is an enormous literature on the A-bomb decision, yet relatively little has been written about the impact of the bomb on Japan's leaders.[6] Robert J. C. Butow's classic monograph, *Japan's Decision to Surrender* (1954), has largely stood the test of time. In fact, his work seemed so definitive that few historians have attempted to go over the same ground. To my knowledge, only two studies since Butow's have analyzed the decision to surrender utilizing Japanese sources. Herbert P. Bix's 1995 article, "Japan's Delayed Surrender," focuses on Emperor Hirohito's responsibility for *delaying* Japan's surrender primarily during the months before Hiroshima, in contrast to this article's argument that the emperor's "sacred decision" in the aftermath of the bombs made it finally possible for a divided government to surrender.[7] Lawrence Freedman and Saki Dockrill, in "Hiroshima: A Strategy of Shock" (1994), argue that the United States pursued "a clear and coherent strategy of "shock," which was successful. The present article attempts to provide much more detailed and comprehensive analysis of the decision-making process in Japan leading to its surrender.[8]

5. The cabinet system, as inaugurated in 1889, in practice required a unanimity of views among its members for any decision making. The army and navy ministers were privileged members and, by resigning and refusing to name their successors, they could overthrow the government.
6. A recent historiographical essay is J. Samuel Walker, "The Decision to Use the Bomb: A Historiographical Update," in *Hiroshima in History and Memory*, ed. Michael J. Hogan (New York: Cambridge University Press, 1996), 11–37.
7. Robert J. C. Butow, *Japan's Decision to Surrender* (Stanford: Stanford University Press, 1954). This book was translated into Japanese and was well received: Butow, *Shushen gaishi: Mujoken kofuku made no keii*, trans. Oi Atsushi (Tokyo: Jiji Tsushinsha, 1958). Herbert P. Bix, "Japan's Delayed Surrender: A Reinterpretation," *Diplomatic History* 19 (1995): 197–225.
8. In Saki Dockrill, ed., *From Pearl Harbor to Hiroshima: The Second World War in Asia and the Pacific, 1941–1945* (New York: St. Martin's Press, 1994), 191–212.

Other broader works that are germane to this article include Barton J. Bernstein's three reflective essays that appeared on the fiftieth anniversary of Hiroshima and Nagasaki.[9] "The Atomic Bombs Reconsidered," in particular, attracted considerable attention in Japan when its translation appeared in the respected monthly journal *Chuo Koron* in February 1995. Leon V. Sigal, in *Fighting to a Finish* (1988), presents a good analysis of bureaucratic politics but minimizes the "psychological impact of the atomic bomb." Paul Kecskemeti's *Strategic Surrender* (1958) contains a shrewd theoretical analysis of the U.S. surrender policy toward Japan.[10]

The review above shows that there are few recent American historians who deal with the impact of the bomb on the Japanese government. Instead they have been preoccupied with the historiographical controversy between "orthodox historians," typified by Herbert Feis,[11] and "revisionists," led by Gar Alperovitz and more recently Martin Sherwin.[12] The former contend that the bomb was necessary as a military means to hasten the end of the war with Japan, while scholars of the latter—the "atomic diplomacy" school—claim the bomb was meant as a political diplomatic threat aimed against the Soviet Union in the emerging Cold War. Bernstein advances a third interpretation, arguing that the bomb, although primarily aimed at the speedy surrender of Japan, had the "bonus" effect of intimidating the Soviet Union. In the heat generated by this

9. Barton J. Bernstein, "The Atomic Bombings Reconsidered," *Foreign Affairs* 74 (1995): 135–52; Bernstein, "Understanding the Atomic Bomb and the Japanese Surrender: Missed Opportunities, Little Known Near Disasters, and Modern Memory," in Hogan, ed., *Hiroshima in History and Memory*, 38–79; and Bernstein, "The Struggle over History: Defining the Hiroshima Narrative," in *Judgment at the Smithsonian*, ed. Phillip Nobile (New York: Marlowe, 1995), 127–256. See also Bernstein, "The Perils and Politics of Surrender: Ending the War with Japan and Avoiding the Third Atomic Bomb," *Pacific Historical Review* 46 (1977): 1–27.

10. Leon V. Sigal, *Fighting to a Finish: The Politics of War Termination in the United States and Japan, 1945* (Ithaca: Cornell University Press, 1988). Paul Kecskemeti, *Strategic Surrender: The Politics of Victory and Defeat* (Stanford: Stanford University Press, 1958).

11. Herbert Feis, *Japan Subdued: The Atomic Bomb and the End of the War in the Pacific* (Princeton: Princeton University Press, 1961). In his revised version, *The Atomic Bomb and the End of World War II* (Princeton: Princeton University Press, 1966), Feis tentatively incorporates some thoughts on anti-Soviet motives of the bombing.

12. Gar Alperovitz, *Atomic Diplomacy: Hiroshima and Potsdam, The Use of the Atomic Bomb and the American Confrontation with Soviet Power* (New York: Simon and Schuster, 1965). Martin Sherwin's most recent position is stated in "Hiroshima at Fifty: The Politics of History and Memory," *IHJ Bulletin* [A Quarterly Publication of the International House of Japan] 15 (1995): 1–10.

debate, American historians have neglected the Japanese side of the picture. Concentrating on the *motives* behind the use of the bombs, they have slighted the *effects* of the bomb.

Strange as it may seem, Japanese historians have written little on this subject. Because of a strong sense of nuclear victimization, it has been difficult until very recently for Japanese scholars to discuss the atomic bombing in the context of ending the Pacific War. The "orthodox" interpretation in Japan has reflected the American "revisionist" view.[13] Long before Alperovitz's *Atomic Diplomacy* appeared in 1965, Japanese historians had come under the influence of British Nobel laureate P. M. S. Blackett, whose *Fear, War and the Bomb* (1949) anticipated Alperovitz's arguments.[14] (Blackett's book was translated into Japanese in 1951 and has often been cited.) Finally in 1995 a Japanese translation of Alperovitz's *The Decision to Use the Atomic Bomb*[15] appeared, but the Japanese reading public paid more attention to the translation of Robert Jay Lifton and Greg Mitchell, *Hiroshima in America: Fifty Years of Denial* (1995), which appeared in the emotionally charged atmosphere of the fiftieth anniversary of Hiroshima and Nagasaki.[16]

Let us sample what Japanese historians have written. A widely read survey by Toyama Shigeki, Imai Seiichi, and Fujiwara Akira, *Showashi* [History of the Showa period] (1959), quotes Blackett approvingly: "The dropping of the atomic bombs was not so much the last military act of the Second World War as the first major operation of the Cold War with Russia."[17] The "atomic diplomacy" thesis has filtered down even to junior high school history textbooks. A typical sample reads, "As the Soviet Union's entry into the war became imminent, the United States dropped the atomic bombs to gain supremacy over the Soviet Union after the war."[18]

13. For a detailed discussion, see Sadao Asada, "The Mushroom Cloud and National Psyches: Japanese and American Perceptions of the A-Bomb Decision, 1945–1995," *Journal of American-East Asian Relations* 4 (1995): 95–116.

14. P. M. S. Blackett, *Fear, War, and the Bomb: Military and Political Consequences of Atomic Energy* (New York: Whittlesey House, 1949).

15. Gar Alperovitz, *The Decision to Use the Atomic Bomb and the Architecture of an American Myth* (New York: Alfred A. Knopf, 1995). Alperovitz's use of Japanese sources via a translator is inadequate.

16. Robert Jay Lifton and Greg Mitchell, *Hiroshima in America: Fifty Years of Denial* (New York: Putnam's Sons, 1995).

17. Toyama Shigeki, Imai Seiichi, and Fujiwara Akira, *Showashi* (rev. ed., Tokyo: Iwanami Shinsho, 1959), 238.

18. Kodama Kota et al., *Chugaku shakai: Rekishiteki bun'ya* [Junior high school/so-

Among monographs, perhaps the most quoted book is Nishijima Ariatsu's *Gembaku wa naze saretaka?* [Why were the atomic bombs dropped?], originally published in 1968 and reissued in 1985. Recapitulating the Blackett thesis, Nishijima argues that "the most important thing" was that Hiroshima-Nagasaki residents were "killed as human guinea pigs for the sake of [America's] anti-Communist, hegemonic policy."[19] Similarly, *Taiheiyo sensoshi* [A history of the Pacific War] (1973), compiled by a group of left-wing historians, states that "500,000 citizens [of Hiroshima and Nagasaki] were utterly meaninglessly sacrificed for America's cruel political purposes."[20] Here, the sense of victimization takes precedence over historical analysis.

This is not to say that more objective scholarship has been absent.[21] In the well-researched joint work edited by Hayashi Shigeru, *Nihon shusenshi* [History of Japan's surrender] (1962), the authors reveal an interesting ambivalence. They quote extensively from Herbert Feis for their narratives of the Manhattan Project and the decision to use the bomb, but, when it comes to assessing the significance of the bomb, they base their interpretation on Blackett. Arai Shin'ichi has drawn on American works and the unpublished Stimson diaries for *Gembaku toka e no michi* [The road leading to the use of the atomic bomb] (1985), which leans toward the "atomic diplomacy" thesis and is the only scholarly monograph written by a Japanese historian. The eminent political scientist Nagai Yonosuke has published a brilliant theoretical analysis of the American decision to drop the bomb, entitled *Reisen no kigen* [The origins of the Cold War] (1978) that tends to support the "orthodox" American interpretation.[22]

One thing is clear: like their American colleagues, Japanese historians have not studied sufficiently the crucial period from Hiroshi-

---

cial studies—History] (Tokyo: Nihon Shoseki, 1986), 197; Kawata Tadashi et al., *Atarashii shakai: Rekishi* [New society: History] (Tokyo: Tokyo Shoseki, 1992), 24.

19. Nishijima Ariatsu, *Gembaku wa naze toka saretaka: Nihon kofuku o meguru senryaku to gaiko* (Tokyo: Aoki Shoten, 1968), 146–48. The author does not seem to have used English language sources.

20. Rekishigaku Kenkyukai, ed., *Taiheiyo sensoshi* (6 vols., Tokyo: Aoki Shoten, 1973), 5:363–66.

21. An early collaborative work is Nihon Gaiko Gakkai, ed., *Taiheiyo senso shuketsu ron* [The termination of the Pacific War] (Tokyo, 1958).

22. Hayashi Shigeru, ed., *Nihon shusenshi* (3 vols., Tokyo: Yomiuri Shinbunsha, 1962), 2:84–93, 94–95; Arai Shin'ichi, *Gembaku toka e no michi* (Tokyo: Tokyo Daigaku Shuppankai, 1985); Nagai Yonosuke, *Reisen no kigen* (Tokyo, 1978), 147–89.

ma to the surrender.[23] It may well be that while the "atomic diplomacy" thesis heightens the Japanese sense of victimization, it also accords with their general unwillingness to come to grips with their responsibility for the Pacific War and its consequences. Consciously or unconsciously, historians have been affected by this climate of opinion—until recently. On August 6, 1995, on the fiftieth anniversary of Hiroshima, the *New York Times* quoted—or actually misquoted—from the embryonic version of this article, calling me, in an ironic twist of logic, a "Japanese revisionist." It observed that such "revisionists" are still "a tiny minority" but "the taboos are breaking down in Japan."[24] The disappearance of the "taboos" coincided, domestically, with Emperor Hirohito's death in 1989 and, externally, with the end of the Cold War.

Because of the nature of Japanese documentary source materials concerning the decision to surrender, historians face enormous handicaps and frustrations. In the weeks before General Douglas MacArthur's arrival, the Japanese government destroyed much of its archives for fear that the materials might be used in the trials of war criminals. In addition to surviving official records, historians are forced to utilize such materials as postsurrender memoirs, testaments, and postwar "interrogations" of Japanese officials. Problematic manuscript sources include "Interrogations" and "Statements" (interviews) of Japanese military and civilian officials conducted from 1948 to 1950 by the Military History Section of G-2 of General MacArthur's General Headquarters (the United States Army, Far East Command). In these "statements," Japanese officials often contradicted themselves, and they were obviously anxious to please their American questioners.[25] They were also eager to defend the emperor and protect the imperial institution.

23. For further discussion on the subject, see Hatano Sumio's thoughtful historiographical essay and his exhaustive bibliography, both contained in volume 6 of Gaimusho [Foreign Ministry], ed., *Shusen shiroku* [Historical record relating to the termination of the war] (6 vols., 1952; Expanded ed., Tokyo: Hokuyosha, 1977–1978), 6:230–53, 259–93.

24. Nicholas D. Kristof, "The Bomb: An Act That Haunts Japan and America," *New York Times*, August 6, 1995. For the nature of this "taboo," see Asada, "The Mushroom Cloud and National Psyches."

25. "Interrogations of Japanese Officials on World War II" (2 vols.; hereafter cited as "Interrogations") and "Statements of Japanese Officials on World War II" (4 vols.; hereafter cited as "Statements"). These interviews were conducted in preparation for General Douglas MacArthur's official war history, *Japanese Operations in the South-*

Among published sources, Kido Koichi's diaries, meticulously edited by a group of scholars at the University of Tokyo, are the most reliable. Kido, as lord keeper of the privy seal, had special access to the emperor. He was a realist par excellence; some would call him an opportunist. In this article he figures as the foremost "peace monger," in Toshikazu Kase's words.[26] A wealth of various source materials—contemporaneous government documents, diaries, memoranda, and excerpts from memoirs—are conveniently collected in Foreign Ministry, ed., *Shusen shiroku* [Historical record of the end of the war], published in 1952 and republished with additions and new annotations in six volumes in 1977–1978.[27] A more critical collection of documents is Kurihara Ken and Hatano Sumio, eds., *Shusen kosaku no kiroku* [Record of the efforts to end the war].[28] Volume 4 of Yomiuri Shimbunsha's edited collection, *Showashi no tenno* [The emperor in the history of the Showa period], based on oral history, is useful.[29] The Japanese army's mentality is revealed in the Army General Staff, comp., *Haisen no kiroku* [A record of the defeat] (1979).[30] Finally, the most important memoir is one by Foreign Minister Togo Shigenori, which has been translated into English.[31] These and other materials

---

west Pacific Area, vol. 2, *Reports of General MacArthur* (Washington, D.C.: U.S. Government Printing Office, 1966). Portions of the original Japanese versions are available at the Library, Military History Department, National Institute of Defense Studies; a complete English translation is available at the U.S. Army Center of Military History, Washington, D.C. For the nature of the problems the historian faces, see Barton J. Bernstein, "Compelling Japan's Surrender without the A-Bomb, Soviet Entry, or Invasion: Reconsidering the U.S. Bombing Survey's Early-Surrender Conclusions," *Journal of Strategic Studies* 18 (1995): 109–37. Butow's *Japan's Decision to Surrender* is an example of what a critical use of these documents can yield. Whenever sources appear dubious and whenever it has been possible, I have attempted to check them with more reliable materials.

26. Kido Koichi Kenkyukai, ed., *Kido Koichi nikki* (2 vols., Tokyo: Toyko Daigaku Shuppankai, 1966). Supplementing these diaries are *Kido Koichi nikki: Tokyo saibanki* [Diaries of Kido Koichi during the period of the Tokyo trials] (Tokyo: Toyko Daigaku Shuppankai, 1980) and *Kido Koichi kankei bunsho* [Papers relating to Kido Koichi] (Tokyo: Tokyo Daigaku Shuppankai, 1966). Toshikazu Kase, *Journey to the Missouri,* ed. David Nelson Rowe (New Haven: Yale University Press, 1950), 55.

27. Gaimusho, ed., *Shusen shiroku,* especially volumes 3–5.

28. Kurihara Hirota and Hatano Sumio, eds., *Shusen kosaku no kiroku* (2 vols., Tokyo: Kodansha, 1975), 33. Yomiuri Shimbunsha, ed., *Showashi no tenno* (30 vols., Tokyo: Yomiuri Shinbunsha, 1968), vol. 4.

29. Shimbunsha, ed., *Showashi no tenno,* vol. 4.

30. Sanbo Honbu, comp., *Haisen no kiroku* (Tokyo: Hara Shobo, 1979).

31. Togo Shigenori, *Jidai no ichimen* [An aspect of the Showa period] (Tokyo: Kaizosha, 1952), translated as *The Cause of Japan,* trans. and ed. Togo Fumihiko and

enable the historian to reinterpret the shock of the bomb and Japan's decision to surrender.

The Atomic Bomb as an "External Pressure"

On August 7 a San Francisco broadcast carried the announcement by President Truman that the United States had dropped an atomic bomb on Hiroshima. As soon as Foreign Minister Togo learned of this through the foreign ministry's shortwave receiver, he tried to get the facts from the army ministry. (Aerial bombings were a purely military matter, and the heads of the armed services exercised sole jurisdiction over reports of air-raid damages.) The army denied that there was any atomic bombing, maintaining that "although the United States claims it to be an atomic bomb, it actually appears to be a conventional bomb with extraordinary destructive power."[32] While Togo recognized the possibility that the United States had exaggerated the bomb for propaganda purposes, he was impressed that American radio broadcasting was "rampant" and "massive." He probably recalled that the Potsdam Declaration of July 26, 1945, had threatened Japan with "prompt and utter destruction." Galvanized by a sense of urgency, he took the initiative in convening an emergency meeting of key cabinet ministers on the afternoon of August 7.[33]

Deliberations at this cabinet meeting can be reconstructed from Togo's memoirs and other sources. The bombing of Hiroshima was the subject of discussion. Togo tried to find a breakthrough to surrender by quoting at great length American radio reports about the bomb. The U.S. government claimed that it had now "added a new and revolutionary increase in destruction," and that, unless Japan surrendered, the United States would keep dropping atomic bombs until Japan was extinct. Togo was resorting to the time-honored device of making the most of "external pressure"—the atomic bomb—

B. B. Blakeney (New York: Simon and Schuster, 1956) (throughout this article I have relied on my own translation).

32. Gaimusho, ed., *Shusen shiroku*, 4:57; Togo, *Jidai no ichimen*, 341–42; Togo, *The Cause of Japan*, 314–15; Kurihara and Hatano, eds., *Shusen kosaku*, 2:354–55.

33. Togo, *Jidai no ichimen*, 342; Togo, *The Cause of Japan*, 315; Togo Shigenori, May 18, 1949, "Statements"; Gaimusho, ed., *Shusen shiroku*, 4:58; Sakomizu Hisatsune, April 21, 1949, "Interrogations."

to counter the army, which was adamant for a "decisive battle on the homeland" against an American invasion. In a line of argument that was to be repeated by the peace party, Togo reasoned that "the introduction of a new weapon, which had drastically altered the whole military situation, offered the military ample grounds for ending the war." He proposed that surrender be considered at once on the basis of terms presented in the Potsdam Declaration. (When those in the peace party talked about "accepting the Potsdam terms," they meant acceptance with one crucial condition: retention of the emperor system.) However, the military authorities refused to concede that the United States had used an atomic weapon. Given the army's intransigence, it was impossible for the cabinet to take up Togo's proposal.[34]

About noon on August 7, Kido Koichi, the emperor's most important adviser ("the eyes and ears of the Throne"),[35] received a report that "the United States had used an atomic bomb against Hiroshima, causing extremely serious damage and 130,000 casualties." In an audience with Emperor Hirohito at 1:30, Kido noted how worried the emperor was. Hirohito, a scientist specializing in marine biology, was quick to grasp the destructive power of the atomic bomb, and he peppered Kido with questions about it.[36] He had been apprised by court attendants of the Hiroshima bomb on the afternoon of August 6 and was informed the following morning that it was an atomic bomb. He demanded more details from the government and the army about the devastation of Hiroshima and was "strongly displeased" that he was not getting enough information.[37]

According to Kido's postwar recollections, Hirohito told him, "Now that things have come to this impasse, we must bow to the inevitable. No matter what happens to my safety, we should lose no time in ending the war so as not to have another tragedy like this."[38] After Kido departed, Hirohito asked his military aide-de-camp al-

34. Togo, *Jidai no ichimen*, 342; Gaimusho, ed., *Shusen shiroku*, 4:57–58, 60; Kurihara and Hatano, eds., *Shusen kosaku*, 2:355–56.

35. Butow, *Japan's Decision to Surrender*, 12.

36. *Kido nikki*, 2:1222; *Kido nikki: Tokyo saibanki*, 421; *Kido kankei bunsho*, 84; Okabe Nagaakiro, *Aru jiju no kaisoroku* [Memoirs of a chamberlain] (Tokyo, 1990), 177–79.

37. Fujita Hisanori, *Jijucho no kaiso* [Memoirs of a grand chamberlain] (Tokyo: Chuo Koronsha, 1987), 126.

38. *Kido nikki: Tokyo saibanki*, 421.

most every hour about the extent of the damage in Hiroshima.[39] The emperor, who had already concluded in June 1945 that the war must end soon, was from this time forward Japan's foremost peace advocate, increasingly articulate and urgent in expressing his wish for peace.

The first to take concrete action to terminate the war was Foreign Minister Togo, a dour-faced, outspoken, and resolute man. On the morning of August 8, with Suzuki's approval, Togo took it upon himself to visit the Imperial Palace and make a direct appeal to the emperor in his underground air-raid shelter. According to his postwar account in September 1945, Togo reported in detail that American and British broadcasts were "most enthusiastically" repeating news of the atomic bomb. Characteristically, he invoked the enemy's broadcast to buttress his case for a prompt surrender. "The atomic bomb," Togo said, "has not only revolutionized modern warfare but has also brought about a great social upheaval and transformation of the daily lives of ordinary individuals as well. This is to be used as the turning point in bringing an end to the war"—on condition, of course, that the emperor system be retained. Emphasizing the urgency of the situation, Togo said that the United States would continue to drop atomic bombs on Japanese cities, as President Truman had warned, unless Japan ended the war at once. As Togo recalled in his memoirs, Hirohito emphatically concurred. "That is just so," he replied, and went on to divulge his own firm determination:

> Now that such a new weapon has appeared, it has become less and less possible to continue the war. We must not miss a chance to terminate the war by bargaining [with the Allied powers] for more favorable conditions now. Besides, however much we consult about [surrender] terms we desire, we shall not be able to come to an agreement. So my wish is to make such arrangements as will end the war as soon as possible.[40]

In these words the emperor expressed his conviction that a speedy surrender was the only feasible way to save Japan. Hirohito urged

39. Yomiuri, ed., *Showashi no tenno*, 4:310–11.
40. Togo, *Jidai no ichimen*, 342; Togo, *The Cause of Japan*, 315–16; Gaimusho, ed., *Shushen shiroku*, 4:60; Kurihara and Hatano, eds., *Shusen kosaku*, 2:356; Fujita, *Jijucho no kaiso*, 126.

Togo to "do his utmost to bring about a prompt termination of the war" and commanded him to apprise Prime Minister Suzuki of his wish. The emperor had deep trust in Suzuki, a seventy-eight-year-old retired admiral, who had served as his grand chamberlain from 1929 to 1936. In compliance with the imperial wish, Togo met Suzuki and proposed that, "given the atomic bombing of Hiroshima, the Supreme War Council be convened with all dispatch." This council was Japan's inner war cabinet, consisting of the "Big Six"—the prime minister, foreign minister, army and navy ministers, and chiefs of the army and naval general staffs. However, there was one full day's delay because some of the military members of the Supreme War Council were not available earlier—a strange, almost criminal excuse when time was so urgent.[41]

On the night of August 8, Suzuki told Sakomizu Hisatsune, the chief cabinet secretary, "Now that we know it was an atomic bomb that was dropped on Hiroshima, I will give my views on the termination of the war at tomorrow's Supreme War Council, and I want you to make preparations for me."[42] After the war Suzuki recalled, "The atomic bomb provided an additional reason for surrender as well as an extremely favorable opportunity to commence peace talks. I believed such an opportunity could not be afforded by B-29 bombings alone."[43] The hitherto vacillating and sphinx-like Suzuki had finally made up his mind. It is important to note that Suzuki did so *before* he was informed of the Soviet entry into the war early on the following day.[44] Sakomizu also felt that "the army will admit that now that the atomic bomb has come into existence, it precludes war between a nation that possesses the atomic bomb and one that does not."[45] However, the army was not to be so easily swayed.

41. Kurihara and Hatano, eds., *Shusen kosaku* 2:356; Gaimusho, ed., *Shusen shiroku,* 4:98.

42. Sakomizu Hisatsune, *Dai Nippon teikoku saigo no 4-kagetsu* [The last four months of the Japanese empire] (Tokyo: Oriento, 1973), 185.

43. Tominaga Kengo, ed., *Gendaishi shiryo, 39: Taiheiyo senso (5)* [Documents on contemporary history: The Pacific War] (45 vols., of which 5 are on the Pacific War, Tokyo: Misuzu Shobo, 1975), 5:756.

44. Sakomizu, May 3, 1949, "Interrogations."

45. "Shusen no shoshofu shusen hiwa" [Imperial rescript on the war's end and the taped recording of Sakomizu's talk] (n.p., [1970]).

Japan's "Longest Day"—and Night

At dawn on August 9, Tokyo intercepted a TASS broadcast that the
Soviet Union had declared war. Within hours the Red Army's mech-
anized forces bypassed or overwhelmed Japanese units on the
Manchurian border and threw the Kwantung Army into confusion.
The Japanese government's panic was now complete. Until the moment of the Soviet entry, Tokyo had been trying to obtain Soviet me-
diation for favorable surrender terms from the United States; now
this last hope was dashed. Prime Minister Suzuki's military estimate
was that Japan would be able to hold out against the Soviets in
Manchuria for at least two months.[46] However, Lieutenant General
Ikeda Sumihisa, who had been transferred from vice chief of staff of
the Kwantung Army to head the cabinet's Comprehensive Planning
Bureau just two weeks earlier, flabbergasted Suzuki by stating that
"Chaochou [capital of Manchukuo] will fall into Russian hands in
two *weeks*"; the Kwantung Army had been reduced to a skeleton after its best troops had been redeployed to the Pacific theater and the
homeland since the latter part of 1944.[47]

The effects of the "twin shocks"—the atomic bombing and the Soviet Union's declaration of war—were profound. Early that morning, Togo visited Suzuki to inform him of the Soviet entry. Suzuki
concurred that the government must end the war at once. On his way
back to the foreign ministry, Togo stopped at the navy ministry and
told Navy Minister Yonai what he had said to Suzuki.[48]

Hirohito, having been apprised of the Soviet entry by Suzuki,
summoned Lord Privy Seal Kido to his underground air-raid shelter
at 9:55 a.m. In light of the Soviet entry, Hirohito said, it was all the
more urgent to find means to end the war. He commanded Kido to
"have a heart-to-heart talk" with Prime Minister Suzuki at once. Co-
incidentally, Suzuki had just arrived at the palace, so Kido immediately conveyed the imperial wish to him, emphasizing the importance of immediately accepting the Potsdam terms. Suzuki assured

---

46. Gaimusho, ed., *Shusen shiroku*, 4:100; Suzuki Hajime, ed., *Suzuki Kantaro jiden*
[Autobiography of Suzuki Kantaro] (Tokyo, 1985), 294–95.
47. Ikeda Sumihisa, *Nihon no magarikado* [Japan at the crossroads] (Tokyo: Chishi-
ro Shuppan, 1968), 206–9; Ikeda Sumihisa, December 23, 1949, "Statements" (my emphasis).
48. Togo, *Jidai no ichimen*, 342; Togo, *Cause of Japan*, 316.

Kido of his determination to end the war speedily, and at 10:55 Kido again had an audience with the emperor to assure him that "the prime minister agrees there is no other way."[49]

Meanwhile, the Supreme War Council had convened at 10:30 a.m., August 9, in an atmosphere of "impatience, frenzy, and bewilderment," as recalled by Fujita Hisanori, the grand chamberlain.[50] It was arguably Japan's most fateful day—and night. All the members of the council recognized that it was impossible to continue the war much longer, but would they be able to come to a decision for surrender? To reach that decision, the government machinery required that the Supreme War Council and the cabinet achieve unanimity of views. If any military member(s) chose to oppose, either no decision would be reached or the Suzuki cabinet would collapse; in either case, a swift surrender would be aborted.

Prime Minister Suzuki opened the meeting with the following observation: "Just when we were smarting from the extremely great shock of the Hiroshima bomb, the Soviet Union entered the war. Continuation of the war is totally impossible, and whether willing or not we have no choice but to accept the Potsdam terms." Foreign Minister Togo, known for his logical mind, forcefully stated that Japan must immediately accept the Potsdam terms with the sole condition being that the Allies "guarantee the emperor's position." He informed the council members of the emperor's conviction that, since the atomic bomb had made its appearance, continuation of the war had become utterly impossible.[51]

What the peace party had been worrying about most was how many more A-bombs the United States had in readiness. Nonetheless, at the beginning of the Supreme War Council meeting, "a rather bullish atmosphere" prevailed, as Admiral Toyoda Soemu, chief of the Naval General Staff, recalled in his memoirs. "To be sure, the damage of the atomic bomb is extremely heavy, but it is questionable whether the United States will be able to use more bombs in rapid succession."[52] Although the proceedings of the council meeting do

49. *Kido kankei bunsho*, 87; *Kido nikki*, 2:1223; Kido Koichi, May 17, 1949, "Statements."

50. Fujita, *Jijucho no kaiso*, 129.

51. Gaimusho, ed., *Shusen shiroku*, 4:107–12.

52. Toyoda Soemu, *Saigo no teikoku kaigun* [The last of the Imperial Navy] (Tokyo: Sekai no Nihonsha, 1950), 206–7.

not exist, it appears that Army Minister Anami indulged in wishful thinking when he said that the bomb dropped on Hiroshima was the only atomic bomb the United States possessed.

At precisely this moment, just before 1:00 p.m., news reached the meeting that a second atomic bomb had been dropped on Nagasaki. The impact of another set of "twin shocks"—Hiroshima and Nagasaki—was devastating. Suzuki now began to fear that "the United States, instead of staging the invasion of Japan, will keep on dropping atomic bombs."[53] Although Japan had measures to cope with the American invasion, nothing could be done about the continuation of atomic bombings.

We must pause here to ask whether the Nagasaki bomb was necessary. The Hiroshima bomb had already jolted Japan's peace party to move toward surrender. The strategic value of a second bomb was minimal. With all land communications severed between Tokyo and Hiroshima, the full extent of the Hiroshima disaster had not yet sunk in among leaders in Tokyo; there had been an interval of only three days between the two bombs. On the other hand, from the standpoint of its shock effect, the political impact of the Nagasaki bomb cannot be denied. Army Minister Anami's wishful thinking was shattered; if two bombs were available, then maybe there were three or even four.[54] In fact, rumor had it that Tokyo would be atomic-bombed on August 12 and that many more cities would be incinerated. The Nagasaki bomb, which instantly killed approximately thirty-five thousand to forty thousand people, was unnecessary to induce Japan to surrender, but it probably had confirmatory effects.[55]

53. Tominaga, ed., *Gendaishi shiryo, 39: Taiheiyo senso (5)*, 5:756.

54. Surprisingly, Army Minister Anami seems to have given some credence to the make-believe account that the United States had a stockpile of one hundred atomic bombs and that Tokyo would be the target for the next atomic bombing. The source of this fabrication was a P-51 fighter pilot by the name of Marcus McDila who had been downed and captured on August 8. (The United States, of course, had completed only two bombs at that time.) Gaimusho, ed., *Shusen shiroku*, 4:119–20; Boeicho Boei Kenshujo Senshi Shitsu [War History Office, Defense Agency], *Senshi sosho: Daihon'ei rikugunbu* [War history series: Imperial General Headquarters, The Army] (Tokyo: Asagumo Shinbunsha, 1975), 10:418, 437. Okura Kimmochi, president of the Technological Research Mobilization Office, also heard a similar rumor (Naisei Kenkyukai and Nihon Kindai Shiryo Kenkyukai, eds., *Okura Kimmochi nikki* [Diaries] [Tokyo: Editor, 1971], 4:321).

55. There was no separate decision to use the second bomb; the local commander was ordered to use additional bombs as they became ready.

The news of the Nagasaki bombing notwithstanding, a heated argument continued at the Supreme War Council. Togo, who strongly urged surrender, with the one condition regarding the emperor system, was supported by Navy Minister Yonai, a taciturn admiral known for his liberal views and avowed connections with the navy's "peace maneuvers" (behind-the-scenes political activities centering on Admiral Okada Keisuke and Rear Admiral Takagi Sokichi). But Army Minister Anami adamantly objected.

It is difficult to grasp Anami's position. In Bernstein's apt expression, he was "the keystone in the arch of power that could lead to peace or prolonged war." Anami was a straightforward man, a typical samurai warrior and a master at archery and swordsmanship. His loyalty to the emperor was unquestioned; he had served as Hirohito's military aide-de-camp from 1929 through 1933. And he knew the emperor wished the war brought to an end. It is on record that he had met Togo at the army minister's official residence on the evening of August 7 from 6:30 to 9:00, had had a heart-to-heart talk with Togo, and had conceded that "defeat was a matter of time."[56] However, when he left his office on the morning of August 9 to attend the Supreme War Council meeting, he told Deputy Chief of the Army General Staff Kawabe Torashiro, "Upon my word I assure you it is going to be a hell of a stormy meeting!"[57]

At the Supreme War Council, Anami in his calmer moments seemed ready to accept the Potsdam terms "in principle" but with certain conditions. At his more belligerent moments, he cried out for a decisive homeland battle. The fact was that Anami, "the darling of the Army," commanded the full confidence of young officers, and he was now under strong pressure from these fire-eating subordinates. Whatever his inner thoughts, Anami insisted not only on the preservation of the imperial institution but also on "three additional conditions": (1) that there be no military occupation of the homeland by the Allies; (2) that the armed forces be allowed to disarm and demobilize themselves voluntarily; and (3) that war criminals be prosecuted by the Japanese government. These were "absolute" condi-

56. Matsutani Makoto, *Dai Tao Senso shushu no shinso* [The truth about terminating the Greater East Asian War] (Tokyo: Fuyo Shobo, 1980), 172–73; Kurihara and Hatano, eds., *Shusen kosaku*, 2:365.

57. Kurihara and Hatano, eds., *Shusen kosaku*, 2:365; Toyoda, *Saigo no teikoku kaigun*, 207–9; Suzuki, ed., *Suzuki Kantaro jiden*, 295–96.

tions, Anami said, and Chief of the Army General Staff Umezu Yoshijiro and Chief of the Naval General Staff Toyoda supported Anami. These military chiefs contended that retention of the emperor system was inconceivable if Japan's homeland were occupied by foreign troops and the Japanese forces disbanded.[58] In reality, however, they were trying to save their own skins. Of course, the "three additional conditions" flew in the face of the Potsdam Declaration, and it was apparent that the United States, its resolve bolstered by the atomic bombs and the Soviet entry into the war, would have rejected these conditions. Insisting on them would have meant fighting to the last.[59] The Supreme War Council failed to break the three-to-three deadlock. Suzuki, Togo, and Yonai insisted on terminating the war on the sole condition concerning the emperor system, while Anami, Umezu, and Toyoda called for a decisive homeland battle unless the United States accepted the three additional conditions as well.

The climax in the final act of the surrender drama came in two emergency cabinet meetings, followed by an imperial conference that lasted into the wee hours of the morning of August 10. At 2:30 p.m., August 9, the first of the cabinet meetings convened but reached an impasse, requiring a second meeting at 6:00 p.m. Suzuki opened the first meeting, and Togo spoke up: there was no hope of obtaining the "three additional conditions." Anami fiercely opposed Togo and Suzuki. In fact, Anami's utterances became almost irrational. As recalled by those who attended the meetings, Anami proclaimed, "The appearance of the atomic bomb does not spell the end of war. . . . We are confident about a decisive homeland battle against American forces." He admitted that "given the atomic bomb and the Soviet entry, there is no chance of winning on the basis of mathematical calculation," but he nevertheless declared that "there will be some chance as long as we keep on fighting for the honor of the Yamato race. . . . If we go on like this and surrender, the Yamato race would be as good as dead spiritually." Such was the mentality of the

58. Gaimusho, ed., *Shusen shiroku*, 4:119–20, 122–23; Toyoda, *Saigo no teikoku kaigun*, 207–9; Shigemitsu Mamoru, *Showa no doran* [Showa: Years of upheaval] (2 vols., Tokyo: Chuo Koronsha, 1952), 2:285–86.
59. Gaimusho, ed., *Shusen shiroku*, 4:118–24; Shimomura Kainan, *Shusen hishi* [The secret history of the termination of the war] (Tokyo: Kodansha, Showa, 1985), 96–103.

Japanese military. Urged by middle-echelon and young officers who were "half mad," Anami would not retreat from making the last sacrificial homeland battle.[60]

During the cabinet meeting in the evening of August 9, Navy Minister Yonai bluntly stated that Japan had no chance and urged a rational decision, pointing out that Japan had lost the battles of Saipan, Luzon, Leyte, Iwo Jima, and Okinawa. Anami retorted that, although Japan had lost battles, it had not yet lost the war. Now on the defensive, Anami said that all he could promise was one massive blow against the invading American forces; what he counted on was that American casualties would be so heavy as to shake American morale and induce a compromise peace. Again, the three-to-three stalemate totally paralyzed the government's decision making.[61]

As the last measure, Suzuki—in accordance with a scenario that he had worked out between Kido, Hirohito, and himself—requested shortly before midnight that an imperial conference be convened in the underground air-raid shelter of the Imperial Palace.[62] Suzuki and Togo, of course, knew where the imperial wish lay. Attending the conference were the members of the Supreme War Council and president of the Privy Council Hiranuma Kiichiro, with Suzuki presiding. Dressed in full army uniform and wearing white gloves, the emperor sat in front of a table covered with a gold-colored tablecloth. In his presence, Togo and Anami reenacted their confrontation. Hirohito patiently heard out the heated arguments for some two hours. Once again, a three-to-three deadlock ensued.[63]

Then, in an act unprecedented in modern Japanese history, the prime minister stepped up to the emperor's seat, bowed deeply, and submitted the matter for an imperial decision. Hirohito saw that only his direct intervention could save the situation. Breaking his customary silence, he made the "sacred decision." Speaking with emotion but in a quiet tone of voice, Hirohito stated that he agreed with Togo, ruling that the Potsdam terms be accepted. "Especially

60. Sanbo Honbu, comp., *Haisen no kiroku*, 283; Gaimusho, ed., *Shusen shiroku*, 4:118–19, 121–25; Ikeda, *Nihon no magarikado*, 174; Hattori Takushiro, *Daitoa senso zenshi* [The complete history of the Greater East Asian War] (8 vols., Tokyo: Hara Shobo, 1953–1956), 8:102; Oki Misao, *Oki nikki* [Oki diaries] (Tokyo, 1969), 335.

61. Gaimusho, ed., *Shusen shiroku*, 4:124.

62. Hata Ikuhiko, *Showa tenno itsutsu no ketsudan* [The five decisions of Showa emperor] (Tokyo: Bungei Shunju, 1994), 71.

63. Gaimusho, ed., *Shusen shiroku*, 4:122–42, 139, 142.

since the appearance of the atomic bomb," he said, continuation of war spelled needless suffering for his subjects and Japan's ruin as a nation. He reprimanded the army and pointed out the discrepancy between its promise and performance, referring to the army's failure to complete defense preparations for the Kujukuri coastal plan, a key point to repel an American invasion of the Kanto (Tokyo) Plain. Thus at 2:30 a.m. on August 10, the "sacred decision" was made to accept the Potsdam terms on one condition: the "prerogative of His Majesty as a Sovereign Ruler."[64] The decision was subsequently ratified by the cabinet. Later the same day, the foreign ministry relayed the message of conditional surrender to the American government through the Swiss and Swedish governments.

As is well known, however, a second intervention by the emperor became necessary on August 14 to resolve the deadlock over the American government's intentionally ambiguous reply, stating that the "authority" of the emperor "shall be subject to" the supreme commander of the Allied powers.[65] Togo was for accepting the American condition, which he said protected the imperial institution, but Anami opposed it most strenuously and demanded a last-ditch homeland battle rather than accepting the American reply. To break the impasse, Hirohito intervened once again, concurring with Togo's view.[66] Finally, at noon on August 15, the emperor broadcast to the nation and to the world at large the rescript of surrender. The war was finally over.

The Atomic Bomb as a "Gift from Heaven"

In a postwar interview in November 1945, Kido explained the decision to surrender in the following words:

The feeling that the emperor and I had about the atomic bombing was that the psychological moment we had long waited for had finally ar-

64. Ibid., 4:139, 142; Sanbo Honbu, comp., *Haisen no kiroku*, 362.
65. On the Japanese reaction, see Hatano Sumio, "'Kokutai goji' to Potsudamu sengen" [The 'national polity' and the Potsdam Declaration], *Gaiko jiho*, no. 1320 (1995): 28–35. For the American side, see Bernstein, "The Perils and Politics of Surrender," 7, 26.
66. Gaimusho, ed., *Shusen shiroku*, 5:17–56; *Kido nikki: Tokyo saibanki*, 443; Togo, *Jidai no ichimen*, 350–58; Toyoda, *Saigo no teikoku kaigun*, 218–22; Sakomizu, *Dai Nihon teikoku*, 233–42; *Kido nikki: Tokyo saibanki*, 443.

rived to resolutely carry out the termination of the war. . . . We felt that if we took the occasion and utilized the *psychological shock* of the bomb to follow through, we might perhaps succeed in ending the war.[67] (my emphasis)

In the same interview Kido went so far as to say that the U.S. government, by using the atomic bomb, actually intended to "assist" Japan's peace party:

I surmise that the atomic bomb was dropped with the intention of posing a grave threat to Japanese leaders and the people at large, forcefully compelling them to end the war. And certainly the bomb had that effect. However, we of the peace party had already been scheming for a termination of the war; and it is not correct to say that we were driven by the atomic bomb to end the war. Rather, *it might be said that we of the peace party were assisted by the atomic bomb in our endeavor to end the war.*[68] (my emphasis)

Unknowingly, Kido proved correct about the intentions of Secretary of War Henry L. Stimson, who considered the bomb a "profound psychological shock." In his memoirs, Stimson wrote that the American leaders had expected the bomb to "produce exactly the kind of shock on the Japanese ruling oligarchy, strengthening the position of those who wished peace, and weakening that of the military party."[69] This "strategy of shock" worked, for it encouraged the peace party to redouble its efforts to bring about the decision for surrender. That Stimson held a high view of Japanese "liberals"—a word that he used interchangeably with the "peace party" and "moderates"—is clear from an important memorandum he submitted to President Truman on July 2, 1945. In it he wrote that Japanese "liberals yielded [to the militarists] only at the point of the pistol" and that after the war they could be "depended upon for [Japan's] reconstruction as a responsible member of the family of nations."[70]

67. *Kido nikki: Tokyo saibanki,* 444.
68. Ibid.
69. Henry L. Stimson and McGeorge Bundy, *On Active Service in Peace and War* (New York: Harper, 1948), 626. Stimson and his colleagues had been following the power struggle within the Japanese government through intercepted Japanese cable messages.
70. Ibid., 620–24, 630–32; Henry L. Stimson diary (on microfilm), entries of June 18 and July 2, 1945, Henry Lewis Stimson Papers, Yale University Library; *Foreign Relations: The Conference of Berlin,* 1:888–92.

Aside from its terrible destructive power at ground zero, then, the bomb was effective in the hands of Japan's peace party as a political expedient. Prime Minister Suzuki called it "a most convenient pretext" for ending the war immediately. In that the peace party needed and obtained America's "assistance" in its struggle against the military to end the war, it may perhaps be said that there was a tacit political "linkage" between conservative American statesmen such as Stimson and Japan's "peace party," which, in Stimson's mind, broadly included such leaders as Togo, Kido, Yonai, former prime minister Konoe Fumimaro, and former foreign minister Shidehara Kijuro. What both groups had in common was the unquestioning acceptance of the atomic bomb as an instrument for terminating the war, and this linkage rested on the atomic devastation of Hiroshima and Nagasaki. Thus viewed, it is understandable that the destruction visited by the bombs did not provoke violent anti-American feelings or a strong sense of victimization among the Japanese leaders in the years immediately following the surrender.

The atomic bomb also saved Japan's ruling elite from an impending domestic crisis. On August 12 Navy Minister Yonai unburdened himself to his trusted subordinate, Rear Admiral Takagi Sokichi, who had been involved in the navy's peace maneuvers.

> Perhaps the way I am putting this is inadequate, but I think that *the use of the atomic bomb and the Soviet entry into the war are gifts from Heaven.* . . . The main reason I have been insisting on saving the situation [surrendering] is neither fear of an enemy attack nor even the atomic bomb and the Soviet entry into the war. Above all, it is the alarming state of domestic affairs. It is good fortune that we can now save the situation without bringing such domestic affairs into the open.[71] (my emphasis)

To call the atomic bomb, which took so many lives, a "gift from Heaven" would seem perverted. Callous as this may sound, Yonai was more alarmed about an impending political crisis, even a military coup d'état (like the February 26 Uprising of 1936), than about

71. Takagi Sokichi, *Takagi kaigun shosho oboegaki* [Memoranda of Rear Admiral Takagi] (Tokyo: Mainichi Shinbunsha, 1979), 351; Takagi Sokichi and Sanematsu Yuzuru, eds., *Kaigun taisho Yonai Mitsumasa oboegaki* [Memoranda of Admiral Yonai Mitsumasa] (Tokyo: Kojinsha, 1978), 153–54.

the atomic bomb.[72] After the war Kido stated that "a large-scale re-volt by the military could easily have been anticipated." Peace ad-vocates such as Kido and Yonai found in the bombs the "external pressure" needed to forestall a domestic commotion. Former prime minister Konoe dreaded a communist revolution if the war contin-ued and the decisive homeland battle took place.[73] To avoid such an eventuality, the peace party used the two sets of "twin shocks"—the atomic bomb and the Soviet entry, Hiroshima and Nagasaki—to bring about speedy acceptance of the Potsdam terms.

The Vacillating Emperor

It must be stressed again that the bomb did not "produce the de-cision" to end the war, nor did it set in motion the political process that led to Japan's surrender. Japan's informal, secret "peace ma-neuvers" had begun as early as March 1943, when Hirohito first in-timated to Kido his wish for peace.[74] But, in the absence of any clear directions from above, nothing came of the various uncoordinated, hesitant "peace feelers" through various foreign channels.[75] In fact, Hirohito himself was vacillating. During the battle of Leyte Gulf in October 1944 he hoped to "give a telling blow to the enemy so that we may find room for a compromise peace."[76] In mid-February 1945 he told Konoe that there still was a chance; he expected to negotiate peace terms after having given the enemy one final blow.[77] By early

72. Takagi, *Takagi kaigun shosho oboegaki*, 227.

73. Tominaga, ed., *Gendaishi shiryo, 39: Taiheiyo senso (5)*, 5:743, 745; Takagi, *Takagi kaigun shosho oboegaki*, 180, 198, 227.

74. *Kido nikki*, 1:28–29, 2:1020; *Kido kankei bunsho*, 46. The position of Hirohito is critically treated in the following works: Tanaka Nobumasa, *Dokyumento showa ten-no*, Vol. 5: *Haisen 2* [A documentary history of Showa emperor, Vol. 5: Defeat] (7 vols., Tokyo: Ryokufo Shuppan, 1988); Yamada Akira and Koketsu Atsushi, *Ososugita sei-dan: Showa tenno no senso shido to senso sekinin* [The sacred decision that came too late: Showa emperor's war guidance and war responsibility] (Tokyo: Showa Shuppan, 1991); and Yoshida Yutaka, *Showa tenno no shusenshi* [A history of Showa emperor's war termination] (Tokyo: Iwanami Shinsho, 1992). Bix's "Japan's Delayed Surren-der" relies heavily on these works.

75. Togo, *Jidan no ichimen*, 329–30; Togo, *Cause of Japan*, 299; Hayashi, ed., *Nihon shusenshi*, vol. 2, *passim*.

76. Terasaki Hidenari and Mariko Terasaki Miller, eds., *Showa tenno dokuhakuroku, Terasaki Hidenari goyogakari nikki* [Monologues of Showa emperor and the diaries of Terasaki Hidenari] (Tokyo: Bungei Shunju, 1991), 101–2.

77. Takagi, *Tahagi kaigun shosho oboegaki*, 227–28.

May, however, he had reversed himself and almost embarrassed Kido by urging a prompt peace: "The sooner the better," he said.[78]

Kido's diary entry of June 9, 1945, contains the first clear indication that Hirohito had decided to think seriously of peace.[79] Distressed by the debacle of the battle of Okinawa, the emperor took an unprecedented step on June 22 when he told the Supreme War Council, "I desire that *concrete plans* to end the war, unhampered by existing policy, be speedily studied and that efforts be made to implement them."[80] (my emphasis) This meant a significant turnabout, but the "Big Six" failed to reach an agreement because Anami, Umezu, and Toyoda insisted that Japan had not yet lost the war and pinned their last hope on a decisive homeland battle.[81] In the end it was the Hiroshima bomb that compelled them to face the reality of defeat.

Thus, the atomic bombing was crucial in accelerating the peace process. The impact of the bomb was such that it brought further urgency to the governmental machinery for achieving peace, enabling the prime minister to bring Hirohito directly into a position where his "sacred decision" for surrender could override the diehards. In the apt words of Robert Butow, the atomic bombing, followed by the Soviet entry, had created "that unusual atmosphere in which the heretofore static power of the emperor could be made active in such an extraordinary way as to work what was virtually a political miracle."[82]

Missed Opportunities

Some have argued that if the United States had only modified its "unconditional surrender" formula and explicitly guaranteed the continuation of the imperial institution, Japan would have surrendered earlier, before the use of the atomic bomb. This was the view of Acting Secretary of State Joseph C. Grew, who urged President

78. Ibid., 228–29; Hosokawa Morisada, *Joho tenno ni tassezu* [Information that never reached the emperor] (2 vols., Tokyo: Dokosha Isobe Shobo, 1953), 2:385.

79. *Kido nikki*, 2:1209–10; *Kido kankei bunsho*, 75–77; Gaimusho, ed., *Shusen shiroku*, 3:91–94.

80. *Kido nikki*, 2:1212–13.

81. Sakomizu, *Dai Nihon teikoku*, 28.

82. *Kido nikki: Tokyo saibanki*, 444; Butow, *Japan's Decision to Surrender*, 231.

Truman to include an announcement to this effect in the Potsdam Declaration. An early draft of the proclamation, submitted to Truman on July 2, contained an explicit assurance of "a constitutional monarchy under the present dynasty." However, this passage was deleted from the final Potsdam Declaration for fear of domestic backlash in the United States and also of strengthening the hands of the military diehards in Japan.[83]

After the war Grew maintained that, had his advice been followed, Japan would have surrendered without the use of atomic bombs, and Stimson agreed in his memoirs.[84] In time the Grew-Stimson view came to be firmly accepted by some American and Japanese historians. For example, Sherwin and Alperovitz argue that the decision to use the bomb "*delayed* the end of war." They contend that, because of the availability of the bomb, Washington delayed modification of the unconditional surrender formula.[85] However, as has been noted, Japan's military chiefs were intransigent about the "three additional conditions" even *after* the two bombs and the Soviet entry into the war. Most likely there was no missed opportunity for an earlier peace.

Another case for an alleged missed opportunity relates to Truman's "failure" to exploit Japan's bumbling efforts in July to seek Soviet mediation for favorable surrender terms. The United States had been eavesdropping on telegraphic exchanges between Foreign Minister Togo and Ambassador Sato Naotake in Moscow through intercepted cable messages. Alperovitz makes much of Togo's cable to Sato dated July 12, which conveyed Hirohito's message "that the war be concluded speedily."[86] In a similar vein, Nishijima Ariatsu contends that Truman, knowing of the Tokyo-Moscow exchanges, lost

---

83. Akira Iriye, *Power and Culture: The Japanese-American War, 1941–1945* (Cambridge: Harvard University Press, 1981), 253–54.

84. Joseph C. Grew, *Turbulent Era: A Diplomatic Record of Forty Years, 1904–1945* (2 vols., Boston: Houghton Mifflin, 1952), 2:1425–28; Stimson and Bundy, *On Active Service*, 628.

85. Gar Alperovitz and Robert L. Messer, "Marshall, Truman, and the Decision to Drop the Bomb," *International Security* 16 (1991/1992): 204–14; Alperovitz, *The Decision to Use the Atomic Bomb*, 634; Alperovitz, *Atomic Diplomacy* (1985 edition), 27–32 (my emphasis).

86. Alperovitz, *The Decision to Use the Atomic Bomb*, 165, 233–37, 248, 412, 519, 536. For Ambassador Sato's negative reaction to this telegram, see Sato Naotake, *Kaiko hachijunen* [Recollection of eighty years] (Tokyo: Jiji Tsushinsha, 1964), 490–91.

"a golden opportunity for a negotiated peace with Japan" and instead dropped the bombs.[87]

What the deciphered Japanese dispatches reveal, however, were indecision and contradiction in Tokyo; the Japanese government could never agree on surrender terms. The cable messages went round and round: Togo, under pressure from the military, repeated that Japan could never accept an unconditional surrender, while the more realistic Sato entreated for "specific" mediation terms and "a concrete plan for terminating the war." As was to be expected, the Soviet response was chilly: Solomon A. Lozovsky, the deputy foreign commissar, replied that the emperor's message "contained mere generalities and no concrete proposal." In the end the Soviet government flatly rejected the Japanese proposal to send the emperor's special emissary, Konoe Fumimaro, to Moscow on the ground that the Japanese proposal was too "opaque" regarding surrender conditions.[88] Through these efforts Japan merely wasted valuable time. There is thus very little likelihood of any missed opportunity here.

If any opportunity were missed, it may have been Japan's failure to accept the Potsdam Declaration of July 26. Togo at once noted from its wording ("The following are our terms . . .") that it actually amounted to a "conditional surrender." Although it said nothing about the emperor system, he interpreted the declaration as offering the basis of a negotiated peace. The upper echelons of the foreign ministry were agreed that the Potsdam terms be accepted at once.[89] However, the Japanese military found the Potsdam terms unacceptable because they contained the "three conditions": (1) Allied trial of Japanese war criminals; (2) demobilization and disarmament of Japanese forces by the Allies; and (3) an Allied military occupation of Japan. Japan's military chiefs had been watching with increasing fear the Allies' stern treatment of Nazi leaders and German war criminals. Likewise, the Potsdam terms demanded the eradication of Japanese "militarism" and the elimination of military leaders.[90]

Apprehensive about the military's opposition, Togo took pains to

87. Nishijima, Gembaku wa naze toka saretaka, 224–26.

88. Sato, Kaiko hachijunen, 481–97; Gaimusho, ed., Shusen shiroku, 3:136–204.

89. Gaimusho, ed., Shusen shiroku, 4:4–5, 13–14, 18; Togo Shigehiko, Sofu Togo Shigenori no shogai [The life of my grandfather Togo Shigenori] (Tokyo: Bungei Shunju, 1993), 373–75.

90. Gaimusho, ed., Shusen shiroku, 4:5, 13–17; Kurihara and Hatano, eds., Shusen kosaku, 2:334–37.

persuade the Supreme War Council and the cabinet on July 27 that nothing be done pending Moscow's reply to Tokyo's mediation proposal. Togo's wait-and-see policy notwithstanding, Prime Minister Suzuki, under pressure from the army and navy command, floundered and announced, to Togo's great dismay, that the Japanese government would "ignore" (*mokusatsu*) the Potsdam terms. (The unfortunate word has been variously translated as "withhold comments," "treat with silent contempt," "ignore with contempt," "unworthy of public notice," and even "reject.")[91] The consequences were swift and devastating: Japan's seeming rejection gave the United States the pretext for dropping the atom bomb.

The Bomb or Soviet Entry?

As to the relative weight of the atomic bombing compared with the Soviet entry in inducing Japan's surrender, there has been lively controversy among historians. While Robert Butow, Herbert Feis, and Barton Bernstein have tended to regard the bomb as the decisive factor in Japan's surrender, Gar Alperovitz and Robert L. Messer have tended to emphasize the Soviet entry.[92] Japanese historians generally regard the Soviet entry as having had "the greatest impact."[93] It is difficult to determine which factor was more important. Because the Soviet entry came on the heels of the Hiroshima bomb, it is hard to separate the impacts of the two events. The foregoing analysis, however, would suggest the primacy of the Hiroshima bomb; the Soviet entry, coming as it did after the bomb had already shaken Japan's ruling elite, served as a confirmation and coup de grace.

From a political and diplomatic viewpoint the Soviet entry was indeed a serious blow to Japan; it dashed the last hope of Soviet peace mediation. But it did not come as a total surprise, which the atomic

91. Gaimusho, ed., *Shusen shiroku*, 4:19–24.
92. For example, Alperovitz and Messer, "Marshall, Truman, and the Decision to Drop the Bomb," 204–6. Among American scholars, Paul Kecskemeti has persuasively argued that the Soviet entry was "the main factor that determined the *timing* of Japan's surrender" (*Strategic Surrender*, 198–99 [my emphasis]).
93. Rekishigaku Kenkyukai, ed., *Taiheiyo s ensoshi*, 5:364, 368–69; Arai Shin'ichi, *Gembaku toka e no michi*, 254–56, 266; Nishijima, *Gembaku wa naze toka saretaka*, 235, 237–38; Arai Shin'ichi, *Dainiji sekai taisen* [World War II] (Tokyo, 1973), 177.

bomb assuredly was. When he received the report of the Soviet declaration of war, Army Minister Anami was heard to remark, "The inevitable has come at last."[94] The army had been aware since the German surrender in May that the Soviets had been transferring powerful forces with offensive equipment to Siberia.

The truth of the matter is that the Soviet entry spelled the strategic bankruptcy of Japan. In late June and early July 1945 the members of the Supreme War Council agreed that Soviet entry into the war would "determine the fate of our Empire."[95] In a similar vein, Kawabe Torashiro, the deputy chief of the Army General Staff, had categorically stated at the imperial conference that "the absolute maintenance of peace in our relations with the Soviet Union is one of the fundamental conditions for continuing the war with the United States."[96] This notwithstanding, when Kawabe was faced with the reality of the Soviet entry, he wrote in his diary, "To save the honor of the Yamato race, there is no way but to keep on fighting. At this critical moment, I don't even want to consider peace or surrender."[97]

From the viewpoint of the shock effect, then, it may be argued that the bomb had greater impact on Japanese leaders than did the Soviet entry into the war. After all, the Soviet invasion of Manchuria gave them an *indirect* shock, whereas the use of the atomic bomb on their homeland gave them the *direct* threat of the atomic extinction of the Japanese people.[98]

The shock of the bomb was all the greater because it came as a "surprise attack." Kawabe later admitted that, although "we have long worried about the question of Soviet entry, a surprise attack with this new [atomic] weapon was beyond our wildest dreams." Oki Misao, the chief secretary of the House of Representatives, wrote in his diary, "There is nothing we can do about the appearance of the

94. Kurihara and Hatano, eds., *Shusen kosaku*, 2:360–61.

95. Sanbo Honbu, comp., *Haisen no kiroku*, 272, 276, 278; Kurihara and Hatano, eds., *Shusen kosaku*, 2:360–61; Boeicho Boei Kenshujo Senshi Shitsu, *Senshi sosho: Kantogun* [War history series: Kwantung Army] (Tokyo: Asagumo Shinbunsha), 3:329.

96. Sanbo Honbu, comp., *Haisen no kiroku*, 276; Miyazaki Shuichi, December 29, 1949, "Interrogations"; Kurihara and Hatano, eds., *Shusen kosaku*, 2:361.

97. Kawabe Torashiro, *Kawabe Torashiro kaikoroku* [Memoirs of Kawabe Torashiro] (Tokyo: Mainichi Shinbunsha, 1979), 154–56; Kawabe, August 23, 1948, "Statements"; Kurihara and Hatano, eds., *Shusen kosaku*, 2:342–43; *Oki nikki*, 334.

98. On this point, see Freedman and Dockrill, "Hiroshima: A Strategy of Shock," in Dockrill, ed., *From Pearl Harbor to Hiroshima*, 205, 207.

atomic bomb. That nullifies everything. All our efforts until now have come to naught."[99]

As noted, even the hitherto vacillating Suzuki said *before* the Soviet entry that he had made up his mind for surrender. In addition, we have Kido's postwar testimony: "I believe that with the atomic bomb alone we could have brought the war to an end. But the Soviet entry into the war made it that much easier."[100] Going a step further, Sakomizu Hisatsune, the chief cabinet secretary, later testified, "I am sure we could have ended the war in a similar way if the Russian declaration of the war had not taken place at all."[101] The foregoing would seem to suggest the relative importance of the bomb's shock.

The A-Bomb Saves the Army's "Face"

From the beginning the army tried to minimize the A-bomb's damage, and Army Minister Anami even denied that it was an atomic bomb. At the cabinet meeting on the morning of August 7, he asked, "Is it not a matter of common knowledge among Japanese physicians that it will take several more years before an atomic bomb can be developed?" Even the representatives of the Technology Board, whose task it was to mobilize the nation's scientific and technological resources, stated, "No matter how advanced American technology may be, it is quite impossible for the Americans to bring such an unstable weapon as an atomic device to Japan, across the Pacific."[102]

However, some army leaders were aware that an atomic bomb had been dropped. As noted before, Miyazaki, the head of the Operation Division, wrote in his diary on August 6, "it may be the so-called atomic bomb."[103] Deputy Chief Kawabe, one of the few army men familiar with Japanese atomic research, suspected that the weapon was an atomic bomb even before he learned of Truman's statement. He recalled having heard about the atomic bomb from Dr. Nishina

99. Kawabe, *Kawabe Torashira kaikoroku*, 155; *Oki nikki*, 334.

100. *Kido nikki: Tokyo saibanki*, 444.

101. Sakomizu, May 3, 1949, "Interrogations."

102. Sakomizu, *Dai Nippon teikoku*, 183; Ikëda Sumihisa, December 23, 1949, "Statements."

103. Miyazaki diary, August 6, 1945; Kurihara and Hatano, eds., *Shusen kosaku*, 2:343.

Yoshio, the leader of the Japanese A-bomb project, and could not help shuddering.[104]

It was hastily decided by the Imperial General Headquarters to dispatch to Hiroshima an investigative commission with Dr. Nishina as an expert member. On the evening of August 8, Nishina reported, "We regret to say that it certainly was an atomic bomb."[105] The full, official report did not reach the Imperial General Headquarters until August 10. The question then became whether or not to acknowledge the A-bomb publicly. The Cabinet Board of Information and the foreign ministry were for announcing the truth, but the military flatly opposed this idea for fear that such an announcement would shake the morale of the people. In the end, the government equivocated and announced that it was just a "new type of bomb"; only after the end of the war did the Japanese people learn the truth about the atomic bomb.[106]

Despite the "twin shocks" of the Hiroshima and Nagasaki bombs, the army men still insisted on a fight to the finish. In the end they accepted surrender partly because the atomic bomb paradoxically helped them save "face." There was a strong feeling among the army's leaders that Japan had been "overwhelmed by America's scientific prowess." On August 8 Miyazaki wrote, "Technically Japan seems about half a century behind" the United States.[107] Colonel Ogata Ken'ichi, the military aide-de-camp to the emperor, unburdened himself in his diary: "Our foe must be given credit for the great power of the atomic bomb and remarkable progress in science and technology. I admit I must admire their achievement."[108]

By saving the army men's "face," such attitudes toward America's scientific achievements smoothed their acceptance of surrender. At the cabinet meeting of August 9, Ishiguro Tadaatsu, the minister of agriculture and commerce, tried to persuade the military: "We have lost a scientific war. The people may be dissatisfied with the military

104. Kawabe, *Kawabe Torashira kaikoroku*, 154; Kawabe, August 23, 1948, "Statements"; Kurihara and Hatano, eds., *Shusen kosaku*, 2:342–43.

105. Arisue Seizo, *Shusen hishi: Arisue kikancho no shuki* [A secret history of the termination of the war: A memoir of Lieutenant General Arisue] (Tokyo: Fuyo Shobo, 1976), 26–33; Sakomizu, *Dai Nippon teikoku*, 183.

106. Gaimusho, ed., *Shusen shiroku*, 4:65–66.

107. Miyazaki diary, August 8, 1945.

108. Yomiuri, ed., *Showashi no tenno*, 4:310.

for the defeat. But if we say we lost a scientific war, the people will understand."[109]

After the war Kido stated, "If military leaders could convince themselves that they were defeated by the power of science but not because of lack of spiritual power or strategic errors, this could save their face to some extent."[110] In fact, some army men accepted the argument that "the Japanese military would never lose a war, but now that Japanese science has been beaten, we must end the war just as soon as possible." Along the same lines, Sakomizu, the chief cabinet secretary, recalled,

> The atomic bomb was a golden opportunity given by Heaven for Japan to end the war. There were those who said that the Japanese armed forces were not defeated. It was in science that Japan was defeated, so the military will not bring shame on themselves by surrendering.

He added that "in ending the war, the idea was to put the responsibility for defeat solely on the atomic bomb, not on the military. This was a clever pretext." From that viewpoint, the endeavor to end the war may be said to have been "a search for ways to save the military's face," although such a face-saving argument was not needed for the highest army officials, Anami and Umezu.[111]

As Sakomizu recollected, "It was commonly understood at that time that the invention of the atomic bomb spelled the end of the war. The power that possessed the atomic bomb will win the war."[112] In point of fact, the Japanese government and the military had embarked on research on the bomb. The wartime prime minister, Tojo Hikeki, took a personal interest in the Japanese bomb project, believing that "the atomic bomb would spell the difference between life and death in this war." It was the consensus among Japan's nuclear physicists, however, that no country would be able to develop an atomic bomb during the course of the war. Since government of-

109. Ikeda, *Nihon no magarikado,* 178; Yomiuri, ed., *Showashi no tenno,* 4:309–10.

110. *Kido nikki: Tokyo saibanki,* 443.

111. Sakomizu, *Shusen no shinso* [The truth about surrender] (Tokyo: privately printed, [1955]); Sakomizu Hisatsune, "Kofukuji no shinso" [The truth about surrender], *Jiyu kokumin* (February 1946): 60–61.

112. Sakomizu, *Shusen no shinso,* 36.

ficials believed this forecast, the Hiroshima bomb caught them completely off their guard.[113]

There is no doubt that the Japanese military would not have hesitated to use the atomic bomb in the unlikely event that Japan had developed one. In his diary, Colonel Ogata confided,

> Is there not somehow a way to invent a new weapon that would forestall the enemy? If we had such a weapon, it will be no problem to attack [and recapture] Iwo Jima, the Ryukyus, and the Marianas. . . . It would then be possible to annihilate the enemy's task force and attack the mainland of the United States, thus turning the tables and affording a golden opportunity to reverse the tide of war. Oh, what a pity![114]

Ogata was engaging in pure fantasy, but what underlies this diary entry is the stark military logic that did not question the legitimacy of using the atomic bomb as a winning weapon.

Conclusion

The above analysis has shown that in August 1945 Japan's peace party made the maximum political use of the atomic bomb to end the war. To them the bomb was "a gift from Heaven," "a golden opportunity," and "a psychological moment" to end the war; they saw the bomb as "assisting" their peace efforts and as a means for the military to save face. But such a utilitarian viewpoint, which regarded the atomic bomb merely as an expedient for inducing surrender, hardly prompted an awareness of the transformation wrought in the fabric of international society by the appearance of the nuclear weapon. Regarding the bomb as if it were a natural calamity also inhibited soul-searching reflection on the war that Japan had started and lost. An embodiment of scientific advances that went beyond their imagination, the super bomb protected Japan's ruling elite from squarely facing the agonies of their nation's unprecedented surrender.

113. Boeicho Boei Kenshujo Senshi Shitsu, *Senshi sosho: Hondo boku sakusen* [War history series: Air defense of the homeland] (Tokyo: Asagumo Shinbunsha, 1968), 632.
114. Yomiuri, ed., *Showashi no tenno*, 4:310.

On August 15, 1945, the day the emperor's rescript of surrender was broadcast, Morobuse Koshin, a liberal journalist of the old generation, lamented that all "responsibility" had been placed on two "unexpected events," the atomic bomb and the Soviet entry into the war. "Nothing is said about the government's ignorance, mistakes, and impotence."[115] The government's responsibility for the war and defeat was thus conveniently shelved.

Although most observers pondered the meaning of the atomic bomb in terms of Japan's surrender, Okura Kimmochi, the president of the Technological Research Mobilization Office, recorded on August 7 his thoughts on the bomb's impact for the next several decades to come:

> As far as I am concerned, I think it is better for our country to suffer a total defeat than to win a total victory in the present Greater East Asian War. During the past ten years the military domination of our country has been flagrant, and the reins of government have been totally controlled by the military. What would happen if Japan were to win the war in such a situation? Inevitably Japan would come under both internal and external attacks and the nation would go to pieces. On the other hand, in case of Japan's total defeat, the armed forces will be abolished, but the Japanese people will rise to the occasion during the next several decades to reform themselves into truly a splendid people. . . . I believe that the great humiliation [of the atomic bomb] is nothing but an admonition administered by Heaven to our country.[116]

Okura was already envisaging the future of a peaceful postwar Japan immediately after he learned about the Hiroshima bomb. However, his vision, which reminds one of Stimson's prospect for a "liberal" postwar Japan, was a minority view. On September 9 an *Asahi* correspondent reported that in America and England there was a rising distrust toward Japan: "Does Japan truly realize that it has been defeated?" Japanese statements, both at home and abroad, do not refer to Japan's war responsibility, attributing the cause of its defeat solely to the atomic bomb."[117] A year later, on August 15, 1946, Mark

115. Morobuse Koshin, *Senso shisho* [Private wartime journal] (Tokyo: Chuo Koronsha, 1990), 330.

116. Naisei Kenkyukai and Nihon Kindai Shiryo Kenkyukai, eds., *Okura Kimmochi nikki*, 4:319.

117. Hayashi, ed., *Nihon shusenshi*, 3:195.

Gayn, an American newsman and eyewitness reporter, shrewdly observed in his diary:

> In vain, on this historic day for Japan, I looked for soul-searching, for
> penitence, for a sign that the lessons of defeat had been taken to heart.
> The Premier has issued a statement filled with generalities. The press
> has contented itself with pious phrases. . . . This would have been a
> good day for the Japanese press to begin telling the people the real and
> complete story of the war and defeat.[118]

Today, fifty-three years after Hiroshima and Nagasaki, the question
of Japan's "war responsibility" still remains with the nation.[119]

Perhaps no account of Japan's surrender decision is complete
without counterfactuals, however risky they may be. This essay has
shown that conventional bombing by B-29s alone would not have
driven Hirohito to say, "we must bow to the inevitable and surrender as speedily as possible." The crucial actor here was the Japanese
military, and only the shock of the bombs followed by the Soviet entry could have thrown them off balance and led to surrender—and
this narrowly.

We must then ask this question: Without the use of the atomic
bomb, but *with Soviet entry* and with continued strategic bombing
and naval blockade, would Japan have surrendered before November 1—the day scheduled for the U.S. invasion of Kyushu?

Available Japanese data do not provide a conclusive answer.[120] In
June 1945 Japanese leaders agreed that food shortages would become critical in the autumn and toward the onset of the cold season;
the country had suffered a "disastrous" failure of its rice crop.[121] On
the other hand, we must consider that fanaticism was not restricted
to the military; the men and women in the street were thoroughly indoctrinated. Women practiced how to face American tanks with
bamboo spears. Perhaps civilian morale had not deteriorated as

118. Mark Gayn, *Japan Diary* (Rutland, Vt.: Tuttle, 1981), 269–71.
119. Ian Buruma, *Wages of Guilt: Memories of War in Germany and Japan* (New York:
Farrar, Straus, and Giroux, 1994). For the changing memory and imagery of the atomic bomb over the past fifty years, see Asada, "The Mushroom Cloud and National
Psyches."
120. Record of the imperial conference of June 8, 1945, in Sanbo Honbu, comp.,
Haisen no kiroku, 256–77; *Kido nikki*, 2:1208–9.
121. Gaimusho, ed., *Shusen shiroku*, 3:135, 208–9; 4:120.

much as the ruling elite had feared. In all probability Japan could not have endured the winter of 1945–1946, but there was a possibility that Japan would not have surrendered before November 1. Most assuredly, Japanese sources do not support the *ex post facto* contention of the U.S. Strategic Bombing Survey (1946) that "in all probability" Japan would have surrendered before November 1 "even if the atomic bombs had not been dropped, even if Russia had not entered the war, and even if no invasion had been planned or contemplated."[122]

To repulse the landing of American forces, the Sixteenth Area Army in Kyushu had been built up to nine hundred thousand soldiers. They were to give a crushing blow to the first wave of an American invasion.[123] In the process, they were to die glorious deaths on the beaches and in the interior—in kamikaze planes as human rockets, in midget submarines as human torpedoes, and in suicide charges by ground units. On the American side, the Army Chief of Staff, General George C. Marshall, began to fear such massive Japanese attacks, causing huge American casualties, and came to consider the tactical use of atomic bombs (six to nine) to assist and support the invading American forces.[124] It may be said that Japan's surrender, coming as it did in August, forestalled sacrifices on both sides far surpassing those at Hiroshima and Nagasaki.

This essay suggests that, given the intransigence of the Japanese military, there were few "missed opportunities" for earlier peace and that the alternatives available to President Truman in the summer of 1945 were limited. In the end, Japan needed "external pressure" in the form of the atomic bombs for its government to decide to surrender. Whether or not the atomic bombing of Hiroshima and Nagasaki was *morally justified* is the question that has been debated ever

122. Cited in Feis, *The Atomic Bomb and the End of World War II*, 191. For a detailed critique, see Bernstein, "Compelling Japan's Surrender," 113–48. See also Robert P. Newman, "Ending the War with Japan: Paul Nitze's 'Early Surrender' Counterfactual," *Pacific Historical Review* 64 (1995): 167–94.

123. Edward J. Drea, *MacArthur's ULTRA: Codebreaking and the War against Japan, 1942–1945* (Lawrence: University Press of Kansas, 1992), 216–25; John Ray Skates, *The Invasion of Japan: Alternative to the Bomb* (Columbia: University of South Carolina Press, 1994).

124. See Barton J. Bernstein, "Eclipsed by Hiroshima and Nagasaki: Early Thinking about Tactical Nuclear Weapons," *International Security* 15, no. 4 (Spring 1991): 149–73; Marc Gallicchio, "After Nagasaki: General Marshall's Plan for Tactical Nuclear Weapons in Japan" *Prologue* 23, no. 4 (Winter 1991): 396–404.

since in Japan and the United States—in fact, the world over—but this is a question that is beyond the scope of this essay and better discussed in the ethical context of just and unjust wars, moral and immoral wars.[125]

125. Michael Walzer, *Just and Unjust Wars: A Moral Argument with Historical Illustrations* (New York: Basic Books, 1977), states, "In the summer of 1945, the victorious Americans owed the Japanese people an experiment in negotiations. To use the atomic bomb . . . without even attempting such an experiment, was a double crime" (263–68). Would such an "experiment" have met conditions demanded by the Japanese military? Martin Sherwin's "Hiroshima at Fifty" offers yet another scenario: Stimson could have declared that "our nation is too moral" to use the atomic weapon and dissuaded President Truman from using it.

The moral ambiguities inherent in the use of the atomic bomb are more judiciously treated by Melvyn P. Leffler, "Truman's Decision to Drop the Atomic Bomb," *IHJ Bulletin* 15 (1995): 1–7. The psychological—and moral—implications of the bomb are discussed at length in Lifton and Mitchell, *Hiroshima in America.*

EDWARD J. DREA

Intelligence Forecasting for the Invasion of Japan
Previews of Hell

O LYMPIC WAS A FITTING CODE NAME for the American invasion of the land of the gods. A massive amphibious assault by nine divisions (six stormed the Normandy beaches) would seize three widely separate landing areas on the southernmost Japanese main island of Kyushu. A tenth would assault offshore islands. More than four hundred thousand American troops were slated for the assault forces.[1] By the spring of 1945 preparations for the invasion were under way. Simultaneously, the Japanese were struggling around the clock to turn Kyushu's beaches into massive killing grounds. The showdown was set for November 1, 1945.

Intelligence forecasts predicted the landing forces would encounter at most ten Japanese divisions throughout all of Kyushu. Planners confidently expected American attackers to outnumber Japanese defenders two or three to one in the southern half of the island. But from early spring to midsummer 1945 the forecast changed dramatically. Intelligence, obtained mainly from reading Japanese military and naval codes, uncovered a Japanese buildup on Kyushu of mind-boggling proportions. By August more than ten Japanese divisions defended southern Kyushu alone. Standard tactics would include widespread suicide attacks on the invasion fleet with everything from kamikazes to human-guided torpedoes.

Countless decrypted messages from the high command in Tokyo underlined Japanese determination to fight to the death against the invaders. Japan's planned defense of Kyushu, unwittingly told to the Allies by the Japanese military in its own words, forecast beach-

1. General Headquarters, U.S. Army Forces, Pacific, "DOWNFALL" Strategic Plan, Annex 3d (I) (C) "Estimate of Troop Lift Requirements," May 28, 1945.

heads running red with American blood. Concern about estimated U.S. losses for the operation runs through American decision makers' thinking. As more and more Japanese troops crowded into Kyushu, there were even suggestions to switch the landing elsewhere in the Japanese home islands. Finally the intelligence forecasts caused serious consideration about the tactical use of atomic bombs to clear Japanese defenders from the landing beaches.

Yet it all began innocently enough. In early April the Joint Chiefs of Staff instructed General Douglas MacArthur to plan and prepare for the invasion of Japan. The same directive named MacArthur commander in chief of U.S. Army forces in the Pacific in addition to commander in chief of the Southwest Pacific area. He controlled almost all American army and air force units and resources in the Pacific. In late May the Joint Chiefs set the date for the invasion, code-named OLYMPIC, for November 1, 1945.

On April 23 Major General Charles A. Willoughby, MacArthur's intelligence chief, submitted his initial estimate of the enemy defenses on Kyushu.[2] Information gleaned from reading Japanese military codes formed the basis of his forecast. Such intelligence was code-named ULTRA. Throughout April ULTRA revealed Japanese anxiety about an imminent invasion of the home islands. Navy messages ordered mining of several Kyushu bays "as soon as possible" and told of the evacuation of civilians from coastal areas, clearly counterinvasion measures.[3] The Japanese vice chief of staff predicted an American invasion of Kyushu sometime after the middle of the year.[4] This apprehension accounted for the urgency of Chief of Army General Staff Umezu's directive to all army commands to discover the time, place, and scale of the Allied invasion of Japan. Japanese overseas commands duly alerted subordinate units to gather intelligence on an Allied invasion.[5]

2. General Headquarters, U.S. Army Forces, Pacific, Military Intelligence Section, G-2, "G-2 Estimate of the Enemy Situation with Respect to an Operation against Southern Kyushu in November 1945," April 25, 1945, RG 4, USAFPAC, Intelligence, General, MacArthur Memorial Bureau of Archives, Norfolk, Va. (hereafter cited as MMBA).

3. War Department, Military Intelligence Service, "'MAGIC' Summary, Far East supplement," April 9, 1945, SRS series, RG 457, National Archives and Records Administration, Washington D.C. (hereafter cited as NARA-DC).

4. War Department, Military Intelligence Service, "'MAGIC,'" April 15.

5. General Headquarters, Southwest Pacific Area, Military Intelligence Section, "Special Intelligence Bulletin," April 27/28, 1945, SRH-203, RG 457, NARA-DC.

ULTRA also identified two combat divisions on Kyushu, the Fifty-seventh in the north and the Eighty-sixth in the south. The total number of troops on the island was estimated at about 230,000 and was expected to increase. Messages from army harbormasters at Pusan were reporting another thirty thousand to sixty thousand Japanese troops embarking from Korean ports and heading for Kyushu.[6] Because Willoughby expected at least six and at most ten combat divisions defending the island, these reinforcements were not cause for alarm. Besides, the Japanese could not know the exact landing beaches, so they would have to protect Kyushu's entire coastline. That meant dispersing their combat divisions equally between northern and southern Kyushu. The Americans would still enjoy overwhelming superiority on the beachheads.

Willoughby predicted three enemy combat divisions, maybe one hundred thousand troops, would be deployed in southern Kyushu by D-day. About two thousand or twenty-five hundred Japanese aircraft would be ready to strike an approaching fleet. Although half the airplanes might be obsolete or trainers, they were still a serious threat, especially if used in kamikaze fashion. The remnants of the once-formidable imperial battle fleet were not considered a significant danger.[7]

Throughout May ULTRA continued to report on the steady, but unspectacular, reinforcement of Kyushu. Japan's Twenty-fifth Division had arrived as predicted from Manchuria and was settling into central Kyushu.[8] An amphibious brigade had been redeployed from the Kurile Islands to southernmost Kyushu.[9] And an unidentified but important headquarters began broadcasting messages from Takarabe to major army command posts throughout Japan.[10] By month's end there were three divisions definitely identified on Kyushu with another three to five either present or expected. The Japanese were making feverish efforts to reinforce Kyushu. Yet the numbers fell within Willoughby's tolerance—the forecasted eight to ten divisions.

The Takarabe headquarters' mystery was solved in June by un-

6. War Department, Military Intelligence Service, "'MAGIC,'" April 13.
7. "G-2 Estimate," April 25, 1945.
8. War Department, Military Intelligence Service, "'MAGIC,'" May 25.
9. War Department, Military Intelligence Service, "'MAGIC,'" May 29.
10. War Department, Military Intelligence Service, "'MAGIC,'" May 16.

veiling the Fifty-seventh Army in south Kyushu. Shortly afterward the Fifty-sixth Army was identified in the north half of the island.[11] Two armies fit Willoughby's original model of Japanese forces on Kyushu, divided between the northern and southern commands. An estimated 280,000 Japanese soldiers were now in Kyushu.[12] Coded addresses on intercepted messages, though, hinted at another major, as yet unidentified, headquarters somewhere in southern Kyushu.[13] Radio messages broadcast from the same region betrayed the Seventy-seventh Division's move from northern Japan to Kyushu.[14] It became the fourth division definitely located on the island.

Decryptions of Japanese naval and air force messages conjured up still fresh and painful memories of mass suicide attacks off the Philippines and Okinawa. The commanding officer of the Twelfth Naval Flotilla based in Kyushu intended to use his nine hundred planes of all types as kamikazes against an Allied landing.[15] Naval air depots throughout Japan were converting more than four hundred biplane trainers into kamikazes, and staging bases were being readied to repel any invasion.[16] Sasebo Naval Base workers on double shifts were building suicide boats, and the command was deploying *kaiten*, the naval version of a piloted torpedo, to bases on the south Kyushu coasts.[17] Suicide weapons en masse would greet any invaders. By mid-June decrypted messages told of Japanese's concern about an Allied landing in southern Kyushu.[18] The Japanese high command did not know the invasion was still months away, but they knew the Allies were coming. They suspected the beaches of Kyushu were the most likely landing areas and were doing everything possible to convert these beachheads into graveyards for American troops.

Japanese army air force communications showed the enemy concentrating all his available aircraft at fields stretching from Shanghai through Korea to Honshu. From bases inside this arc, Japanese air-

11. War Department, Military Intelligence Service, "'MAGIC,'" June 1/7.
12. War Department, Military Intelligence Service, "'MAGIC,'" June 7.
13. General Headquarters, "Special Intelligence Bulletin," June 10/11.
14. General Headquarters, "Special Intelligence Bulletin," June 13/14.
15. General Headquarters, "Special Intelligence Bulletin," June 11/12; and War Department, Military Intelligence Service, "'MAGIC,'" June 11.
16. General Headquarters, "Special Intelligence Bulletin," June 9/10, 14/15.
17. War Department, Military Intelligence Service, "'MAGIC,'" June 17.
18. General Headquarters, "Special Intelligence Bulletin," June 14/15.

craft were well within range of Kyushu's beaches, especially for their one-way missions.[19] Army construction battalions were busy working on underground aircraft hangers and concealing dispersal airfields throughout Kyushu.[20] With fourteen hundred suicide training planes in the homeland augmented by four thousand other aircraft of varying quality, the prospect loomed of a bitter and protracted air war over the home islands for the next several months. Allied air attacks would destroy hundreds of Japanese planes before the scheduled invasion. Even so, MacArthur's latest intelligence estimates forecast serious damage to invasion shipping from enemy air attacks. ULTRA was telling two stories. One was a straightforward rendition of Tokyo's hurried efforts to transform Kyushu into a mighty bastion. The other was even more frightening. Nowhere in the enemy's mindset could ULTRA detect pessimism or defeatism. Instead Japan's military leaders were determined to go down fighting and to take as many Americans with them as possible.

Marshall's preview of invasion beaches laced with mines, barbed wire, pillboxes, and thousands of Japanese defenders stiffened by massive numbers of kamikazes troubled him. Before discussing OLYMPIC with President Truman and the other Joint Chiefs on June 18, he cabled MacArthur. What was MacArthur's estimate of American casualties for OLYMPIC? The response was prompt: 105,500 battle casualties for the first ninety days of fighting plus 12,600 more nonbattle losses.[21] Such unacceptably high estimates shocked Marshall. How long could a democracy be keyed up to fight a foreign war, especially with large numbers of dead and wounded?[22] He told MacArthur of his concern and added, "[The] President is very much concerned as to the number of casualties we will receive in OLYMPIC operation." MacArthur now understood what Washington wanted. He reassured Marshall. The earlier estimate it turned out was "purely academic and routine," and he had not even seen it. This was disingenuous. Nothing left MacArthur's headquarters, let alone a message to the chief of staff, without review and approval.

19. General Headquarters, "Special Intelligence Bulletin," June 15/16.
20. General Headquarters, "Special Intelligence Bulletin," June 6/7, 8/9.
21. Marshall to MacArthur, War Department (WD) 1050, June 16, 1945; and MacArthur to Marshall, WD 1052, June 17, 1945; RG 4, USAFPAC, folder 4 (WD 1001–1095) April 29/August 2, 1945, MMBA.
22. Forrest C. Pogue, *George C. Marshall: Statesman 1945–1959* (New York: Viking, 1987), 6.

Personally, MacArthur continued, he doubted losses would be that high. Besides, Soviet intervention "sufficiently ahead of our target date" would prevent Japanese troops on the Asian mainland from reinforcing the home islands. OLYMPIC was a solid plan. No change was needed.

Within minutes of reading MacArthur's cable, Marshall went to see the president and other joint chiefs. Afterward he cabled MacArthur. "Your message," Marshall wrote, "arrived with 30 minutes to spare and had determining influence in obtaining formal presidential approval for OLYMPIC."[23] It was not mere flattery. During the momentous meeting, Marshall had quoted verbatim an entire section of MacArthur's estimate supporting an invasion.[24]

American casualties remained a concern, but the invasion was on. Within weeks casualties became an obsession because of the changing intelligence picture of Japanese defenses on Kyushu. The forecast turned ominous for two reasons. First, Japanese army and navy codebooks captured on Luzon and Okinawa enabled Allied cryptanalysts to read the enemy's most important codes.[25] Second, newly mobilized Japanese divisions were organizing on Kyushu. Every day their radio operators tapped out a steady flow of messages to coordinate redeployments, to issue orders, and to administer all the other things involved in preparing a new unit for operations. In other words, the appearance in radio communications of the new divisions coincided with the Allies' newfound ability to decipher the Japanese army's most secret messages. The result was startling.

As far as Marshall knew when he met the president, all the Japanese reinforcements earmarked for Kyushu were already there. That meant a maximum of eight enemy divisions would defend Kyushu. ULTRA had alerted the chief of staff about additional divisions being raised in Japan. Still, American air and naval attacks, he told Truman, made further reinforcement of Kyushu suicidal. The Japanese would lose so many men and so much equipment that the attempt

23. Marshall to MacArthur, WD 1056, June 19, 1945; MacArthur to Marshall, WD 1057, June 19, 1945; Marshall to MacArthur, WD 1060, June 19, 1945, MMBA.

24. U.S. Department of State, *Foreign Relations of the United States: The Conference of Berlin (The Potsdam Conference), 1945* (Washington D.C.: U.S. Government Printing Office, 1960), 1:906.

25. Memorandum, Lieutenant Colonel A. W. Sanford, general staff, to commander in chief, Australian Military Forces (Blamey), June 30, 1945, in SRH-219, 64, RG 457, NARA-DC.

was just not worth it. Throughout July ULTRA made mockery of Marshall's estimate.

The Japanese navy was busy converting two thousand biplane trainers, fighters, and floatplanes into kamikazes. Pilots were practicing for night attacks. Biplanes might sound ridiculous, but American radar could not detect the flimsy wood-and-fabric machines. By striking in darkness, determined suicide pilots might gain an edge. As if to underline their deadlines, suicide biplanes sank one U.S. destroyer and damaged another in a moonlight attack in late July.[26] Staging bases on Kyushu were being assigned for kamikaze units. ULTRA located new, secret airfields being built, underground storage dumps being constructed, and aircraft being camouflaged and dispersed.[27] There was so much military construction under way in Kyushu that there were not enough airfield construction battalions to go around,[28] and appeals for thousands more men to fill labor battalions were sent as far away as central China.[29]

One reason for the labor shortage was so many men had been mobilized to form new divisions. During 1945, Japanese strength in the homeland doubled from 980,000 on January 1 to 1,865,000 on July 10.[30] Allied intercept operators listened to the reverberations of the mass mobilization in southern Japan. Early in July two more divisions, the 206th and the 212th, were identified in Kyushu.[31] A week later the 154th Division was positively located on the south-central coast. Within a few days ULTRA exposed two tank regiments and three independent mixed brigades there. An estimated 380,000 Japanese troops now garrisoned Kyushu.[32] Shortly afterward, Allied eavesdroppers overheard the 156th Division broadcasting orders to its subordinate regiments,[33] and another division, the 146th, was pinpointed in southernmost Kyushu along with three tank brigades.[34] ULTRA now confirmed nine divisions already on the is-

26. War Department, Military Intelligence Service, "'MAGIC,'" August 3.

27. General Headquarters, "Special Intelligence Bulletin," July 3/4.

28. General Headquarters, "Special Intelligence Bulletin," July 10/11.

29. General Headquarters, "Special Intelligence Bulletin," August 1/2.

30. General Headquarters, "Special Intelligence Bulletin," July 15/16.

31. General Headquaarters, "Special Intelligence Bulletin," July 8/9, and War Department, Military Intelligence Service," "'MAGIC,'" July 13.

32. War Department, Military Intelligence Service, "'MAGIC,'" July 20.

33. General Headquarters, "Special Intelligence Bulletin," July 15/16, 23/24.

34. General Headquarters, "Special Intelligence Bulletin," July 28/29, 25/26.

land. The estimate of Japanese troops by July 21 ballooned to 455,000.[35]

But the most important ULTRA find was a newly organized Fortieth Army headquarters in southwestern Kyushu. No longer was the Japanese high command regarding northern and southern Kyushu as equally liable for invasion. Two army headquarters in the south meant the Japanese had decided the invaders would hit the southern beaches. That was where they were concentrating their divisions. The Allies had counted on Japanese defenders being dispersed throughout Kyushu. That was no longer true. The Kyushu reinforcements were swarming into the very areas designated for the OLYMPIC landings. Estimates of Japanese troops swelled to 525,000 by the end of July.[36]

What the high command expected from its soldiers was also chillingly explicit. In early July the general staff completely reversed Japanese defensive doctrine. ULTRA provided, in Tokyo's own words, a preview of Kyushu's defense. According to Imperial Headquarters' guidance, air and sea forces had to annihilate the invaders at sea. If the Allies were bold enough to risk a landing on Japan proper, a full-scale offensive would be launched. Fighting at the water's edge was a dramatic reversal of defensive doctrine, a return to the abandoned doctrine of 1943–1944. Japanese ground forces would expose enemy weaknesses at the water's edge, then destroy him on the coast. If the enemy managed to establish a lodgment, mobile troops would counterattack and smash it by repeated attacks. Coastal troops would cover the concentration of the mobile units into attack assembly areas. No matter what tactically important points the Allies took, Japanese divisions deployed along the coast could not retreat. Continual counterattacks were the order of the day, and Japanese soldiers could not depend on passive defensive tactics. From the high command to the lowest private soldier, everyone would act boldly, aggressively, and decisively.[37] Either Japanese soldiers would die in their pillboxes and foxholes dotting Kyushu's beaches, or they would die attacking the invaders. But they were expected to die defending their sacred homeland.

35. War Department, Military Intelligence Service, "'MAGIC,'" July 21.
36. War Department, Military Intelligence Service, "'MAGIC,'" July 30.
37. General Headquarters, "Special Intelligence Bulletin," July 14/15, and War Department, Military Intelligence Service, "'MAGIC,'" July 12.

The number one target on the beaches during an invasion was enemy tanks. Armor was the backbone of Allied ground units, and without it they would falter. Japanese units would build antitank defenses in depth from the water's edge inland. Engineers would demolish all coastal roads forcing tanks into rugged terrain where they would be vulnerable to attack by small suicide units. Tokyo ordered all officers and men, regardless of branch or service, to carry out such suicide attacks.[38]

Navy pilots, too, would join the fighting at the water's edge. For them, success depended on crashing into Allied attack and landing craft while the transports were still loaded with troops. The float-plane kamikaze pilots, previously identified by ULTRA, were known to be practicing shoreline attacks. Their mission was to smash into landing craft headed for shore.[39] Of the 2,700 navy suicide training planes, 773 were already deployed somewhere in Kyushu.[40] Naval authorities claimed air and sea kamikazes could sink 30 to 40 percent of the invading convoy—more if the invasion came after August, because there would be more ships and thus more targets. Army staff officers were more conservative, but still expected 10 or 20 percent losses.[41]

The Japanese high command made the purpose of these suicidal measures brutally explicit. ULTRA told of the Japanese military's intention to inflict severe losses on the Allies. In so doing they expected to prolong the war and thereby convince the Allies of the futility of further bloody fighting.[42] These stark military objectives paralleled efforts by elites at the imperial court and the foreign ministry to obtain a negotiated peace for Japan.

ULTRA even let the Allies peer over their enemies' shoulders as Japanese commanders war-gamed the defense of the homeland. These practice maneuvers correctly predicted an Allied landing in

38. General Headquarters, "Special Intelligence Bulletin," July 29/30.
39. General Headquarters, "Special Intelligence Bulletin," July 15/16.
40. General Headquarters, "Special Intelligence Bulletin," July 17/18.
41. Supreme Commander for the Allied Powers, *Japanese Operations in the Southwest Pacific Area*, vol. 2, *Reports of General MacArthur* (Washington, D.C.: U.S. Government Printing Office, 1966), pt. 2, 652 and 654. Boeicho Boei Kenshujo senshishitsu, *Senshi sosho*, vol. 51, *Hondo kessen jumbi*, pt. 1, *Kyushu no boei* [Official military history, vol. 51. Preparations for the decisive battle of the homeland: Defense of Kyushu, pt. 1] (Tokyo: Asagumo shimbunsha, 1972), 500.
42. War Department, Military Intelligence Service, "'MAGIC,'" June 29.

southern Kyushu, D-day was forecast for August 20. By D plus 15 the tabletop maneuvers had ten U.S. divisions ashore in southern Kyushu, but heavy fighting on the beaches still contained the invaders' amphibious lodgment. In this scenario, two American airborne divisions had dropped behind Japanese lines, but mobile forces had quickly counterattacked to check them.[43] From these June map maneuvers, Tokyo concluded a third of the assault troops could be destroyed at sea and another 15 to 20 percent of the first assault wave killed by artillery or beach defenses.[44]

As ULTRA continued to uncover more and more Japanese divisions in southern Kyushu, the forecast for the invasion steadily worsened. Six more Japanese divisions appeared in Kyushu during June and July, and even more reinforcements were on the way. The odds were against the invaders, because the defenders would soon equal or outnumber the attackers on the beaches. This was, as Willoughby candidly put it, "hardly a recipe for success."[45] On August 1, because of the accelerated buildup of Japanese reinforcements on the island of Kyushu, General Headquarters ordered an immediate air campaign to destroy bridges, railroads, barges, ports, and anything moving on Kyushu's roads.[46] It came too late to stop, or even slow down, the movement of troops.

During the first week of August, ULTRA identified four new divisions in Kyushu. The 312th Division had deployed there from central Japan. Washington now credited 545,000 Japanese soldiers on Kyushu.[47] ULTRA confirmed two other divisions, the 216th and the 303rd, four days later.[48] In between a 351st Division was mentioned in messages passed from Imperial Headquarters to the Sixteenth

43. War Department, Military Intelligence Service, "'MAGIC,'" July 26; and General Headquarters, "Special Intelligence Bulletin," August 3/4.

44. David Westheimer, *Downfall: The Top-Secret Plan to Invade Japan* [originally published as *Lighter Than a Feather*] (New York: Bantam, 1972), 447. Senshi kenkyu gurupu, "Hondo kessen moshi okonawarereba" [What if the decisive battle of the homeland had occurred?] *Rekishi to jimbutsu* 1 (August 1977): 344.

45. General Headquarters, "Special Intelligence Bulletin," July 29.

46. General Headquarters, U.S. Army Forces, Pacific, G-2 (Willoughby) to G-3 (Sutherland), "SUBJECT: Kyushu Reinforcement," July 28, 1945; and Sutherland to commanding general Far East Air Forces, "SUBJECT: Destruction of Enemy Lines of Communication and Enemy Forces in Kyushu," August 1, 1945, S. J. Chamberlain Papers, U.S. Army Military History Institute, Carlisle Barracks, Pa.

47. War Department, Military Intelligence Service, "'MAGIC,'" August 2.

48. War Department, Military Intelligence Service, "'MAGIC,'" August 7.

Area Army in charge of the overall defense of Kyushu.[49] By now ULTRA had divulged thirteen of the fourteen Japanese divisions defending Kyushu. Besides the infantry divisions, the Fourth Artillery Command appeared in southwestern Kyushu to complement the First Artillery Command located on the southeastern half of the island.[50] As artillery coordination centers, they controlled at least six medium artillery regiments as well as two heavy artillery battalions.[51] Rocket gun units assigned to infantry regiments in the newly organized infantry divisions increased their firepower, making them seem quite formidable.[52] Washington's estimate of Japanese troops on the island jumped to 560,000.

These numbers were far beyond the original estimates used to plan the invasion. More troubling than the sheer number of divisions was their steady attraction to southernmost Kyushu. It was as though the beaches selected for the OLYMPIC landings were magnets pulling the Japanese to them. Following electronic footprints left by routine radio transmissions from mobile headquarters, Allied intelligence experts tracked the Eighty-sixth Division from central Kyushu to Ariake Bay, where Eleventh Corps would land. The 146th and 206th divisions had moved to the beaches of the southwest coast where Fifth Amphibious Corps would invade. As mobile reserves, the Seventy-seventh Division would have to contend with rugged terrain but might move against either landing area. In any case, it sat perched on Kagoshima City, the Fifth Amphibious Corps' objective. And the 212th was readying to move farther south into the First Corps landing zone.[53] This buildup, stacking enemy troops on the very landing beaches, the accompanying tactics, and the overall Japanese objective of inflicting as many Allied casualties as possible were Marshall's preview of hell. A professional soldier could easily visualize the bloody carnage along the beachheads. The assault troops needed every weapon America possessed to get them across the beaches and inland with the fewest possible losses. By now these weapons included the atomic bomb.

49. General Headquarters, "Special Intelligence Bulletin," August 5/6.
50. General Headquarters, "Special Intelligence Bulletin," August 4/5.
51. General Headquarters, "Special Intelligence Bulletin," July 6/7.
52. General Headquarters, "Special Intelligence Bulletin," August 5/6.
53. War Department, Military Intelligence Service, "'MAGIC,'" August 4, and General Headquarters, "Special Intelligence Bulletin," August 9/10.

Sometime earlier Marshall had asked Major General Leslie Groves, director of America's atomic bomb program, about using atomic bombs as tactical weapons. On July 30 Groves's written report of the bomb's tactical possibilities reached Marshall. The bomb blast alone could wipe out enemy resistance over an area two thousand feet in diameter, paralyze it seriously over a mile in diameter, and hinder it seriously over an area of five miles in diameter. The blast effect would kill soldiers in slit trenches within eight hundred feet of the explosion, but troops sheltering in deep caves a mile or so from ground zero would survive to fight. Eleven or twelve bombs might be ready by the invasion date.[54] In the meantime the bomb would be used as a strategic weapon against Japan's cities. Many thought the evidence of its awesome destructiveness would be enough to force Japan's surrender.

The first atomic bomb exploded on Hiroshima but without the results Marshall expected; it did not shock Japan's leaders into surrender. Code breakers read dispassionate eyewitness Japanese military assessments from Hiroshima downplaying the enormous destruction. One vivid ULTRA description of one hundred thousand casualties actually seems to have affected Truman more than it did Japan's warlords. While they looked for countermeasures for atomic bombs, he secretly ordered no more bombs to be used without his express approval.[55] Marshall saw Hiroshima against a larger backdrop of strategic bombing. According to a deciphered message, an earlier air raid had killed one hundred thousand Japanese people in the capital of Tokyo in a single night, but seemingly had no effect whatsoever on Japanese determination to fight on. Even worse destruction to Hiroshima yielded no surrender. Japan seemed determined to fight. An invasion was still likely.[56] Indeed, ULTRA had located three more Japanese divisions on Kyushu the day the Hi-

54. Barton Bernstein, "Eclipsed by Hiroshima and Nagasaki: Early Thinking about Tactical Nuclear Weapons," *International Security* 15, no. 4 (Spring 1991): 161.

55. Ibid., 164.

56. Larry I. Bland, ed., *George C. Marshall: Interviews and Reminiscences for Forrest C. Pogue* (Lexington, Va.: George C. Marshall Research Foundation, 1991), 423. The figure of one hundred thousand killed in the Tokyo bombing was known to the Allies via a decrypted message by early April. This ULTRA was likely the source for Marshall's figure. See Joint Intelligence Center Pacific Ocean Area, "Summary of ULTRA Traffic," April 7, 1945, SRMD-007, RG 457, NARA-DC.

roshima bomb was dropped. The Sixteenth Area Army now had six hundred thousand troops on Kyushu and expected even more.

The quality of the Japanese divisions defending Kyushu varied enormously. There were first-class outfits, such as the Twenty-fifth and Fifty-seventh Divisions. Many of the newer ones though were desperately short of equipment, even uniforms. Training often consisted of slogans, because weapons were lacking. Certainly soldiers in line units knew little about higher headquarters' grand operational plans. One young lieutenant had the vague notion that three days after the enemy landing his company would be thrown against the beachhead. It would be, their division commander assured them, a most splendid death.[57] A conscript in another newly raised formation saw a vicious cycle of corruption undermining discipline, as soldiers openly traded gasoline for food on the black market. When the division commander arrived to inspect his brand new unit, his staff car, a luxury in itself, was crammed full of fresh meat, poultry, and vegetables. A recalled veteran of the China front wondered aloud if the general had come to inspect the officers' wives.[58] Other recruits, many previously graded 4-F, resorted to black humor, referring to themselves as victim units.[59] But it was one thing to be sullen and insubordinate, quite another to be openly defeatist. Except for the war minister, no Japanese soldier had any inkling about Japan's efforts to end the war. Besides, for a frontline soldier or sailor to surrender was a court-martial offense punishable by death. So the Kyushu reinforcements were a mixed bag, some just ragtag units. Yet, they were already digging in along the very beaches where the Americans would land. The invasion would be costly. The enemy would be fighting in prepared positions, for their homes, and for their families. They had nothing to gain by surrender, and everything to lose by defeat. And bitter experience from Guadalcanal to Okinawa made clear that they could be expected to fight to the death.

Seen or, more accurately, listened to from afar, the deficiencies of the new divisions were not that apparent. A special War Department analysis of the new Japanese divisions reached Marshall around Au-

57. Senshi kenkyu gurupu, "Hondo kessen moshi okonawarereba," 341.
58. Hosokawa Morisada, *Hosokawa nikki, ge* [The Hosokawa diary], vol. 2 (Tokyo: Chuko bunko, 1979), 378.
59. Westheimer, *Downfall: The Top-Secret Plan,* 437.

gust 6. From 1937 to 1943, the Japanese army mobilized an average of eight divisions per year. In 1944, thirty were formed. But in the first seven months of 1945, at least forty-two were activated, twenty-three in Japan itself. And Japan had the potential manpower to create even more divisions, as many as sixty-five infantry and five armored by the time of the invasion. Equipment, especially artillery, was deficient, but the Japanese use of rocket units made up for their lack of artillery. According to decrypted messages, a single twenty-four-round volley from a rocket gun produced the equivalent in weight to 120 155-mm U.S. projectiles.[60] A bored naval watch officer in Hawaii noted in his log with malicious delight that all the "experts" on the Japanese army were quietly burning their estimates on enemy ground strength for late 1945 or early 1946.[61] To Marshall it was no laughing matter. The Japanese army was still expanding and would continue to do so right up to the invasion.

On August 7, the day after the Hiroshima bombing, Marshall sent an "Eyes Only" message to MacArthur. He said he was frankly worried by intelligence reports about the large enemy buildup both of divisions and of air forces in Kyushu and southern Honshu. Marshall also foresaw the likelihood of discussions in Washington about the reported Japanese reinforcements. Did it make sense to attack into the teeth of the Japanese defenses? Maybe it was better to shift OLYMPIC to less well-fortified places such as Tokyo, Sendai, and Ominato? What did MacArthur think? Imagine Marshall sending such a cable to Eisenhower asking him to consider switching the Normandy invasion to Norway just three months before D-day! MacArthur's reply, received two days later, dismissed reports of reinforcements as "greatly exaggerated." Besides there was no reason to change OLYMPIC in the slightest. Overwhelming logistical difficulties, exacerbated by his air campaign, would isolate and weaken Japanese forces on Kyushu before the invasion.[62]

MacArthur's determination to lead the greatest amphibious operation in history blinded him to ULTRA's disclosure of the growing risks of invasion. Indeed, throughout the war, MacArthur had paid

60. War Department, Military Intelligence Service, "'MAGIC,'" July 15.
61. "Summary of ULTRA Traffic," August 7, 1945.
62. Marshall to MacArthur, War 31897, August 9, 1945; MacArthur to Marshall, War 31897, August 9, 1945. Photocopies in author's possession.

scant attention to intelligence forecasts urging caution or delay. He once remarked that there were only three great intelligence officers in the history of warfare "and mine is not one of them."[63] So far, talent, generalship, and good luck had allowed him to treat intelligence in such a cavalier fashion.

After Hiroshima (August 6), the Soviet declaration of war against Japan (August 8), and Nagasaki (August 9), the Japanese still offered only a conditional surrender (August 10). A rapid series of shock actions—each one thought capable by itself of forcing immediate capitulation—had failed to produce Japan's unconditional surrender. Grave doubts had replaced the certainties of a week before. Atomic bombs had not forced the Japanese to surrender, nor had the Soviet entry into the war. Thirteen divisions, not the anticipated ten, now protected Kyushu, and more were thought to be en route to the island fortress. Expected counteramphibious doctrine was completely reversed, calling for all-out bloodletting on the beaches. The Imperial Army was mobilizing new divisions at a record pace. What other surprises could the Japanese have waiting for the Americans?

As far as Marshall, or anyone else, knew, it would still take an invasion to subdue Japan. Impressions of blood-soaked Omaha Beach enabled him to picture the hell awaiting GIs on Kyushu's shores. MacArthur told him that to postpone or change the invasion was unacceptable. ULTRA told him the Japanese defenders were still massing on the proposed landing beaches. Groves told him the bomb could be used as a tactical weapon. Marshall needed some way to reverse the preview of hell on Japan's beaches. If the bombs could not shock the Japanese government into surrender, and judging from ULTRA reports and Japanese public braggadocio, they could not, then the bombs could be used to soften invasion beaches before the American landings.

On August 10 Marshall instructed Groves that the third atomic bomb, which would be ready by the sixteenth, would not be dropped without the express authority of the president.[64] Truman was appalled at the thought of "wiping out" another "100,000 people," and according to a confidant, he did not want to drop another atomic

63. Cited in Edward J. Drea, *MacArthur's ULTRA: Codebreaking and the War against Japan, 1942–1945* (Lawrence: University Press of Kansas, 1992), 187. An evaluation of MacArthur's use of intelligence appears on pages 230–31.

64. Marc Gallicchio, "After Nagasaki: General Marshall's Plan for Tactical Nuclear Weapons in Japan," *Prologue* 23, no. 4 (Winter 1991): 397.

bomb on a Japanese city.[65] The next day Marshall told Groves not to ship more fissionable material to the Pacific. Then the head of army intelligence, Major General Clayton Bissell, told Marshall not to expect atomic bombs to have a decisive effect in the next thirty days.[66] Believing further atomic attacks against Japanese cities would not force capitulation—and the days passed without any sign of Japan's unconditional surrender—Marshall reconsidered using the bomb as a tactical weapon. On the thirteenth, Lieutenant General John E. Hull, the assistant chief of staff for operations and plans, phoned Groves's aide, Colonel L. E. Seeman. Hull told Seeman about Marshall's idea for using atomic bombs in direct support of operations.[67]

Seeman said seven bombs might be available by the OLYMPIC invasion date. Then they talked about tactical bombs to support the landing forces. Seeman confirmed what Groves had earlier told Marshall. With U.S. soldiers and marines on ships about six miles offshore, atomic bombs would clear beaches by blast effect. A few days later the invaders would land. If the Japanese decided to continue the war, Hull, echoing the army's G-2's estimate, doubted another atomic attack against a city would convince them to surrender.[68] In other words, Marshall now regarded the tactical use of atomic bombs to support the Kyushu invasion as a realistic alternative to the continued pounding of Japanese cities.[69]

Japan's seeming unwillingness to surrender unconditionally did shape Marshall's thinking. But the driving force behind his emerging plan to use atomic bombs on Japan's beaches was the intelligence sneak preview of thousands and thousands of Japanese infantrymen awaiting American GIs and marines on the landing beaches. ULTRA made Marshall well aware of the tough Japanese infantrymen waiting patiently for the invasion in their concrete pillboxes, camouflaged earth-and-log revetments, tunnels, caves, and rifle pits behind obstacle-strewn beaches and shorelines sowed with mines. Only their emperor or death could move them. Marshall's ULTRA-derived forecast gives special meaning to his later comment: "We

65. Cited in Bernstein, "Eclipsed by Hiroshima and Nagasaki," 164–65.
66. Major General Clayton Bissell to chief of staff, "Estimate of Japanese Situation for the Next 30 Days," August 12, 1945, WD, general and special staffs, OPD, file 2, box 12, RG 165, NARA-DC.
67. Gallicchio, "After Nagasaki," 400.
68. Ibid., 401.
69. Ibid., 402.

had to visualize very heavy casualities unless we had enough atomic bombs at the time to supplement the troop action, if the bomb proved satisfactory for that purpose."[70] Japan's surrender made such decisions unnecessary. But what if the militarists had insisted on a fight to the bitter end?

An atomic attack on such a scale along Kyushu's shores would have rendered Hiroshima and Nagasaki mere footnotes to history. The atomic hell on the beaches, however, would have seared both ways. Thousands of Japanese troops, not to mention numerous Japanese civilians, would have immediately died on or near the beaches. But for those who survived the blast, including the American GIs and marines who would land on the radioactive beaches, a personal agony of radiation poisoning might just be beginning. Because no one yet understood the full implications of radioactive fallout, an atomic hell on the beaches would have been followed by a lingering one for veterans of both sides for decades. OLYMPIC would not have invaded the land of the gods but the world of the dead.

70. Cited in Bernstein, "Eclipsed by Hiroshima and Nagasaki," 151–52.

D. M. GIANGRECO

"A Score of Bloody Okinawas and Iwo Jimas"

President Truman and Casualty Estimates for the Invasion of Japan

MORE THAN A DECADE HAS PASSED since controversy erupted over the display of the *Enola Gay* at the National Air and Space Museum (NASM). There were no winners in that sad affair, which left in its wake tarnished careers, the dismissal of NASM's director, Martin Harwit, and a torrent of angry words. Countless articles have appeared in the press and scholarly journals, and no fewer than ten books deal wholly or in part with events on the Mall.[1]

Harwit, who had tried vainly to keep his footing at the center of the melee, wrote after his dismissal from the NASM that the contro-

---

1. Diary entry, August 10, 1945, Henry Lewis Stimson diaries (microfilm edition, reel 9), Henry Lewis Stimson Papers (hereafter cited as Stimson Papers), Yale University Library, from microfilm at Harry S. Truman Presidential Museum and Library (hereafter cited as Truman Library), Independence, Mo. Martin Harwit, *An Exhibit Denied: Lobbying the History of the Enola Gay* (New York: Springer-Verlag, 1996); Edward T. Linenthal and Tom Engelhardt, eds., *History Wars: The Enola Gay and Other Battles for the American Past* (New York: Metropolitan, 1996); Kai Bird and Lawrence Lifschults, *Hiroshima's Shadow: Writing on the Denial of History and the Smithsonian Controversy* (Stony Creek, Conn.: Pamphleteer's Press, 1997); Michael J. Hogan, ed., *Hiroshima in History and Memory* (New York: Cambridge University Press, 1996); Steven C. Dubin, *Displays of Power: Memory and Amnesia in the American Museum* (New York: New York University Press, 1999); *The Enola Gay Debate: A Collection of Materials Documenting the Public Debate between Veterans and the National Air and Space Museum Concerning the Proposed Enola Gay Exhibit* (Arlington, Va.: Air Force Association, 1995); Philip Nobile, ed., *Judgment at the Smithsonian* (New York: Marlowe, 1995); John T. Correll, *The Smithsonian and the Enola Gay: Air Force Association Special Report* (Arlington, Va.: Air Force Association, 2004); Charles T. O'Reilly and William A. Rooney, *The Enola Gay and the Smithsonian Institute* (Jefferson, N.C.: McFarland, 2005), and Robert P. Newman, *The Enola Gay and the Court of History*, (New York: P. Lang, 2004).

versy was a battle between a "largely fictitious, comforting story" presented by the veterans and the "event as revealed in trustworthy documents now at hand in the nation's archives," which the veterans "feared ... could cast into doubt a hallowed, patriotic story."[2] Many in the academy support this contention. For example, Laura Hein praises the "contemporary historical scholarship" displayed in the original exhibit script and maintains that "a great many U.S. soldiers in the Pacific in 1945 believed the bombs brought the war to a speedy end, but they were not in a position to know."[3]

This presumes, however, that assumptions based on these "trustworthy" documents are themselves correct and are derived from a comprehensive understanding of the material. In the case of NASM, critical decisions about the principal hot-button issue, casualty estimates for the invasion of Japan, were based on highly qualified—and limited—U.S. Army projections printed in a variety of briefing documents. Scholars involved in the *Enola Gay* exhibit did not realize that these estimates usually represented only the initial thirty days in what was envisioned in 1945 as a series of campaigns extending throughout 1946. Nevertheless, both the planners creating the documents and the senior officials receiving them, including Secretary of War Henry L. Stimson, Army Chief of Staff General George C. Marshall, White House Chief of Staff Admiral William D. Leahy, and also President Harry S. Truman, understood them well.[4]

Truman's much-derided accounts of massive casualties projected for the two-phase invasion of Japan are richly supported by U.S. Army, White House, Selective Service, and War Department documents produced before the use of nuclear weapons against Japan and stretching back through the last nine months of the Roosevelt administration. Moreover, the casualty estimates were not secreted away in obscure Pentagon departments to be seen only by the eyes

2. Harwit, *An Exhibit Denied,* viii, 426.
3. Laura Hein, "Remembering the Bomb: The Fiftieth Anniversary in the United States and Japan" *Bulletin of Concerned Asian Scholars* 27 (April/June 1995), esp. 4, 12.
4. Harry S. Truman, a highly respected full colonel in the Reserve Officer Corps, had only recently transitioned from the active to inactive reserve. He served as a battery commander in World War I and rose through the ranks to command National Guard field artillery regiments as a full colonel during the 1930s. He was completely versed in both the methodology and practical application of military planning and did not require the detailed explanations that some scholars today desire to find in the historical record.

of anonymous junior officers. A recently discovered exchange of memoranda shows that Truman himself was warned that the invasion could result in "the expenditure of 500,000 to 1,000,000 American lives" more than one month before the Potsdam Conference.[5] He personally acted on this information by ordering his senior advisers to prepare a written analysis before coming to discuss it face to face.[6] None of these civilian advisers batted an eye at the casualty estimate, and Truman promptly ordered a meeting with the secretaries of the army and navy and the Joint Chiefs of Staff (JCS) to discuss "the losses in killed and wounded that will result from an invasion of Japan proper."[7] This outcome is quite different from what has become the conventional wisdom today. But how has this come to pass?

Historians looking into the reasons behind the decision to drop the atomic bombs have been hampered by a lack of understanding of how the U.S. Army's casualty projections were formed, or even that specific methodologies existed for their creation. Complicating the situation even further for modern scholars is the fact that the army's strategic, medical, and logistics planners used a form of verbal shorthand in their communications and shared similar data on the relative strengths and weaknesses of the opposing U.S. and Japanese forces. Consequently, World War II planning documents frequently have been misinterpreted. Together with a lack of research below the "top layer" of documents, this has led many historians to the conclusion that Truman's assertion that he expected huge losses during an invasion was fraudulent; similarly, some argue that his claim that "General Marshall told me that it might cost half a million American

5. Herbert Hoover, "Memorandum on Ending the Japanese War," in Stimson "Safe File" Japan (After 7/41), box 8, Records of the Secretary of War, RG 107, National Archives and Records Administration, College Park, Md. (hereafter cited as NARA-MD).

6. Exchange of memos between Truman and Secretary of War Henry L. Stimson; Acting Secretary of State Joseph C. Grew; Director of the Office of War Mobilization and Reconversion Fred M. Vinson; and former secretary of state Cordell Hull in State Dept., WWII, White House Confidential File (WHCF), box 43, Harry S. Truman Papers, Truman Library. Includes Hoover's "Memorandum on Ending the Japanese War" with annotation by Truman.

7. William D. Leahy to members of the Joint Chiefs of Staff (JCS), the secretary of war and secretary of the navy, Memo SM-2141, June 14, 1945, in U.S. Department of Defense, *The Entry of the Soviet Union into the War against Japan: Military Plans, 1941–1945* (Washington, D.C.: U.S. Department of Defense, 1955), 76.

lives to force the enemy's surrender on his home grounds" was a "postwar creation" to justify dropping the bombs.[8]

From its inception during the Revolutionary War, the U.S. Army made efforts to estimate probable losses. Its leaders had to know approximately how many men would still be fit for duty by the last battle of the campaign season (i.e., before winter) after casualties from accidents, planned and unforeseen clashes, the erratic flow of recruitment, and disease drained the army of men.[9]

The U.S. Army's methodologies for estimating casualties during World War II were rooted in the experience of World War I when American divisions of twenty-seven thousand men each fought the German army in France. Postwar military planners drew on this experience to compile detailed analyses of the average costs to manpower, by percentage, from a wide variety of tactical settings—information they collected to serve as a starting point, or baseline, for casualty estimates when using appropriate projection parameters, factoring in the size ratio of the opposing forces and types of situations U.S. combat units might face. Army officers during the 1920s and 1930s received this information as part of their advanced instruction at the Command and General Staff School at Fort Leavenworth, Kansas, and the Infantry School at Fort Benning, Georgia.

Military planners realized that even the most careful estimate derived from the best data was still only an educated guess. During Marshall's tenure as academic director of the Infantry School (1927–1932), he drove home this principle. In a book that Marshall edited in 1934 and 1939, he titled the opening chapter "Rules," yet pointedly emblazoned the legend "Combat situations cannot be solved by rule" immediately underneath. Casualty projection studies came (and still come) with the warning that tables used in field manuals

8. Harry S. Truman, *Memoirs by Harry S. Truman: Year of Decisions* (2 vols., Garden City, N.Y.: Doubleday, 1955), 1:417; Barton J. Bernstein, "A Postwar Myth: 500,000 Lives Saved," *Bulletin of the Atomic Scientists* 42 (June/July 1986), 38–40.

9. Mary C. Gillett, *The Army Medical Department, 1775–1818* (3 vols., Washington D.C.: U.S. Government Printing Office, 1981), 1:3, 8; John Clement Fitzpatrick, ed., *The Writings of George Washington from the Original Manuscript Sources, 1745–1779* (39 vols., Washington, D.C.: U.S. Government Printing Office, 1931–1944), 7:149–50; Worthington Chauncey Ford, ed., *Journals of the Continental Congress, 1774–1789* (34 vols., Washington, D.C.: U.S. Government Printing Office, 1904–1937), 7:134.

and instructional materials were to be used solely "as the basis from which planning can begin." Moreover, if a young officer wading through a staff course had not already perceived the ambiguous nature of the subject because of the deceptively specific baseline percentages, his field manual spelled it out for him: such material "clearly indicates that the estimation of probable casualty rates in advance is not a simple matter that can be reduced to a general formula." Of particular importance in terms of casualty estimates for the invasion of Japan is this fundamental principle: "The longer the conflict progresses, the more comprehensive the statistical base will become. Accurate estimates of losses should, therefore, improve over time as the unique aspects of the conflict become readily apparent."[10]

Early in the Pacific War, medical and campaign planners built their casualty estimates using tables constructed from the U.S. Army's World War I experience, factoring in projected troop strength, operational plans, and intelligence estimates of Japanese capabilities, terrain, and relative firepower. By the time of the invasion of the Philippines in 1944, planners within General Douglas MacArthur's headquarters were able to replace the World War I baseline figures with data compiled from the battles on and around New Guinea, while Pentagon planners turned to the recent fighting on Saipan to gain a more realistic idea of how the fighting would play out in Japan's home islands. Several sets of casualty estimates would emerge from these exercises that might or might not be completely synchronized, depending on the individual interpretations of intelligence data and the level of coordination between the different staffs within a command. In general, the resulting estimates fell into three categories:

(1) *Medical estimates* were used for logistical purposes by the staffs charged with preserving the lives of the wounded.

10. C. T. Lanham with George C. Marshall, ed., *Infantry in Battle* (Washington, D.C.: The Infantry Journal, 1939), vii, 1; and FM [Field Manual] 101–10 1/2: *Staff Officers' Field Manual: Organizational, Technical, and Logistical Data Planning Factors* (Washington, D.C.: U.S. Government Printing Office, 1987), vol. 2, chap. 4, sec. 4, subsection 5–27 to chap. 5, sec. 6, subsection 5–17; esp. chap. 4, sec. 4, subsection 4–9, 4–13, and chap. 5, sec. 1., subsection 5–5. For a more simplified explanation of the "tactical points" used as casualty projection variables, see Dr. Michael E. DeBakey (colonel, U.S. Army) and Capt. Gilbert W. Beebe, *Battle Casualties: Incidence, Mortality, and Logistic Considerations* (Springfield, Ill.: Thomas, 1952), 14–15. Much of the material in this work was produced during DeBakey's World War II service with the U.S. Army's Surgical Consultants Division. See also Colonel John R. McLean, "Personnel Losses and Replacement Requirements," *Military Review* 29 (August 1949): 53–62.

(2) *Manpower estimates* were used as the basis for estimating the number of replacements needed after a short battle or to maintain the combat strength of the force during a lengthier fight.

(3) *Strategic estimates,* compiled at higher staff levels by theater commands and planners in Washington, were created in an effort to understand how future operations would fit into overall objectives and what might be the possible costs of options a staff either proposed or was directed to plan for or comment on.

Thus, at least three sets of casualty projections—and frequently more—would be created by staffs at most command levels, from division, corps, army, army group/theater on up through the strategic and logistics planners in Washington. These staffs were not producing the estimates for the benefit of historians but to meet the needs of their own unit and chain of command. Moreover, they spoke their own language with all that implies for individuals sifting through documents today. Casualty projections were seldom listed directly as such or carried titles convenient for researchers such as "Estimated Losses for Operation 'X'." They were obliquely stated, in terms of "requirements" for manpower, or have to be extrapolated, using contemporary formulae, from stated medical needs. Complicating matters even further is the fact that there were four organizations in Washington that contained groups of staff planners: the War Department, Navy Department, Joint Chiefs of Staff, and Combined Chiefs of Staff.

Only a comparatively small portion of this complex and interconnected planning structure is directly relevant to understanding the formulation of the casualty projections that reached the highest levels of government. These latter estimates were produced by three War Department organizations: the Army Service Forces, Medical Corps, and Operations Division of the War Department General Staff, as well as various committees and staff groups within the JCS, a policy-setting body formed in the first critical months after Pearl Harbor. When Truman became president, the JCS consisted of Army Chief of Staff Marshall, Chief of Naval Operations Admiral Ernest J. King, General Henry H. Arnold of the army air forces, and the president's personal representative on the body, Admiral Leahy.[11]

11. Ray S. Cline, *Washington Command Post: The Operations Division* (Washington, D.C.: Office of the Chief of Military History, Dept. of the Army, 1951), 98.

The first campaign to present Pentagon planners with a convincing model for combat against large Japanese field armies was the June 1944 invasion of the Marianas, which involved 125,000 U.S. troops taking the islands of Guam, Saipan, and Tinian. Operations on Saipan were thought to be particularly relevant to future operations in Japan since the joint army-marine force conducted both an opposed landing and a ground offensive on a corps (multidivision) frontage against a very large enemy force defending terrain similar to that in Japan, all on an island that contained large numbers of enemy civilians.[12]

Well before the invasion of Saipan, the JCS's Joint Planning Staff in the Pentagon had been working on a document outlining its concept of the final stages of the Pacific War. JPS 476, "Operations against Japan Subsequent to Formosa," was released for comment on June 6, 1944, approved for submission to the Joint Chiefs on June 30, 1944, as JCS 924 (midway through the month-long battle for Saipan), and regularly updated.[13]

At Saipan, the cost of 3,426 U.S. dead plus 13,099 wounded to kill 23,811 Japanese defenders had a sobering effect on the JCS's Joint Strategic Survey committee that presided over the refinements made to "Operations against Japan Subsequent to Formosa."[14] Through the spring of 1945, long after its name was rendered obsolete by events, this document was used as the primary outline for planning the series of campaigns to culminate on Japan's soil—Operation

12. *History of the Medical Department of the United States Navy in World War II* (28 vols., Washington, D.C.: U.S. Government Printing Office, 1953), 1:74; and Maurice Matloff and Edwin M. Snell, *Strategic Planning for Coalition Warfare, 1943–1944* (Washington, D.C.: Office of the Chief of Military History, Dept. of the Army, 1953–1959), 488.

13. JPS 476, "Operations against Japan Subsequent to Formosa," June 6, 1944; and JCS 924, "Operations against Japan Subsequent to Formosa," June 30, 1944, ABC [American-British Conversations] 381 Japan (8–27–42), sec. 7, box 353, Records of the Office of the Chief of Staff, RG 165, NARA-MD. These records are also in Geographic File 1942–1945, CCS [Combined Chiefs of Staff] 381 Pacific Ocean Area (6–10–43), sec. 5, box 683, Records of the United States Joint Chiefs of Staff, RG 218. Copies of each annex were sent to the recipients of the original document, and additional copies became part of a central pool of classified materials to be checked out for specialized use by individuals and organizations within the Pentagon. The last annex added to this document was JCS 924/16, May 2, 1945. The Saipan ratio was also used to project casualties for other proposed operations.

14. Henry I. Shaw Jr., Bernard C. Natly, and Edwin T. Turnbladh, *Central Pacific Drive: History of U.S. Marine Corps Operations in World War II* (Washington, D.C.: Historical Branch, G-3 Division, Headquarters, U.S. Marine Corps, 1966), 346.

OLYMPIC against the southernmost island of Kyushu in late 1945 and Operation CORONET against Tokyo itself in spring 1946.[15] In the document's August 30, 1944, annex, the planners estimated the number of Japanese troops that could be made available to defend the home islands at 3.5 million. An extrapolation of that number against a not-yet-complete count of the destroyed Japanese garrison on Saipan led them to conclude: "In our Saipan operation, it cost approximately one American killed and several wounded to exterminate seven Japanese soldiers. On this basis it might cost us half a million American lives and many times that number wounded . . . in the home islands."[16]

This "Saipan ratio" suggested that defeating Imperial Japan would be at least as costly as the defeat of Nazi Germany, and this set the standard for strategic-level casualty projections in the Pacific. Marshall personally used it to estimate casualties in upcoming operations at precisely the time when the army's manpower requirements for the coming year (1945) were being formulated and before Truman became vice president.[17] The army would not move beyond preliminary studies for 1946 requirements until the spring of 1945.[18]

Together with the experience of combat attrition of line infantry units in Europe, the Saipan ratio provided the basis for the U.S. Army and War Department manpower policy for 1945 and became a critical factor in both (1) the ratcheting up of Selective Service inductions from sixty to one hundred thousand men per month in order to feed the "replacement stream" for what would be a "one front" war

15. The Central Intelligence Agency's former deputy director for intelligence, Douglas J. MacEachin, explains that JCS 924, "incorporate[ed] various modifications [and] articulated the JCS consensus on an invasion of Kyushu" (*The Final Months of the War with Japan: Signals Intelligence, Invasion Planning, and the A-Bomb Decision* [Washington, D.C.: Central Intelligence Agency, 1998], 1–2).

16. JCS 924/2 "Operations against Japan Subsequent to Formosa," August 30, 1944, 120.

17. For example, the OPD estimated that an invasion of Formosa would cost 88,600 American casualties, including approximately 16,000 dead, which George C. Marshall rounded out to "approximately 90,000 casualties" in a September 1, 1944, memo to Joint Strategic Survey chief Lt. Gen. Stanley C. Embick, in Larry I. Bland and Sharon Ritenour Stevens, eds., *The Papers of George Catlett Marshall* (4 vols., Baltimore: Johns Hopkins University Press, 1996), 4:567–69.

18. For an analysis of the lead time required to draft, process, train, and ship soldiers overseas in preparation for combat operations, see D. M. Giangreco, "Casualty Projections for the U.S. Invasion of Japan, 1945–1946: Planning and Policy Implications," *Journal of Military History* 61 (1997): 521–81, esp. 564–69.

against Japan then projected to last throughout 1946; and (2) the corresponding expansions of the training, supply, and medical infrastructures to support increased manpower needs. All of this took place as the war in Europe was winding down and, indeed, "the capacity of Army Ground Force replacement training centers reached a wartime peak of 400,000 in June 1945," nearly two months after U.S. Army divisions pulled to a halt along Germany's Elbe River.[19]

Later in the summer of 1945, General MacArthur's staff would develop a formula dubbed the "sinister ratio," based on the most recent Pacific fighting.[20] But the practical side of the August 1944 Saipan ratio was that, whether or not a very general analysis of that type would hold up in the final analysis—at least two-and-a-half years in the future—it indicated that very high troop strengths would have to be maintained in the face of an increasing public demand that the longest-serving troops be returned home after the defeat of Germany. The War Department and army's solution was to tighten draft deferments on such groups as agricultural workers and expand the categories of those to be inducted, while simultaneously initiating a "points system" that allowed soldiers to be released after a specified amount of time in combat combined with length of service.[21]

Months before public demands peaked in May 1945 for what was essentially a partial demobilization in what was then believed to be the middle of the war, the Roosevelt administration and the army struggled with how to juggle America's dwindling reserves of eligible manpower. Because of the time it takes to train soldiers then ship them overseas, men previously inducted during the final months of 1944 would join those retained and reassigned from European the-

19. Robert R. Palmer, Bell J. Wiley, and William R. Keast, *The Procurement and Training of Ground Combat Troops* (Washington, D.C.: Historical Division, Dept. of the Army, 1948), 216–25.

20. Maj. Gen. Charles A. Willoughby, "Occupation of Japan and Japanese Reaction," *Military Review* 26 (June 1946): 3–4, in an appreciation written for field grade and general officers produced in late 1945. See also Giangreco, "Casualty Projections," 549, 574–77.

21. Lt. Gen. Lewis B. Hershey, prepared by Lt. Col. Irving W. Hart, *Selective Service and Victory: The 4th Report of the Director of Selective Service, July 1, 1944, to December 31, 1945* (Rev. ed., Washington, D.C.: U.S. Government Printing Office, 1960), 53–59, 70–71, 85–88. The army's finely tuned program was structured in such a way that public demands might be placated while still allowing the army to retain a sizable core of veterans for the upcoming campaigns on the Japanese home islands.

ater units being demobilized in the summer of 1945 with both groups being used primarily as replacements for men expected to be released under the points system. These replacements were the soldiers who would fill out the units making the initial assaults on Japan in late 1945 and the spring of 1946. Yet more troops would be needed to take the place of battle and nonbattle casualties lost during the fighting against Japan.[22]

The January 3, 1945, telegram from Selective Service director Brigadier General Louis B. Hershey to the state Selective Service directors reached to the heart of the matter. It tied proposed and directed changes in various deferments to long-term needs rather than to a passing crisis precipitated by the Germans' December 1944 counterattack in the Ardennes. The message, quoting a letter from the director of the Office of War Mobilization, future secretary of state James F. Byrnes, read in part:

> The Secretaries of War and Navy have advised me jointly that the calls from the Army and Navy to be met in the coming year will exhaust the eligibles in the 18 through 25 age group at an early date. The Army and Navy believe it is essential to the effective prosecution of the war to induct more men in this age group.[23]

Letters outlining the military's critical manpower needs were sent from Roosevelt, Marshall, and King to Chairman Andrew J. May of the House Military Affairs Committee and released to the *New York Times* and other newspapers on January 17, 1945. The public was informed in front-page articles that "The Army must provide 600,000 replacements for overseas theaters before June 30, and together with the Navy, will require a total of 900,000 inductions by June 30."[24]

Even as the army's monthly Selective Service call-up increased from sixty to eighty thousand in January 1945, it was decided to raise it yet again in March to one hundred thousand men per month in anticipation of the invasion of Japan.[25] The army planned the expansion of the number of training regiments to thirty-four in order to form a ready pool of replacements and, as noted earlier, army

22. Giangreco, "Casualty Projections," 564–66.
23. Ibid., 112.
24. *New York Times*, January 18, 1945, 1.
25. *Selective Service and Victory*, 595.

ground-force replacement training centers were expanded to a wartime peak of four hundred thousand in June.[26]

What this meant in terms of the planned invasions of Japan was essentially this: starting in March 1945, when levies were increased to one hundred thousand per month for the U.S. Army alone (the navy and marine corps counted separately and brought the total March call-up to 141,200), nearly every man inducted would enter the "replacement stream" now oriented for a one-front war that was estimated to last at least through the latter part of 1946.[27] The army did not sugarcoat the prospect of a long war for the soldiers in the field and new inductees; in June 1945 it warned that various "major factors—none of them predictable at this stage of the game—will decide whether it will take one year, two years or longer to win the Far East war."[28]

Not everyone in the Pentagon believed the fighting would last that long. With the end of the war in Europe in sight and Japan's Imperial Army soon to bear the full weight of American might, some strategic planners were clearly more optimistic about how potential losses against the Japanese might play out than were their colleagues whose thinking paralleled that of the manpower and medical planners. It would not be accurate to characterize the manpower and medical planners as pessimists, since there is virtually no record that any doubted that the war would end in anything other than victory for the United States. However, their basic functions within the army revolved not around the strategic planners' educated guesses but practical realities—the hard numbers generated by the escalatory nature of the fighting then taking place in the Pacific, which demon-

26. The terribly costly battles of Iwo Jima and Okinawa were fought even as draft quotas were nearly doubled. For a war-weary American public, this was a bitter pill, but it was made more palatable by the imminent return of the first soldiers under the points system; the Senate (with Vice President Truman as its presiding officer) balking on a House bill to draft women nurses aged twenty to forty-four; and both houses' passage of a law that eighteen-year-olds could not be sent into combat unless they had finished a minimum of six months of training. See *Selective Service and Victory*, 21, 23.

27. Ibid., 596–96. See also Giangreco, "Casualty Projections," 564–66.

28. This quotation is from the cover story of a particularly widely disseminated and read article: "How Long Will We Have to Fight the Jap War?" *Yank* 4 (June 8, 1945): 2. *Yank*'s circulation was currently 2.6 million per edition. For a useful look at the political context in which this U.S. Army's "information campaign" was made, see John W. Dower, *War without Mercy: Race and Power in the Pacific War* (New York: Pantheon Books, 1986), esp. 15–32.

strated that casualty ratios were drawing dangerously close to one to one as the war moved closer to the home islands in the spring of 1945.[29]

Up to this point, the spring of 1945, casualty projections for the invasion of Japan had only been examined and discussed at senior planning levels within the army and the War Department. As operations on the home islands loomed closer, it became necessary to inform the troops and the public at large of what was expected. A change occurred in how those projections were framed for public dissemination—a change that in some ways paralleled the recent shift in how current casualties from the overall war effort were being presented to Americans.[30]

The estimate from the Saipan ratio that subjugating Japan "might cost us half a million American lives and many times that many wounded" appeared, in the long run, to be unrealistically high to a cross section of strategic planners and senior leaders in Washington. After all, it seemed reasonable to assume U.S. forces would learn how to cope better with Japanese defensive techniques through hard-learned battle experience. The implied top-end figure of ap-

29. An analysis outlining this trend was published by DeBakey and Beebe in *Health* (May 31, 1945), box 613, Monthly Progress Reports, Office of the Commanding General, Records of Army Service Forces, RG 160. *Health* was a classified army publication distributed to senior military planners by the U.S. Army Surgeon General's office. The analysis was further disseminated to Truman and top administration officials through subsequent reports in June and July of 1945 including the June 18, 1945, meeting between the president, the JCS, and service secretaries. See page 103 for ratio table below.

30. D. M. Giangreco, "Spinning the Casualties: Media Strategies during the Roosevelt Administration" *Passport* 35 (December 2004): 22–30. Early in the war, the army established a policy under which virtually the entire flux and flow of manpower was disseminated on a monthly basis through public relations channels to the press and through its own organs to its troops. The artificially large numbers represented in these releases were gained by lumping together losses through purely administrative matters, such as separations from the service due to age or infirmity, with battle and nonbattle deaths, prisoners, and missing (but not wounded for certain security reasons); these ultimately became a political liability during the 1944–1945 "casualty surge." After the steep jump in casualties commensurate with the increased tempo of operations in June 1944, released figures for total army losses neared the 1.5 million mark in the fall of 1944 and, beginning in November, the army publicly experimented with various formulas that narrowed the criteria for the casualty data it released. A commonality of these new formulas was that they all had the effect of both (1) restarting the publicly released casualty counts from new, lower baselines, and (2) masking the rate of growth. The army did not settle on a new standard for public releases of casualty figures until February 1945.

proximately two million battle casualties, built on the Saipan ratio, was slashed to a best-case scenario figure of five hundred thousand, a number that was not so huge as to make the task ahead appear insurmountable and even lower than the already-released figure of six hundred thousand men needed for replacements.[31]

Use of the five hundred thousand battle casualty figure became "the operative one at the working level" among strategic planners during the spring of 1945.[32] Future general and West Point superintendent Andrew J. Goodpaster, then a young officer with the Strategy Section of the JCS's Joint War Plans Committee (JWPC), noted that "Secretary Stimson used the number regularly" and the figure—now representing total casualties and not just deaths—was given in briefings at such diverse locations as the U.S. First Army Headquarters in Weimar, Germany, B-29 training bases in the southwestern United States, and to newly assigned planning personnel at the Pentagon.[33] This smaller figure was not constructed from either previous or ongoing combat operations and appears to have been based purely on the assumption that the U.S. military would certainly learn to better counter Japanese tactics. Whether bravado or racism figured most heavily in its creation is beyond the scope of this study, but the assumptions nonetheless neglected the fact that, as evidenced by the casualty ratios then emerging from Iwo Jima and Okinawa, the Imperial Japanese Army was riding its own learning curve.

The low five hundred thousand number for total battle casualties, used widely in briefings, was not used for ongoing operational purposes, and it had no effect on the nearly doubled Selective Service call-up, the expansion of the army's training base, or the plans of the Transportation Corps, Medical Corps, and other U.S. Army organizations. For example, at the same time that the lower figure came into use in briefings, the Army Service Forces under Lieutenant General Brehon B. Somervell was working with estimates of "approximately" 720,000 for the projected number of replacements needed

31. *New York Times,* January 18, 1945, 1.
32. Samuel Halpern to Barton J. Bernstein, July 16, 1990, in *The Enola Gay Debate,* chap. 10.
33. "Strategic Bombing Symposium on the Atomic Bombing of Japan," Smithsonian Institution, Air and Space Museum, July 12, 1990, author's telephone interview with former superintendent of the U.S. Military Academy Gen. Andrew J. Goodpaster, May 7, 1997. See also Giangreco, "Casualty Projections," 537–38.

for "dead and evacuated wounded" through December 31, 1946—numbers that included only U.S. Army and Army Air Force personnel and did not include navy and marine corps losses.[34] Yet, while the low figure originated as simply a "public information" tool divorced from actual planning, it was nevertheless a very large number and long term. Pentagon planner Samuel Halpern said forty-five years later that the five hundred thousand figure "made a deep, indelible impression on a young man, 23 years old. It is something I have never forgotten."[35]

As if out of the blue, a seemingly unlikely character now entered the discussion of projected losses for the invasion of Japan, former president Herbert Hoover. Condemned to a political wilderness by his own party and the Roosevelt administration, Hoover was well outside the Washington mainstream in spite of his frequent assistance to congressional committees. Even this limited activity, however, brought him to the attention of what the editor of Truman's personal papers, Robert H. Ferrell, has described as "a Pentagon cabal of smart colonels."[36]

This group, according to one of its members, believed it their duty to ensure that "vital facts [and] intelligence reports" from a wide variety of different agencies were "acted upon rather than ignored." Their method, quite simply, was to get the material into the hands of a "certain few senators [and congressmen] who were both totally trustworthy as intelligence receivers, and highly able to get actions —without letting the sources of their facts become known." The recipients of their highly classified offerings included Howard Smith, chairman of the House Rules Committee and powerful Special Committee to Investigate Executive Agencies, as well as Republican senators Styles Bridges, George Malone, John W. Bricker (Thomas E.

34. "Summary of Redeployment Forecast," March 14, 1945, 6, Demobilization Branch, Plans and Operations Division, Army Service Forces, call no. N8864. Combined Arms Research Library (hereafter cited as CARL), Fort Leavenworth, Kans.; there are no folder or box numbers, only call numbers, at CARL.

35. Halpern to Bernstein, August 27, 1990, *The Enola Gay Debate*.

36. Robert H. Ferrell, from panel discussion following "What Did They Know and When Did They Know It? Intelligence Assumptions before the Invasion of Japan" at the annual meeting of the Society for Military History, Pennsylvania State University, April 16, 1999. For Ferrell's presentation, see "The Bomb—the View from Washington," in his *Harry S. Truman and the Cold War Revisionists* (Columbia: University of Missouri Press, 2006), 37–43.

Dewey's running mate in 1944), and one lone Democrat, the chairman of the Senate Special Committee to Investigate the National Defense Program, Harry S. Truman. Several of the colonels also made periodic trips to the former president's "high lair atop the Waldorf Towers in Manhattan . . . to discuss selected items." The briefings received by Hoover were all classified, and the colonels found that Hoover, in spite of his outsider position, "was always able to securely use them for the Republic's good."[37]

A close examination of Hoover's papers makes it clear that he had a comprehensive understanding not only of ongoing military matters unknown to the general public but also of developing high-level policy considerations. Indeed, it was his knowledge and insight that placed him in such demand by the congressional committees.[38] In addition to the colonels, Hoover regularly received richly detailed reports from *Army and Navy Journal* publisher John Callan O'Laughlin, who obtained his information—nearly all of which was top secret—from a wide variety of senior officers up to and including Army Chief of Staff Marshall.[39]

After Truman became president, Stimson, who had formerly served as Hoover's secretary of state, sought to bring the two statesmen together, but Hoover would not visit the White House without an invitation. On May 15, two days after a lunch and afternoon meeting at Stimson's Long Island estate, Hoover provided him with a memorandum outlining his views on ending the war with Japan. In

37. William LaVarre to Ivan D. Yeaton, January 10, 1978, box 4, "increment" folder, Papers of Ivan D. Yeaton, Hoover Institution Library, Stanford, Calif., copies from Herbert Hoover Presidential Library (hereafter cited as Hoover Library), West Branch, Iowa. This letter, recently discovered by the Hoover Library's senior archivist, Dwight M. Miller, reveals that this revolving group contained both European and "Asiatic" intelligence specialists, coalesced as early as 1942, was known to or utilized by a number of senior Pentagon officials such as Major General Clayton L. Bissell, assistant chief of staff for intelligence, and had at least four officers at its core including Colonels Peter Vischer, Truman Smith (an intimate of General Marshall's), Joseph A. Michela, and Percy G. Black. Yeaton also may have been a part of this group of officers.

38. Maurice Matloff, "The 90-Division Gamble," in *Command Decisions, The United States Army in World War II*, ed. Kent Roberts Greenfield (Washington, D.C.: U.S. Government Printing Office, 1960), 370.

39. See Ferrell, "What Did They Know?"; Miller to Ferrell, August 3, 1999; Ferrell to author, August 7, 1999; and Miller to author, October 8, 1999. John Callan O'Laughlin's relationship with Marshall—and their mutual friend Gen. John J. Pershing—is presented in Bland and Stevens, ed., *The Papers of George Catlett Marshall*, 1:475, 520–21; 2:153–54, 277–78; 287–88, 287.

this document and another prepared for Truman later that month, Hoover suggested that the invasion could cost "500,000 to 1,000,000 lives," an estimate that pointedly warned of up to twice as many deaths then postulated by the army in JCS 935. Stimson sent the paper to Marshall's staff for comment and hid its origins, stating only that it had been authored by "an economist."[40] Had Hoover come up with this larger top-end number himself, or had it come via the "smart colonels"?

Hoover's figures matched the revised estimates then being pushed upward from the mid-1944 estimate in JCS 924 that U.S. forces would face approximately 3.5 million Japanese troops. As further analysis of Japan's manpower and training capabilities demonstrated, the Imperial Army's two-tiered mobilization system was on its way to producing at least five million trained and properly equipped soldiers—a force far surpassing what U.S. specialists originally believed probable.[41] The estimates of larger Japanese forces invariably changed the projections of how many American casualties those Japanese might be able to inflict.[42] As navy invasion planner George L.

40. Undated and untitled May 15, 1945, memorandum by Hoover and accompanying June 1, 1945, memorandum from Maj. Gen. Thomas T. Handy to Lt. Gen. John E. Hull, National Archives Collection, reel 115, item 2656, George C. Marshall Library (hereafter cited as GCM Library), Lexington, Va. For Hoover's cover letter to the undated and untitled paper, see Hoover to Stimson, May 15, 1945 (microfilm edition, reel 12), Stimson Papers.

41. "Japanese Military Manpower," *Military Research Bulletin,* April 25, 1945 (Washington, D.C., 1945), 5–9. In the final analysis, the upwardly revised estimate of five million was short by nearly five hundred thousand in the initial invasion area and 1.5 million overall. The total number of Japanese armed forces personnel demobilized by the U.S. military government in Japan proper after the surrender was 6,465,435 (see *MacArthur in Japan: The Occupation, Military Phase,* vol. 1, supplement, *Reports of General MacArthur* [Washington, D.C.: U.S. Government Printing Office, 1966], 266). See also "Japanese Military Manpower Potential for 1945," *Military Research Bulletin,* July 4, 1945, 1–4; and "The Japanese System of Defense Call-Up," ibid., July 18, 1945, 1–3.

42. The new information on Japanese manpower trends was not yet widely disseminated—even within higher headquarters' organizations. Military intelligence analysts would have been among the very first personnel working the revised figures against the Saipan ratio (plus other ratios developed from more recent operations). Members of this same close-knit community made up Hoover's Pentagon pipeline. Increases in Japanese troop strength were also being leaked by a headquarters far removed from Washington—Admiral Chester W. Nimitz's press organization. One of these articles ("Palmer Warns No Easy Way to Beat Japs," *Los Angeles Times,* May 17, 1945, 5) specifically tied an estimate of up to one million American dead to future combat with five to six million Japanese troops. See also Ferrell, *Harry S. Truman and the Cold War Revisionists,* 42; and Frank McNaughton and Walter Hehmeyer, *Harry Truman: President* (New York: Whittlesey House, 1948), 3.

McColm put it in 1996, "every time" Japan's troop strength increased, "they had to revise the [casualty] numbers up."[43]

Two days after the May 13 meeting between Stimson and Hoover, Stimson again failed to persuade Hoover to visit Truman without a specific invitation. He did, however, finally succeed in convincing Truman of the need for a meeting. Against the pointed advice of some of his political staff from the Roosevelt administration, Truman, on May 24, invited Hoover to the White House. The two finally met on May 28. Before they parted, Truman requested that Hoover prepare memoranda on the issues discussed.[44]

Upon his return home to New York, Hoover prepared extensive notes on the meeting. He then produced four memoranda on "1. The European Food Organization; 2. The Domestic Food Organization; 3. The Creation of a War Economic Council; [and] 4. The Japanese Situation." In memo 4, a brief work less than seven hundred words in length, Hoover stated twice that the cost to America from an invasion of Japan could run from "500,000 to 1,000,000 lives," and thus implied total casualties far beyond the acceptable all-causes losses represented by the current 100,000-men-per-month induction rate.[45] It and the other memos were sent to Truman via the president's longtime friend, Press Secretary Charley Ross, to avoid possible mischief from the Roosevelt holdovers. Hoover's letter left New York on either May 30 or May 31.

The existence of Hoover's May 15 and May 30 memos, a well as the two subsequent Pentagon analyses of memo 4 requested by Stimson, are well known, and all have been noted in a variety of venues.[46]

43. From a summary of a March 26, 1996, telephone interview with George L. McColm, the U.S. Navy agriculture and weather specialist who served as chief of the agriculture section in the JCS Working Group (Presidio, Calif.) planning for the invasion and occupation of Japan. Quotation was examined and approved by McColm on April 17, 1996.

44. "Stimson, Henry L., 1945–1950," and "Truman, Harry S., 1945," Post Presidential Individual File, Hoover Papers, Hoover Library; President's Secretary's Files (PSF), Truman Library. See also Timothy Walch and Dwight M. Miller, eds., *Herbert Hoover and Harry S. Truman: A Documentary History* (Worland, Wyo.: High Plains Publishing, 1992), 37.

45. Ibid., 43–53, esp. 50–53.

46. In addition to Bernstein's "A Postwar Myth," 39, where the author of the memorandum is referred to as a "layman" instead of by name or former occupation, other examples include Richard B. Frank, *Downfall: The End of the Imperial Japanese Empire* (New York: Random House, 1999), 133; and Gar Alperovitz, *The Decision to Use the Atomic Bomb and the Architecture of an American Myth* (New York: Alfred A. Knopf, 1995), 43–45, 350–51, 520.

What has virtually never been discussed, however, is Truman's reaction to the memos. Recently discovered documents at the Harry S. Truman Library shed light on this question.

Truman acknowledged the receipt of Hoover's memos on June 1, yet the existence of this material is hardly the same as evidence that they were actually read by the president. But, in fact, Truman seized upon memo 4 and ordered his senior advisers each to prepare a written analysis before coming in to discuss it face to face.

Truman received the material from Ross and, after writing "From Herbert Hoover" across the top, he forwarded the original of memo 4, "Memorandum on Ending the Japanese War," to the new director of the Office of War Mobilization and Reconversion, Fred M. Vinson, on or about June 4. Truman's manpower czar did not bat an eye over the casualty estimate when he responded on June 7. He returned the original memorandum with his own memo suggesting that Hoover's paper be sent to Stimson, Acting Secretary of State Joseph C. Grew, and former secretary of state Cordell Hull. Truman agreed and had his staff type up additional copies of memo 4 on June 9 (carbon copies were also made) and sent them to all three men. Truman asked each for a written analysis of the memo and told Grew and Stimson that he wished to discuss their individual analyses personally after they submitted their papers. The request for a meeting was not made of Hull who was then hospitalized at the Bethesda Naval Medical Center.[47]

Grew immediately initiated an oral and written exchange on the memo with long-time Roosevelt adviser and speech writer Judge Samuel L. Rosenman, who was then serving as Truman's special counsel.[48] Stimson, meanwhile, sent his copy to the army's deputy

47. The original copy of Hoover's "Memorandum on Ending the Japanese War" (memo 4 of 4, May 30, 1945) with Truman's notation, the White House retypes/carbon copies of this document, and the subsequent exchange of memos among Truman, Grew, Cordell Hull, Stimson, and Vinson are under State Dept., WWII, in box 43 of the White House Confidential File (WHCF), Truman Library. The memorandum had been modified substantially in form, but not content, from the document that Hoover sent to Stimson after their May 13, 1945, meeting. Both versions of the memorandum are well known with the May 30, 1945, version frequently cited. After locating the copy with Truman's annotation and the subsequent exchange between Truman and his senior civilian advisers, I supplied copies to numerous scholars, including Robert Ferrell and Robert Newman, as well as to various institutions. The Truman Library also received copies of the documents cited in notes 48, 57, and 59 below, which were added to its archives' vertical file.

48. Grew to Rosenman, June 16, 1945, in Stimson "Safe File," NARA-MD. The lack of a cover letter for the carbon copy of Grew's memo to Rosenman in Stimson's possession suggests that memo 4 was also personally discussed by Stimson and Grew.

chief of staff, Lieutenant General Thomas J. Handy, because he wanted to get "the reaction of the [Operations Division] Staff to it." Stimson also mentioned in his diary that he "had a talk both with Handy and with Marshall on the subject" and subsequently received from Grew a carbon copy of Grew's memo to Rosenman.[49]

Cordell Hull responded first. He branded memo 4 Hoover's "appeasement proposal" in his June 12 letter and did not take issue with the casualty estimate. Grew, in his June 13 memorandum to Truman, confirmed that the Japanese "are prepared for prolonged resistance," adding that "prolongation of the war [will] cost a large number of human lives."[50] Grew, like Vinson, also returned Truman's original, signed directive, as well as his White House retype of "Ending the Japanese War"—standard operating procedure in the days before retention of copies became a fetish among government officials. It should also be noted that Grew had earlier "received competent military opinion to the effect that the military operations in Japan cannot be anything but costly in terms of human lives," and that his answer would not have come as any surprise to the president.[51] Grew told both Truman and Rosenman (ironically just hours after the meeting with Hoover) that "The Japanese are a fanatical people capable of fighting to the last man. If they do this, the cost in American lives will be unpredictable."[52] One can readily surmise that Hoover's and Grew's statements, hitting virtually back-to-back, were not of much comfort to the new commander in chief.

Grew's memorandum and Cordell Hull's letter both arrived on June 13, and Truman subsequently met with Admiral Leahy on the matter.[53] In addition to serving as the president's White House chief of staff, the admiral was also his personal representative on the Joint Chiefs and acted as unofficial chairman at their meetings. The morning after the Hull and Grew messages arrived, Leahy sent a memorandum stamped "URGENT" to the other JCS members as well as to

49. Stimson diary entry, June 11, 1945, Stimson Diaries (microfilm edition reel 9), Stimson Papers, from microfilm at Truman Library; Grew to Rosenman, Stimson "Safe File," NARA-MD.

50. Cordell Hull and Grew memos in WHCF, Truman Library.

51. Grew to Rosenman, Stimson "Safe File," NARA-MD.

52. Daily sheets, May 28, 1945, Truman's Appointments File, PSF, Truman Library; and Joseph C. Grew, *Turbulent Era: A Diplomatic Record of Forty Years, 1904–1945* (2 vols., Boston: Houghton Mifflin, 1952), 2:1429.

53. Daily Sheets, June 13, 1945, Truman's Appointments File, PSF, Truman Library.

Stimson and Secretary of the Navy James Forrestal. The president wanted a meeting the following Monday afternoon, June 18, where he would be, in effect, "reopen[ing] the question of whether or not to proceed with plans and preparation with Olympic . . . a campaign that was certain to take a large price in American lives and treasure."[54] Leahy informed them that the commander in chief wanted some very specific information:

> He desires an estimate of the time required and an estimate of the losses in killed and wounded that will result from an invasion of Japan proper.
> He desires an estimate of the time and losses that will result from an effort to defeat Japan by isolation, blockade, and bombardment by sea and air forces.
> He desires to be informed exactly what we want the Russians to do.[55]

Leahy's memo stated unequivocally that "It is his intention to make his decision on the campaign with the purpose of economizing to the maximum extent possible in the loss of American lives. Economy in the use of time and in money cost is comparatively unimportant."[56]

This directive to the Joint Chiefs and service secretaries was issued before the president received Stimson's written response to Hoover's memo 4, although the secretary had spoken with Marshall about it on June 11 and received a carbon copy of Grew's June 16 memo to Rosenman. While the record-keeping structure of the White House during this period leaves open the possibility that the president and Stimson discussed the matter over the telephone or during a brief, unscheduled meeting—and it seems highly unlikely that the secretary of war would ignore his commander in chief's request to get back to him—Stimson apparently made no written state-

54. Grace Person Hayes, *The History of the Joint Chiefs of Staff in World War II: The War against Japan* (Annapolis, Md.: Naval Institute Press, 1982), 706. This source originated as a classified document generated in 1953 by the Historical Section, JCS.

55. Leahy to JCS members Marshall, Henry H. Arnold, and Ernest J. King; Secretary of War Stimson; and Secretary of the Navy James Forrestal, Memo SM-2141, June 14, 1945, in U.S. Department of Defense, *Entry of the Soviet Union into the War against Japan*, 76.

56. Ibid.

ment on the casualties question until after the June 18 meeting with Truman.[57] He did, however, receive the "Staff opinion" he had requested from General Handy.

As noted earlier, the upper end of Hoover's estimate of five hundred thousand to one million U.S. dead was fully double the mortality figure used in JCS 924 and far beyond the cumulative—and acceptable—total of the army's 100,000-men-per-month replacement stream that was, by now, several months into its implementation.[58] Consequently, Marshall endorsed the comments by the staff officer who said that the estimate "appears to deserve little consideration." The previous week Marshall also received an apparently different officer's comments on the same estimate in Hoover's earlier May 15 memorandum submitted directly to Stimson after their Long Island meeting. The two analyses displayed varied approaches to Hoover's points. From Marshall's perspective, each was a sound analysis, completely in line with army doctrine yet carrying different interpretations. He signed both.[59]

The May 15 memorandum traveled the same path as the May 30 memorandum requested by Truman: Lieutenant General Handy down to Brigadier General George A. Lincoln's Strategy and Policy Group, then back up the chain with its accompanying commentary to Stimson, who forwarded neither set of documents to Truman. The staff officer responding to the May 15 memorandum agreed that Hoover's casualty estimate was "entirely too high," yet the pointed

57. Truman to Stimson, original in Stimson "Safe File," NARA-MD; copy in Vertical File, Truman Library.

58. The estimate of five hundred thousand to one million dead implied, as the staff officer commenting on the May 30 memorandum correctly noted, that total casualties could run in the area of two million to as many as five million. These numbers were in line with casualties suffered by the war's other major combatants, who had entered hostilities much earlier than the United States, and in themselves were not unimaginable, if the intent was to conquer virtually all resisting Japanese on the home islands by force of arms. Such, however, had never been the intent or desire of planners, who firmly believed that effective "military control" of all Japan could be "obtained by the securing of a relatively few vital coastal areas" on Honshu, and that the opening invasion of Kyushu would entail only seizing enough land to serve as a base to launch the Honshu invasion against Tokyo in 1946 (*Daily Summary of Enemy Intelligence*, no. 1209, July 26–27, 1945, 8, Military Intelligence Section, General Staff, United States Army Forces, Pacific, call no. 6377, CARL).

59. National Archives Collection, reel 115, item 2656, GCM Library; also available in RG 165, NARA-MD, and Vertical File, Truman Library.

disclaimer that immediately follows—"*under the present plan of campaign*"—is regularly deleted from accounts of the analyses even though, excluding headlines, it is the only portion of the 550-word response with a typed underline.[60] This emphatic qualifier turned out to be a perceptive one because, after three years of fighting, the Japanese had a clear understanding of U.S. methods and logistic requirements.[61] They correctly inferred that southern Kyushu would likely be the next invasion target and were already moving quickly and decisively to reinforce Kyushu with a massive number of troops before it could be cut off by U.S. air and sea power.[62]

Stimson was willing to expose others' thoughts to the president, unfiltered by his own analysis, as when he forwarded the letter of Manhattan Project engineer Oswald C. Brewster to Truman, but he apparently saw nothing in the staff comments that warranted the chief executive's direct examination.[63] Other than Stimson's oral statements during the June 18 meeting with the JCS, Navy Secretary Forrestal, and Truman, there is no record that he directly addressed the casualties question to the president until his memorandum of July 2, 1945, a report that became well known largely because it was later published within a high-profile article in *Harper's*. In it he stated that U.S. forces will face "a more bitter finish fight than in Germany [and] we shall incur the losses incident to such a war."[64] With American casualties directly related to combat then topping one and 1.25 million, the bulk of which had been suffered during the war against Germany in just the previous year, Truman would not have

60. Ibid., emphasis in original.

61. Alvin D. Coox, "Japanese Military Intelligence in the Pacific: Its Non-Revolutionary Nature," in Walter Theodore Hitchcock, *The Intelligence Revolution: A Historical Perspective* (Washington, D.C.: Office of Air Force History, U.S. Air Force, 1991), 200; Edward J. Drea, *MacArthur's ULTRA: Codebreaking and the War against Japan, 1942–1945* (Lawrence: University Press of Kansas, 1992), 202–25. See also Drea, "Previews of Hell," *Military History Quarterly* 7, no. 3 (Spring 1995): 74–81.

62. "Amendment No. 1 to G-2 Estimate of the Enemy Situation with Respect to Kyushu," G-2, AFPAC, July 29, 1945, call no. N6377, CARL. See also Giangreco, "Casualty Projections," 574- 77.

63. D. M. Giangreco and Kathryn Moore, eds., *Dear Harry . . . , Truman's Mailroom, 1945–1953: The Truman Administration through Correspondence with "Everyday Americans"* (Mechanicsburg, Pa.: Stackpole Books, 1999), 282–90.

64. For the full text of the July 2, 1945, memo, see Henry L. Stimson, "The Decision to Use the Atomic Bomb," *Harper's Magazine* 194 (February 1947): 97–107. First, second, and final drafts in Stimson "Safe File," NARA-MD.

found such an unambiguous statement from his secretary of war to be encouraging.[65]

This discussion of army staff comments *not* shown to President Truman may appear out of place in an essay discussing his knowledge of U.S. casualty estimates for the planned invasion of Japan. But unlike the Truman-Grew-Hull-Stimson-Vinson exchanges in the aftermath of Hoover's memo 4, which remained unknown to historians until its recent discovery, the "staff opinions" cannot be ignored because they have figured heavily in the discourses of both critics and defenders of Truman's decisions. These documents provide a window to the thinking of strategic planners in General Lincoln's Strategy and Policy Group, but it must be noted that the views were not shared by all strategic planners, the Pentagon's logistic and medical planners, or by the relevant echelons within MacArthur's headquarters. In fact, these officers' opinions and the plethora of informal exercises conducted in the spring of 1945 had no impact at all within the army hierarchy and the War Department's already-implemented manpower policy for that year—nor were they intended to do so.[66]

---

65. *Army Battle Casualties and Nonbattle Deaths in World War II, Final Report, 7 December 1941/December 1946* (Washington, D.C.: Statistical and Accounting Branch, Office of the Adjutant General, Dept. of the Army, 1987). The final total of army and army air force casualties stands at 945,515, but while this figure includes nonbattle deaths, it does not include categories that drained the army of manpower and were closely monitored by senior leaders. These included disability discharges due to nonbattle injuries in combat zones, such as loading accidents, totaling 50,520; losses due to disease including 862,356 discharges; combat-related psychiatric breakdowns accounting for 312,354 discharges; and 101,600 American prisoners of war who survived their captivities and were counted as casualties *during* the war (Frank A. Resiter, ed., *Medical Department, United States Army: Medical Statistics in World War II* [Washington, D.C.: Office of the Surgeon General, Dept. of the Army, 1975], 13–14, 43). Also part of the wartime totals were a minimum of 201,937 navy, marine corps, coast guard, and merchant marine battle casualties. See Giangreco, "Casualty Projections," 540n.

66. Many scholars who have studied the 1945 invasion planning and related casualty estimates have given undue and misleading emphasis to the plethora of staff comments and briefing papers that had no effect within the army hierarchy or on the War Department's manpower policy for that year. See, for example, John Ray Skates, *The Invasion of Japan: Alternative to the Bomb* (Columbia: University of South Carolina Press, 1994), 77–80; J. Samuel Walker, *Prompt and Utter Destruction: Truman and the Use of Atomic Bombs against Japan* (Chapel Hill: University of North Carolina Press, 1997), 38–39, 118–19n12; Rufus E. Miles Jr., "Hiroshima: The Strange Myth of Half a Million Lives Saved," *International Security* 10 (Fall 1985): 121–40, esp. 133–38; Bar-

The president never saw other army documents about possible casualties during the invasion operations. Produced exclusively as possible briefing papers during the frenzy of activity preceding the June 18 meeting, virtually all were superfluous, technically flawed, or contained portions structured in a form that was contrary to army doctrine (which rendered them ambiguous and thus unusable). Consequently, Marshall, who personally pieced together and read the meeting's opening statement, did not include them in either his opening remarks or the detailed outline of invasion plans then being produced for use at the upcoming Potsdam Conference.[67] Nor did the briefing papers have any effect on the army's complex manpower policy for 1945. By this period, the summer of 1945, Stimson and Marshall had long since moved on and were in the midst of examining manpower needs for the following year's invasion near Tokyo and explaining those needs to the relevant congressional committees.[68] Nevertheless, the documents must also be briefly discussed since, just like the staff comments to Stimson, they have been

---

ton J. Bernstein, "Reconsidering Truman's Claim of 'Half a Million American Lives' Saved by the Atomic Bomb: The Construction and Deconstruction of a Myth," *Journal of Strategic Studies* 22 (March 1999): 54–95, esp. 61–64. Errors in the above are thus largely due to their authors' lack of understanding of how planning documents are created, connected, and used. One notable exception is Frank's *Downfall.* Although the author's understanding of army doctrine and the practicalities of constructing workable logistic and manpower estimates is limited and he focuses on materials generated long after the relevant manpower decisions were made and implemented, Frank demonstrates a better grasp of the factors affecting casualty projection analysis than has been displayed in other book-length works.

67. JCS 1388/4, "Details of the Campaign against Japan," July 11, 1945; Marshall's remarks and extracts of the president's meeting with the JCS, Stimson, and Forrestal in the June 18, 1945, "Joint Chiefs of Staff Corrigendum to JCS 1388," Records of the Joint Chiefs of Staff: Part 1, 1942–1943: The Pacific Theater, reel 2, CARL.

68. House Subcommittee on Appropriations, *Hearings on the Military Establishment Appropriations Bill for 1946,* conducted May 25, 1945, 79th Cong., 1st sess., 1945, 1–18. When Marshall and Stimson were questioned by Congress, separately, about this highly charged manpower issue, the transcripts show that their testimonies were off the record, and private discussions of the matter with legislators at the Pentagon and in Stimson's office were also not recorded. Only many years later did references to what was discussed surface in other congressional testimony. Aside from his off-the-record testimony before the House Appropriations Committee during discussion of the "inadvisability of war of attrition" and elsewhere, Marshall spoke of "the terrific losses which we would sustain when we invaded Japan" before the House Military Affairs Committee. See the transcript of Charles E. Bohlen's testimony before the Senate Foreign Relations Committee on March 2, 1953, in Charles E. Bohlen, *Witness to History: 1929–1969* (New York: Norton, 1973), 317.

featured prominently in previous works as proof that high casualty figures were a "postwar creation."[69]

The first of these is JWPC 369. Leahy's memo about the June 18 meeting had stressed that Truman's first priority was to minimize the loss of American lives.[70] The night before the momentous meeting, Truman wrote in his diary that the decision whether to "invade Japan [or] bomb and blockade" would be his "hardest decision to date."[71]

In compliance with the president's request, Marshall and Admiral King asked for additional information from their staffs and from subordinate commands in the Pacific in order to obtain the most current data. Marshall received papers submitted by the Joint Planning Staff; the Strategy and Policy Group's Joint War Plan's Committee (JWPC) of Brigadier General William W. Bessell Jr.; and other staffs, with one from Bessell's group, "Details of the Campaign against Japan," supplying much of the language and analysis that would go into Marshall's opening remarks and the accompanying "Memorandum for the President."[72]

It was apparent that the staffs were required to produce hard, specific numbers. This was a highly unusual task for the strategic planners, but they did their best. The JWPC's paper, edited by Lincoln, stated that "it would be difficult to predict whether Jap resistance on Kyushu would more closely resemble the fighting on Okinawa or whether it would parallel the Battle of Leyte." They placed quotation marks around the term *educated guess* when they presented a "best estimate" made up of hard numbers for battle casualties from several possible sequences of operations in the home islands and extending out for ninety days.[73]

69. A much-quoted example is Bernstein, "A Postwar Myth," 38–40. Other versions of this article were published under the titles "The Myth of Lives Saved by A-Bombs," *Los Angeles Times*, July 28, 1985, and "The Bombing Did Not Save Lives," *Nuclear Arms 1985 Supplement* (St. Paul, Minn., 1986), 139.

70. Leahy to JCS members Marshall, Henry H. Arnold, and Ernest J. King; Secretary of War Stimson; and Secretary of the Navy James Forrestal, Memo SM-2141, June 14, 1945, in U.S. Department of Defense, *Entry of the Soviet Union into the War against Japan.*

71. Truman diary entry, June 17, 1945, PSF, Truman Library. See also Robert H. Ferrell, ed., *Off the Record: The Private Papers of Harry S. Truman* (New York: Harper and Row, 1980), 47.

72. "Memorandum for the President," in JWPC 369/1, "Details of the Campaign against Japan," June 15, 1945; JCS 1388, "Details of the Campaign against Japan," June 16, 1945, call no. N20903.1, CARL.

73. JWPC 369/1, "Details of the Campaign against Japan," June 15, 1945, call no. N20903.1, CARL.

The JWPC's figures were based primarily on the ratio of American-to-Japanese losses from Leyte. The choice resulted in lower casualty estimates than those produced by navy planners, who had selected Okinawa as their model.[74] Yet another element within the Strategy and Policy Group, probably Colonel Max S. Johnson's Strategy Section, also produced "an involved calculation based primarily on Okinawa."[75] But while Marshall used much of the JWPC's language, he discarded its hard-number figures. This had less to do with the probability that the navy's estimate was more likely to be appropriate (in light of the terrain and recent experience) than that "prediction of battle casualties is hazardous at best."[76] Marshall, Lincoln, and Bessell's JWPC was opposed to presenting hard numbers that could be rendered worthless by any number of factors, such as unforeseen weather or terrain conditions, or even modest changes in the force structures of the opposing armies. Instead, they preferred to stick to standard army doctrine and present ratios to predict a range that could be modified to account for changing circumstances, such as the extensive Japanese reinforcement of Kyushu, which would not become clear for over a month.[77]

74. While the JWPC estimated thirty thousand battle casualties for the first thirty days, the navy's estimate for the same period was forty-nine thousand ("Joint Staff Study: Olympic, Naval, and Amphibious Operations, Commander-in-Chief, U.S. Pacific Fleet and Pacific Ocean Areas [CINCIPOA]," June 18, 1945, 70, call no. R11623, CARL). Admiral King's effort to get this figure into the detailed outline of invasion plans then being produced for the president's use at the upcoming Potsdam Conference, JCS 1388/4, was rebuffed by Marshall (see JCS 1388/1- /2-/3, "Details of the Campaign against Japan," call no. N20903.1, CARL), who stated that it was "unnecessary and undesirable for the Joint Chiefs of Staff to make estimates which can be at best only speculative." The unused JWPC estimates for total ground-force battle casualties from both Operations OLYMPIC and CORONET were 193,500 including 43,500 killed and missing—roughly that of the first four months of American battle casualties in France.

75. Memorandum to Lt. Gen. John E. Hull from Brig. Gen. George A. Lincoln, June 16, 1945, microfilm: "GHQ, SWPA, 1941–1945: Chronological Index and Summary of Communications," University Publications of America, reel 12, courtesy Edward J. Drea.

76. DeBakey and Beebe, *Battle Casualties*, 13.

77. It has been suggested by Frank (in *Downfall*, 145–46) that Truman was "systematically denied information about the huge [casualty] projections"; he states that "reconciling Marshall's matchless overall record of probity with his conduct here is troubling." Marshall was intent on providing an answer that conformed with army doctrine and in a form with which all the participants in this process—including the president (see note 4)—were intimately familiar. Marshall was fully aware of Truman's military background and abilities. From Marshall's standpoint, the only honest alternative to providing ratios upon which inevitable changes in the opposing force structures, factors unknown, and the questionable duration of the combat

The JWPC paper specifically advised against using any hard-number strategic estimates—which obviously included the very material it was ordered to create. Marshall did not need much convincing. He deleted their hard-number estimates without further comment. Instead, he used a second, more standard JWPC table presenting known casualties from recent operations as a baseline from which a series of ratios was applied.[78]

In addition to JWPC 369's hard-number tables, Marshall also discarded casualty projections from MacArthur's headquarters in Manila; consequently, Truman never saw them. The rushed nature of Marshall's request for estimates and a series of misunderstandings and miscommunications resulted in figures that were based on medical staff planning being sent to the Pentagon. While correct for the specific aspect of the Operation OLYMPIC casualty evacuation program they dealt with, the data's structure clearly indicated that the estimates were generated too far down the chain of command to be appropriate for the upcoming meeting with the president. In fact, they were just as ambiguous as earlier material from MacArthur's headquarters, which had prompted Lincoln to complain that "we cannot, from the data I have seen, deduce his estimated battle casualties."[79]

When it came time for the meeting with Truman, Marshall distributed copies of the JWPC's briefing paper—minus the ninety-day estimates. The only table included with the paper was the aforementioned standard ratio table displaying known casualties from recent, large-scale operations used as baselines:[80] the text of the paper was presented orally by Marshall himself.

---

could be applied would be estimates at the extreme range of best-case and worst-case scenarios. An example of this can be found in the president's 1953 letter to James L. Cate, in which he stated Marshall's opinion that the invasion of Japan would have cost a "minimum" of 250,000 casualties and "might" have cost up to one million (Giangreco and Moore, eds., *Dear Harry*, 466–76).

78. This table was derived from the DeBakey and Beebe material in *Health* (see note 29).

79. War Department transmissions W-17477 and W-18528; Commander in Chief, Army Forces, Pacific (CINCAFPAC) transmissions C-19571 and C-19848, box 17, War Department Messages No. 1001 to 1095, April 29/August 2, RG 4, MacArthur Memorial Archive, Norfolk, Va.; and Memorandum, Lincoln to John Hull, June 15, 1945, microfilm: "GHQ, SWPA," courtesy Edward J. Drea. For a detailed analysis of this exchange, see Giangreco, "Casualty Projections," 545–50.

80. Extracts from the June 18, 1945, meeting here and below are from "JCS Corrigendum to JCS 1388."

Casualties. Our experience in the Pacific War is so diverse as to casualties that it is considered wrong to give any estimate in numbers. Using various combinations of Pacific experience, the War Department staff reaches the conclusion that the cost of securing a worthwhile position in Korea would almost certainly be greater than the cost of the Kyushu operation. Points on the optimistic side of the Kyushu operation are that: General MacArthur has not yet accepted responsibility for going ashore where there would be disproportionate casualties. The nature of the objective area gives room for maneuver, both on the land and by sea. As to any discussion of specific operations, the following data are pertinent:

CAMPAIGN	US CASUALTIES Killed, Wounded, Missing	JAP CASUALTIES Killed and Prisoners (not inc. wounded)	RATIO US to Jap
Leyte	17,000	78,000	1:4.6
Luzon	31,000	156,000	1:5
Iwo Jima	20,000	25,000	1:1.25
Okinawa	34,000 (Ground) 7,700 (Navy)	81,000 (Uncompleted count)	1:2
Normandy (1st 30 days)	42,000	[ ]	[ ]

The record of General MacArthur's operations from March 1, 1944 through May 1, 1945 (northwestern New Guinea and the Philippines) shows 13,742 U.S. killed compared to 310,165 Japanese killed, or a ratio of 22 to 1 [*sic*].[81]

It is at this point in the discussion that historians—military and civilian alike—invariably lose track of exactly what the meeting's participants were saying to each other. The table's numbers, representing U.S. to Japanese casualties during the most recent campaigns, were used solely as a base to establish ratios that might be applicable to the fighting ahead. Ratios from recent campaigns comparing U.S. battle casualties with enemy killed (which the Japanese casualties almost invariably were) were presented for comparative

81. Ibid., 2. The numbers are transposed, so this ratio should read "1 to 22." None of the meetings' participants would have misunderstood the meaning of Marshall's statement and , if they even noticed the transposition, would have immediately recognized that the numbers were simply flipped.

purposes, as well as a U.S. casualty total for the first third of the fighting in the Normandy campaign with no ratios given because of uncertainties in the corresponding number of German casualties.

Throughout the meeting, its participants made references to operations or portions of operations. These do not refer to the baseline figures, which are frequently quoted by authors and historians, but to the ratios they spawned and that only *suggest* how battle casualties from the much larger Japanese and U.S. forces involved in the first of the two lengthy invasion operations on Japanese soil might play out. This was explicitly stated by Lincoln in a memo to his chief, Lieutenant General John E. Hull, during the formulation of the JWPC paper: "about 30,000 for the first 30 days (which are the casualties we have experienced in Luzon to date [160 days]) is about a balanced estimate."[82] The one exception to this came when Admiral Leahy questioned the baseline figure for Okinawa, which he believed to be incomplete. The intensity of the fighting and length of time that units were required to stay in combat had resulted in roughly as many nonbattle casualties as direct battle casualties, primarily because of psychiatric breakdowns (commonly, and euphemistically, referred to as "battle fatigue").[83] Leahy believed that, by not including nonbattle casualties, the baseline figure for Okinawa had been made artificially low, thus skewing the ratio.

Marshall continued,

82. Memorandum, Lincoln to John Hull, June 18, 1945, microfilm "GHQ, SWPA," courtesy Edward J. Drea. Readers may better grasp the phraseology in this memo as well as the significance of the Marshall JWPC wording if they know that, although the month-long siege of Manila ended on March 3, 1945, Luzon remained the scene of intense fighting until the surrender of Japan. For example, during the campaign to secure a series of northern Luzon passes from April through late May, 1,510 men from the U.S. Twenty-fifth and Thirty-second Infantry divisions were killed and 4,250 were wounded. Their troops also suffered an excessively large number of psychiatric breakdowns—the inevitable result of inadequate numbers of troops committed to a lengthy operation. The Sixth Infantry Division battling for the critical dams east of the capital in April saw roughly three soldiers lost to psychosis or disease for each of its 1,335 killed or wounded. Further airborne and amphibious operations on Luzon were only days away when Truman met with the JCS and service secretaries. See Rafael Steinberg, *Return to the Philippines in the United States Army in World War II* (Alexandria, Va.: Time-Life Books, 1979), 176–93.

83. "U.S. Tenth Army Action Report, Ryukyus, 26 March to 30 June 1945," vol. 1, chap. 11, sec. 1, 12, call no. N11432, CARL; Thomas M. Huber, *Japan's Battle for Okinawa, April/June 1945* (Fort Leavenworth, Kans.: Combat Studies Institute, 1990), 119–20. See also Giangreco, "Casualty Projections," 539–40.

There is reason to believe that the first 30 days in Kyushu should not exceed the price we have paid for Luzon. It is a grim fact that there is not an easy, bloodless way to victory in war and it is the thankless task of the leaders to maintain their firm outward front which holds the resolution of their subordinates. Any irresolution in the leaders may result in costly weakening and indecision in the subordinates.[84]

Marshall's "price," one American battle casualty for every five Japanese, represents only a fraction of the casualties accrued during the smaller operation in Luzon. The limitation of the estimate to "the first 30 days" of the planned ninety-day drive to a "stop line" one-third of the way up the island was made because the ratio could very easily change as U.S. soldiers and marines started to fight their way into the mountains against additional Japanese divisions moving down from northern Kyushu. Detailed speculation beyond thirty days could come back to haunt Marshall, and even the first thirty-day projection was hedged by the qualifier, "there is reason to believe." The minutes describe Marshall's opening remarks ending with the following conclusions:

> General Marshall said that it was his personal view that the operation against Kyushu was the only course to pursue. He felt that air power alone was not sufficient to put the Japanese out of the war. It was unable alone to put the Germans out. General [Ira C.] Eaker and General [Dwight D.] Eisenhower both agreed to this.[85] Against the Japanese, scattered throughout mountainous country, the problem would be much more difficult than it had been in Germany. He felt that this plan offered the only way the Japanese could be forced into a feeling of utter helplessness. The operation would be difficult but no

84. "JCS Corrigendum to JCS 1388," 2.
85. Gen. Ira C. Eaker had also received a copy of the JWPC paper the day before the meeting. See memorandum to Eaker, June 17, 1945, microfilm: "GHQ, SWPA," courtesy Edward J. Drea. There is no record at either the Marshall Library or Dwight D. Eisenhower Presidential Library, Abilene, Kans., of Marshall's querying Eisenhower on this matter before the June 18 meeting. However, in an October 21, 2001, letter to the author, *Marshall Papers* editor Larry Bland noted that when Eisenhower flew in from Europe on the 18th, Marshall met him at the airport at 11 o'clock and that they had approximately ten minutes in which they could speak privately in the car on the way to the Pentagon. The rest of Eisenhower's time with Marshall before the 3:30 meeting with the president was taken up with celebrations (see "Million Roar D.C. Tribute to Eisenhower; Buckner Killed as Okinawa Fall Nears," *Washington Post*, June 19, 1945, 1).

more so than the assault in Normandy. He was convinced that every individual moving to the Pacific should be indoctrinated with a firm determination to see it through.[86]

Discussion of the tactical land operational aspects surrounding the opening invasion of Kyushu, the southernmost of Japan's home islands, followed, with the emphasis on their effects on U.S. casualties. One portion of that discussion would have a great impact on the *Enola Gay* debate five decades later.

> Admiral Leahy recalled that the President had been interested in knowing what the price in casualties for Kyushu would be and whether or not that price could be paid. He pointed out that the troops on Okinawa had lost 35 percent in casualties. If this percentage were applied to the number of troops to be employed in Kyushu, he thought from the similarity of the fighting to be expected, that this would give a good estimate of the casualties to be expected. He was interested therefore in finding out how many troops are to be used in Kyushu.[87]

Leahy did not believe that the narrow, presented figure of thirty-four thousand ground-force battle casualties offered a true picture of losses on Okinawa, which, depending on the accounting method used, actually ran from 63,631 to 72,000 largely because of psychiatric breakdowns.[88] He used the total number of casualties to formulate the 35 percent figure. Since Leahy, as well as the other participants including Truman, already knew that ground-force casualties on Okinawa were far higher than thirty-four thousand and approximately how many men were to be committed to the Kyushu

86. "JCS Corrigendum to JCS 1388," 3. The statement that "the problem would be much more difficult than it had been in Germany" is telling. It is supported by the follow-up statement that "the operation would be difficult but not more so than the assault in Normandy," which saw incremental advances through the tangled hedgerow country as American forces positioned themselves for a breakout from the Normandy Peninsula. Excluding the considerable number of "other losses," there were 133,316 U.S. and 92,003 British battle casualties during the Normandy campaign, June 8 through August 31, 1944. U.S. casualties are from *Army Battle Casualties*, 32; the British total is from L. F. Ellis et al., *Victory in the West* (2 vols., London: H. M. Stationery Off., 1962–1968), 1:488, 493.

87. "JCS Corrigendum to JCS 1388," 4.

88. "U.S. Tenth Army Action Report," vol. 1, chap. 11, sec. 1, 12; Huber, *Japan's Battle for Okinawa*, 119–20; and Giangreco, "Casualty Projections," 539–40.

fight, he was obviously making an effort—commonly done in such meetings—to focus their attention on the statistical consequences of the disparity. Fifty years later, Leahy's use of the 35 percent figure from Okinawa as a way to gain a better understanding of potential casualties during OLYMPIC was to be controversial.[89]

The table of organization strength (TOE) of strictly ground-force combat units at the commencement of Operation OLYMPIC was 190,000 troops. Dividing the TOE by one-third results in a thumbnail casualty estimate of approximately sixty-three thousand for the first month. Indeed, Leahy noted in both his diary and autobiography his impression that Marshall was "of the opinion" that this same number represented likely casualties from some undefined portion of the invasion.[90] However, even though sixty-three thousand is in line with a one-month estimate derived from the TOE, one can only guess at what the number actually represents. Because it is not in evidence in the meeting transcript—and Leahy attached no parameters to the estimate—it has been discarded by military historians who have instead used more properly documented estimates.

None of the meeting's participants found Leahy's approach in the least unusual or took issue with his statement that 33 percent "would give a good estimate of the casualties to be expected." Indeed, Marshall had the data at hand and answered Leahy's question by presenting the most recent figure for the troop commitment forty-five days into the invasion, 766,700.[91] He then allowed those around the table, including Leahy, to draw their own conclusions as to long-term implications. The meeting's participants also understood that

89. The sixty-three thousand figure was ultimately adopted by the National Air and Space Museum at the insistence of Barton Bernstein, as the total number of casualties expected by the U.S. military during the invasion of Japan. Use of this artificially low figure further inflamed veterans' passions during the *Enola Gay* controversy and contributed directly to Harwit's dismissal. See Harwit, *An Exhibit Denied,* 345–46, 380.

90. Diary entry, June 18, 1945, William D. Leahy Diaries, 1897–1956 (microfilm edition, reel 4), interlibrary loan, Naval War College, Newport, R.I., to CARL. See also William D. Leahy, *I Was There: The Personal Story of the Chief of Staff to Presidents Roosevelt and Truman Based on His Notes and Diaries Made at the Time* (New York: Whittlesey House, 1950), 384.

91. Marshall's figure of 766,700 differs only slightly from that of MacArthur's headquarters, which gave 766,986 as the number of men to be landed within a month and a half of the invasion in "Staff Study, 'Olympic,' Operations in Southern Kyushu," May 28, 1945, Appendix B, Annex 4, Commander in Chief, Army Forces, Pacific, call nos. N11619 and N11619-B, CARL.

Marshall's figure did not include replacements for losses, who would themselves become part of the equation and subject to the ratios because of the extended length of Operation OLYMPIC.

They then discussed the sizes of the opposing Japanese and American forces, which was fundamental to understanding how the ratios might play out. Finally, Truman, who had been monitoring the rising casualty figures from Okinawa on a daily basis, frequently with Leahy at his side, cut to the bottom line: "The President expressed the view that it was practically creating another Okinawa closer to Japan [Tokyo], to which the Chiefs of Staff agreed."[92]

More discussion ensued. Truman asked, "if the invasion of Japan by white men would not have the effect of more closely uniting the Japanese?" Stimson stated that "there was every prospect of this." He added that he "agreed with the plan proposed by the Joint Chiefs of Staff as being the best thing to do, but he still hoped for some fruitful accomplishment through other means." The other means included a range of measures from increased political pressure brought to bear through a display of Allied unanimity at the upcoming conference in Potsdam to the as-yet-untested atomic weapons that it was hoped would "shock" the Japanese into surrender.

Continued discussion touched on military considerations and the merits of unconditional surrender. The minutes record the end of the meeting as follows:

> The President reiterated that his main reason for this conference with the Chiefs of Staff was his desire to know definitely how far we could afford to go in the Japanese campaign. He had hoped that there was a possibility of preventing an Okinawa from one end of Japan to the other. He was clear on the situation now and was quite sure that the Joint Chiefs of Staff should proceed with the Kyushu operation.[93]

Truman's multiple references to Okinawa—specifically his comment of the invasion operations representing "an Okinawa from one

92. For Leahy's frequent accompaniment of Truman, see George M. Elsey to author, March 30, 1997. See also Elsey's lengthy introduction to "Blueprints for Victory," *National Geographic* 187 (May 1995): 55–77, for information on Leahy's and Truman's visits to the White House Map Room. See also Elsey's *An Unplanned Life: A Memoir by George McKee Elsey* (Columbia: University of Missouri Press, 2005), 80–82, 89, 99.

93. Ibid., 5.

end of Japan to the other"—indicate clearly what he believed would be the magnitude of the fighting. The Japanese navy was essentially destroyed, but Japanese air power was being preserved for kamikaze flights during the invasions. More importantly, intelligence estimates clearly demonstrated that Japan's field armies in the home islands were swelling rapidly, and there was ample time to train and arm recruits not only for the defense of the Tokyo area in 1946 but also for the defense of Kyushu in the coming winter. Future wars along the Asian littoral would demonstrate the limitations of America's industrial dominance when applied against enemies fighting an infantry-intensive war on rugged home ground. The situation facing the armed forces was painfully evident to the secretary of war. Stimson summed up his view of the meeting and the casualties question in his July 2, 1945, memo to the president:

> There is reason to believe that the operation for the occupation of Japan following the landing may be a very long, costly and arduous struggle on our part. The terrain, much of which I have visited several times, has left the impression on my memory of being one which would be susceptible to a last ditch defense such as has been made on Iwo Jima and Okinawa and which of course is very much larger than either of those two areas. According to my recollection it will be much more unfavorable with regard to tank maneuvering than either the Philippines or Germany [because of the extensive network of dikes, canals, and rice paddies].
>
> If we once land on one of the main islands and begin a forceful occupation of Japan, we shall probably have cast the die of last ditch resistance. The Japanese are highly patriotic and certainly susceptible to calls for fanatical resistance to repel an invasion. Once started in actual invasion, we shall in my opinion have to go through with an even more bitter finish fight than in Germany. We shall incur the losses incident to such a war and we shall have to leave the Japanese islands even more thoroughly destroyed than was the case with Germany. This would be due both to the difference in the Japanese and German personal character and the differences in the size and character of the terrain through which the operations will take place.[94]

Stimson had been a colonel of artillery during the brutal fighting of World War I, and Truman would not take lightly his appraisal of

94. Memo in Stimson, "The Decision to Use the Atomic Bomb," 102–4.

the targeted Japanese terrain gained from direct examination on multiple occasions between the wars. On the subject of casualties, the president did not need to have it explained to him what Stimson meant by "an even more bitter finish fight than Germany" since he and everyone else who had taken part in the June 18 meeting knew that it had cost roughly a million American all-causes casualties to defeat the Nazis, and that U.S. casualties were actually small when compared to those of the major allies. Moreover, Marshall told the president the same thing at the meeting when he stated that, because of Japan's mountainous terrain, "the problem would be much more difficult than it had been in Germany." Stimson's warning in his July 2, 1945, memo to Truman that "we shall incur the losses incident to such a war" was equally clear. For anyone not understanding the reference, Stimson spelled it out in his high-profile *Harper's* article after the defeat of Japan: "We estimated that if we should be forced to carry this plan to its conclusion, the major fighting would not end until the latter part of 1946, at the earliest. I was informed that such operations might be expected to cost over a million casualties."[95]

The belief that total casualties "might" exceed a million men—roughly the same number that had been experienced by America in the war against Germany—was far below the two to three million implied by Hoover's memoranda yet was double the five hundred thousand figure being briefed to Pacific-bound servicemen and being used by Stimson himself at least through May 1945. Were the escalating estimates of Japan's manpower potential and its widely trumpeted mobilization responsible for Stimson's change, or was he simply restating the Saipan ratio?

Stimson's fears aside, the casualty estimates coming from "always conservative" planners were grim enough.[96] "There were all kinds of estimates as to the cost of it in manpower," said Lieutenant General John Hull, chief of the Operations Division, "and had the Japanese continued fighting and fought as hard for their homeland as

95. Ibid., 102.

96. In an August 9, 1943, memorandum from Marshall to Handy, Marshall recounted that President Roosevelt had told him that "Planners were always conservative and saw all the difficulties, and that more could usually be done than they were willing to admit" (Bland and Stevens, eds., *The Papers of George Catlett Marshall*, 4:85).

you would expect them to . . . it would have been a bloody operation. . . . The casualty estimates ran everything from a few hundred thousand to a million men to do the thing."[97]

Truman's postwar published statement in the official air force history has also been called into question. The president wrote air force historian James Lea Cate:

> When the message came to Potsdam that a successful atomic explosion had taken place in New Mexico, there was much excitement and conversation about the effects on the war. . . . I asked General Marshall what it would cost in lives to land on the Tokyo Plain and other places in Japan. It was his opinion that such an invasion would cost at a minimum one quarter million casualties, and might cost as much as a million, on the American side alone.[98]

To some, the president's statement of what was said in an oral presentation seemed insufficient, and an examination of the historiography and a very small selection of some of the more readily accessible documents led Kai Bird to conclude in his *New York Times* article "The Curators Cave In" that "No scholar of the war has ever found archival evidence to substantiate claims that Truman expected anything close to a million casualties, or even that such large numbers were conceivable."[99]

When it later turned out that there was, in fact, a considerable amount of documentation available, the question was recast by Barton Bernstein as "fundamentally about what *top* U.S. officials—not lower and middle-level people—believed." Bernstein wrote, "No scholar has been able to find any *high-level* supporting archival documents from the *Truman months* before Hiroshima that, in unalloyed form, provides even an explicit estimate of 500,000 casualties, let alone a million or more."[100] However, the relevance of this narrow

97. Interview with Lt. Gen. John E. Hull (no interviewer cited), April 8, 1974, 22, Senior Officer Oral History Program, vol. 2, sect. 7, tape 1, U.S Army Military History Institute, Carlisle Barracks, Pa.

98. Wesley Frank Craven and James Lea Cate, *The Army Air Forces in World War II* (7 vols., Chicago: University of Chicago Press, [1948–1958]), insert between pages in 5:712–13.

99. Kai Bird, "The Curators Cave In," *New York Times*, October 9, 1994, 15.

100. Emphasis in originals. Barton Bernstein to the editor, *Journal of Military History* 63 (January 1999): 247; and "Truman and the Bomb: Targeting Noncombatants, Using the Bomb, and Defending the 'Decision,'" in ibid., 62 (July 1998): 552. In a let-

focus on the period after Truman became president appears questionable since it ignores the fact that the government's manpower policy for 1945 was formulated in the winter of 1944–1945 and that the huge hikes in Selective Service inductions were publicly announced and implemented months before Truman took the oath of office.[101] Nevertheless, the Hoover memorandum of May 30, 1945, and the subsequent memos between President Truman and his most senior civilian advisers—the Truman-Grew-Hull-Stimson-Vinson exchange—unquestionably meet the evolving criteria of critics.

Truman's statement in the air force history was found wanting on other grounds as well. A lack of references to a "formal" meeting on the atom bomb in the diaries of several participants at the Potsdam Conference led Bernstein to discount it as "Truman's postwar, dubious claim of Marshall's *alleged* pre-Hiroshima casualty estimates," and he maintains not only that "no such meeting took place at Potsdam" but that "there is no record of such a discussion or such an estimate."[102]

However, references in the "Log of the President's Trip to the Berlin Conference," multiple Truman diary entries, and British diplomatic papers all indicate that such a meeting did indeed take place on July 18, 1945.[103] In addition, it was immediately after Truman "conferred with the Secretary of State and a number of his advisers" at this meeting that he brought Winston Churchill the telegrams de-

---

ter to the editor, *Pacific Historical Review* 69 (2000): 352, Bernstein states, "some of my recent work [specifically "The Alarming Japanese Buildup on Southern Kyushu, Growing U.S. Fears, and Counterfactual Analysis: Would the Planned November 1945 Invasion of Southern Kyushu Have Occurred?" ibid., 68 (1999): 561–609] critically examines Truman's pre- and post-Hiroshima thinking, but that work does not repudiate those quoted 1986 words or thoughts about the myth of a half-million U.S. lives saved." Bernstein maintains in his letter, "[T]here is no reliable evidence that in mid-1945 [Truman] anticipated 500,000 or a million U.S. casualties."

101. Ferrell contends that, since Truman was presiding officer of the Senate and, presumably, a reader of the *New York Times,* "large military call-ups had to come to [Truman's] attention for they were politically sensitive" ("Intelligence Assessments and Assumptions," [paper, annual meeting of the Society for Military History, Pennsylvania State University, April, 6, 1999]). See also note 25; and D. M. Giangreco and Kathryn Moore's essay in this volume, "Half a Million Purple Hearts."

102. Emphasis in originals. Bernstein, "Truman and the Bomb," 551, 153; Barton J. Bernstein, "Writing, Righting, or Wronging the Historical Record: President Truman's Letter on His Atomic-Bomb Decision," *Diplomatic History,* 16 (1992): 171.

103. Giangreco and Moore, eds., *Dear Harry,* 466–76. The first printing of this book contains an error in the endnotes to these pages. Endnotes 8 to 13 should be renumbered 9 to 14, and the printed endnote 14 removed.

tailing the successful atom bomb test in the New Mexico desert.[104] Following their working lunch, the prime minister wrote in a memorandum that the president was weighted down by the "terrible responsibilities that rested upon him in regard to the unlimited effusion of American blood" expected during the invasion.[105] Ironically, this was one month to the day after the White House meeting with the Joint Chiefs, Stimson, and Forrestal.

Truman has also been taken to task for the wide variety of figures he later gave for possible American casualties resulting from an invasion of Japan. "Truman's own postwar claims," Bernstein has written, "oscillated so widely that no responsible analyst should trust any particular recollection on this subject."[106] The criticism also begs a question: Why should one expect Truman to be any more skilled at counterfactual analysis than the scholars criticizing him many decades after the fact?[107] There is far more utility in examining the projected, or profactuals—the many variables and unknowables that leaders and planners during World War II had to consider when planning *ahead* in time for the effects of weather, opposition, logistics, and so on. This must not be confused with counterfactual

104. William M. Rigdon, "Log of the President's Trip to the Berlin Conference, 6 July 1945 to 7 August 1945," 23, Truman Library.

105. Winston Churchill memorandum of conversation, July 18, 1945, *Documents on British Policies Overseas* (3 vols., London: Stationery Office, 1984), 1291. See also Truman diary entry, December 2, 1950, PSF, Truman Library. In the midst of China's stunning entry into the Korean War and the grim conflict with MacArthur over the direction of military strategy and foreign policy, the president wrote, "Now [MacArthur's] in serious trouble. We must get him out if we can. The conference [with Dean Acheson and Gen. Omar Bradley] was the most solemn one I've had since the Atomic Bomb conference in Berlin. We continue in the morning. It looks very bad" (Giangreco and Moore, eds., *Dear Harry*, 474). This private reference to an A-bomb-related meeting at Potsdam was penned two years before Truman's letter to Professor Cate.

106. Bernstein, "Truman and the Bomb," 553.

107. Robert James Maddox, from "What Did They Know?" See also Maddox, *Weapons for Victory: The Hiroshima Decision Fifty Years Later* (Columbia: University of Missouri Press, 1995). In addition to Bernstein, "Truman and the Bomb," see also Bernstein's "The Alarming Japanese Buildup on Southern Kyushu, Growing U.S. Fears, and Counterfactual Analysis"; Bernstein, "Reconsidering 'Invasion Most Costly': Popular History Scholarship, Publishing Standards, and the Claim of High U.S. Casualty Estimates to Help Legitimize the Atomic Bombings," *Peace and Change* 24 (1999): 220–47; Bernstein, "Reconsidering Truman's Claim of 'Half a Million American Lives' Saved by the Atomic Bomb: The Construction and Deconstruction of a Myth," *Journal of Strategic Studies* 22 (March, 1999): 54–95.

analysis and is exactly what both American and Japanese military staffs were—and still are—paid to do.

The newly discovered exchange between Truman and his most senior civilian advisers in the wake of the Hoover memorandum, and his subsequent meeting with Marshall and the other Joint Chiefs, should make Truman's priorities clear. Yet the answer to what Truman actually "believed" will never find universal concurrence. The primary participants in these events were long gone before the *Enola Gay* controversy, but key people from their personal staffs remember well the context in which decisions affecting the lives of millions had to be made. President emeritus of the American Red Cross, George M. Elsey, was then a "watch officer" for the White House Map Room, where the progress of the war was graphically charted and updated daily. He notes the close attention paid to growing Japanese troop strength and remembers "Admiral Leahy discussing the invasion plans with the President in the Map Room prior to our departure for Potsdam." Elsey emphasized "the concern they both had as to the size of the Japanese forces available to oppose us" and that during the course of "many conversations" with the president that fateful summer, Truman made it very clear that he "was deeply worried about the casualties that would inevitably be incurred in an invasion."[108]

And while Marshall's beliefs have also been called into question, it is important to note that he certainly never refuted, even obliquely, Truman's statements that he was the source of the casualty estimates the president used in his memoirs and the air force history. What Marshall told his biographer, Forrest Pogue, was that conquering Japan by invasion would have been "terribly bitter and frightfully expensive in lives and treasure." He said that claims the war would have ended soon, even without the use of atomic weapons, "were rather silly" and maintained that "it was quite necessary to drop the bomb to shorten the war," adding "I think it was very wise to use it."[109] As to whether this reflected Marshall's true beliefs or was simply an effort to cover his commander in chief, one

---

108. Elsey to author, March 30, 1997. See also Elsey's *An Unplanned Life,* 89–90.
109. Forrest C. Pogue, *George C. Marshall: Statesman, 1945–1959* (New York: Viking, 1987), 23.

of Marshall's key assistants in the immediate postwar period, George F. Kennan, maintains, "I have no doubt that our leaders, General Marshall among them, had good reason to anticipate a casualty rate of dreadful and sickening proportions in any invasion of Japan."[110]

110. George F. Kennan to author, October 6, 1997.

Half a Million Purple Hearts

I N EARLY 1989, JUST AS NATO WAS stepping up its bombing campaign in Kosovo, the news broke that the United States was manufacturing nine thousand new Purple Hearts, the decoration that goes to American troops wounded in battle and the families of those killed in action. To the media, this seemed a clear indication that despite its pledge not to send in ground forces, the United States was planning to do just that. "Why in good God's name are we making Purple Hearts if we are not in a war and we don't expect casualties?" asked the *New York Post.*

But in fact the run of medals had nothing to do with imminent combat; rather, it cast light backward on a long-ago war. For this was the first large-scale production of the decoration since World War II: for more than half a century, American casualties have been receiving Purple Hearts stockpiled for the invasion of Japan. All the other implements of that war—tanks and LSTs, bullets and K rations— have long since been sold, scrapped, or used up, but these medals, struck for their grandfathers, are still being pinned on the chests of young soldiers. More than 370,000 Purple Hearts have been issued between the outbreak of the Korean War through the current peacekeeping operations in Bosnia and Kosovo. Remarkably, some 120,000 more are still in the hands of the armed services, not only stockpiled at military supply depots, but kept with major combat units and at field hospitals so that they can be awarded without delay. But although great numbers of the World War II stock are still available and ready for use, those controversial nine thousand new ones were ordered for the simplest of bureaucratic reasons: so many medals had been transferred to the armed services that the government organization responsible for procuring them, the Defense Supply Center Philadelphia, had to replenish its own inventory.

Established as the Badge of Military Merit in 1782, the decoration was General George Washington's way around congressional unwillingness to reward ordinary soldiers for extraordinary deeds. In the eighteenth century, the traditional practice among all armies of the world was to present decorations only to officers. Early in the war, the new American army used promotion to reward exceptional gallantry, but as money dwindled the military found such promotions to be a hard sell with Congress.

In the hard-pressed Continental Army, there were often no funds to pay a soldier at his existing rank, let alone for a promotion. Still, some way had to be found, said Inspector General Baron von Steuben, to recognize "soldiers who have served with fidelity." Washington's answer was to order narrow strips of cloth added to the lower left sleeve of a uniform to denote length of service (these are commonly referred to today as *hash marks*) and the creation of the Badge of Military Merit for "singularly meritorious action" as well as for "extraordinary fidelity and essential service." Washington stipulated that the decoration be worn over the left breast and be created in "the figure of a heart of purple cloth, or silk, edged with narrow lace or binding." The general himself presented the first two.

The decoration fell into disuse after the Revolution, and efforts to revive it in the wake of World War I by Army Chief of Staff Charles P. Summerall failed. Summerall's successor, Douglas MacArthur, had better luck, largely because his campaign coincided with the run-up to the bicentennial of George Washington's birth in 1932. MacArthur changed its name to the Purple Heart and, at the last minute, expanded its franchise to include wounds received as a result of enemy action. In 1942 this became the sole criterion—a separate medal had been established for wartime meritorious achievement—and other services later adopted the award.

The demands of global warfare played havoc with the first 633,000 Purple Hearts produced during the fighting of World War II, and a variety of manufacturers and contracting agencies attempted to standardize mass-production techniques. To the delight (or consternation) of collectors, there were four major variations of the medal before all the parties involved settled on the attributes making up the decorations still being presented today. Although the vast majority of these early types were awarded long before the war ended, the nature of the medal's distribution resulted in some being returned to the central pool; medals struck in 1942—with a six-digit serial number—appeared as late as the Vietnam War.

In all, some 1,506,000 Purple Hearts were made for the war effort with production reaching its peak as America geared up for the invasion of Japan. The unexpected ferocity of the Pacific fighting led to last-minute scrambling by the navy to have awards ready for the invasion of the home islands. The navy had believed that its initial 1942 order for 135,000 Purple Hearts would be sufficient for all wartime needs but found that it had to order twenty-three thousand more in October 1944—and, alas, fifty thousand more in the spring of 1945. These orders could not be fulfilled until as late as the next year—months after soldiers and marines were expected to fight their way ashore while sailors battled fresh waves of kamikazes. The director of the mint, Nellie Tayloe Ross, reprimanded her Philadelphia facility, which was responsible for producing the medal's central components: "Think of the 20,000 heroes at Iwo Jima, due to receive the Purple Hearts which we are unable to supply!" The navy brass swallowed hard and made arrangements with the army to "borrow" sixty thousand decorations.

And then the war ended. The most wonderful of all its surplus: 495,000 unused Purple Hearts.

By 1976 roughly 370,000 of these had been earned by servicemen and women who fought in America's Asian wars as well as in trouble spots in the Middle East and Europe. This total included a significant number issued to World War II and even World War I veterans whose paperwork had finally caught up with them. That year also saw a small production run of additional Purple Hearts before a warehouse load—125,000 decorations—of decades-old inventory was rediscovered after falling off the books.

Increasing terrorist activity in the late 1970s and 1980s resulted in mounting casualties among service personnel, and a decision was made to inspect the remaining stock. Thousands of these decorations were labeled "unsalvageable," but thousands more were refurbished and repackaged between 1983 and 1991. By the end of 1999, most of the refurbished medals had been shipped to other government customers, and the Defense Supply Center Philadelphia entered into contracts with Graco Industries of Tomball, Texas, for the first large-scale production of Purple Hearts since World War II.

NATO had begun its bombing campaign in Kosovo less than two months earlier, and in the volatile political climate of the day, it was unlikely the order would escape notice in the press. It didn't. Nor was it missed by certain World War II veterans who five years earlier had worked with the Smithsonian Institution on the fiftieth anniversary display of the *Enola Gay*, the B-29 that dropped the atom bomb on Hiroshima. Controversy had erupted over the presentation at the National Air and Space Museum when veterans protested that the exhibit portrayed the Japanese as victims of a needless slaughter.

The veterans came under heavy criticism for insisting that the bomb had ended the war quickly and ultimately saved countless thousands of American—and Japanese—lives. Their opponents maintained that military men had later invented projected casualty numbers in order to justify the use of the weapon on a wholly beaten nation.

Bill Rooney, a former intelligence officer with the B-29s, said that if the information about Purple Heart production had been more widely known during the controversy, "the notion that Truman simply made up huge casualty estimates after the fact to justify dropping the bombs would have been more effectively countered." James Pattillo, then president of the Twentieth Air Force Association, stated that "detailed information on the kind of casualties expected would have been a big help in demonstrating to modern Americans that those were very different times." Medical and training information in "arcanely-worded military documents can be confusing," said Pattillo, "but everyone understands a half-million Purple Hearts."

GIAN PERI GENTILE

Advocacy or Assessment?

The United States Strategic Bombing
Survey of Germany and Japan

Based on a detailed investigation of all the facts and supported by the testimony of the surviving Japanese leaders involved, it is the Survey's opinion that certainly prior to 31 December 1945, and in all probability prior to 1 November 1945, Japan would have surrendered even if the atomic bombs had not been dropped, even if Russia had not entered the war; and even if no invasion had been planned or contemplated.

USSBS, *Summary Report (Pacific War)* (1946)

With the project now effectively finished, the USSBS came to an end, having performed, to my mind, a difficult and demanding task with energy, objectivity and dispatch.

Paul Nitze, *From Hiroshima to Glasnost* (1989)

ECRETARY OF WAR Henry L. Stimson officially established the United States Strategic Bombing Survey (USSBS) in November 1944 to analyze the effects of strategic air power in the European theater. Later, President Harry S. Truman expanded the survey's scope to study all types of aerial war against Japan, including the effects of the atomic bombing. In an attempt to keep the survey's findings impartial, prominent civilians, instead of military officers, were appointed as directors of the survey's divisions. The key directors were Franklin D'Olier (chairman), Henry Alexander (vice chairman), George Ball, Paul Nitze, Theodore Wright, Fred Searls, and John Kenneth Galbraith.[1] The final studies, officially

1. David MacIsaac, *Strategic Bombing in World War II: The Story of the United States Strategic Bombing Survey* (New York: Garland, 1976), x, 54, 107–8; Gordon Daniels, *A*

completed and released for printing in the summer of 1946, numbered more than 330 reports and annexes; the massive amount of research and statistical data is staggering.

The survey contains conclusions that have influenced scholars and strategies since its reports were first published in 1946. Analysts such as Bernard Brodie and P. M. S. Blackett have used the survey's conclusions and evidence to support their ideas on nuclear strategy and postwar defense policy and organization. The survey's findings also played a role in the postwar debate over President Truman's decision to drop the atomic bombs on Hiroshima and Nagasaki. Beginning with Henry L. Stimson, and continuing up through at least Herbert Feis and Gar Alperovitz, writers have used portions of the survey to support their position in the debate over the combat use of the bomb.

The survey has readily adapted itself to the wide range of arguments found in this amalgam of postwar writings. The USSBS reports are collectively, and at times individually, very malleable sources. Their sometimes competing conclusions and even contradictions, and their not-infrequent ambiguities, have made the reports a pliant source for scholars, pundits, and journalists alike. This essay will critically analyze key survey reports to explain how and why they have accommodated such diverse conclusions.[2] In addition, it will show how these influential documents have been used in postwar thinking on strategic bombing, military strategy, and the atomic bombing of Japan in 1945.

One way to get at the diverse nature of the survey's reports is to take some of its stated conclusions and then illustrate how the evi-

---

Guide to the Reports of the United States Strategic Bombing Survey (London: Offices of the Royal Historical Society, 1981), xxi/-xxiii. In the foreword of each survey report is a paragraph indicating that the survey was established by "the Secretary of War on 3 November 1944, pursuant to a directive from the late President Roosevelt."

2. Using a different approach, David MacIsaac has argued in "What the Bombing Survey Really Says," *Air Force Magazine* 56 (June 1973): 63, that studies of strategic bombing in World War II should rely predominantly on the survey reports published under the auspices of the chairman's office, and not on the ancillary reports. That approach, however, would force analysts, every time a contradiction or ambiguity occurred in one of the ancillary reports, to return to the chairman's reports for the survey's "consensus" opinion. Such a process, by focusing only on the official opinions in the chairman's reports, would overlook the many contradictions, ambiguities, and conflicting evidence to be found elsewhere in those reports. For an argument similar to MacIsaac's, see Guido R. Perera, *Leaves from My Book of Life,* vol. 2: *Washington and War Years* (Boston: privately printed, 1975), 183.

dence used, or not used, by survey authors to support their conclusions can lead to alternative findings. A well-known and often-cited conclusion from the survey is that "Japan would have surrendered even if the atomic bombs had not been dropped, even if Russia had not entered the war, and even if no invasion had been planned or contemplated." The authors further asserted that the surrender would have occurred "certainly prior to 31 December 1945, and in all probability prior to 1 November 1945." The survey's implicit argument is that in the final stages of the war conventional (nonatomic) strategic air power was the decisive factor that forced Japan to surrender "unconditionally."[3]

This conclusion appears in a report from the Pacific Survey, issued by the chairman's office and entitled *Japan's Struggle to End the War*. The report provides a detailed narrative of the events leading to Japan's capitulation on August 14, 1945. The survey emphasized that, as early as 1943, the Japanese military and political leaders had begun to believe that their country could not win the war. A string of military setbacks at various points in the Pacific War convinced them that defeat was inevitable. In November 1944, the United States Army Air Forces (AAF) initiated its aerial campaign against the Japanese home islands. The bombing grew with ferocious intensity in March 1945 when the AAF made the population in Japanese cities its primary bombing target. As a result of the aerial campaign, the narrative states, "Those [Japanese leaders] responsible for the decision to surrender felt the twin impact of our [air] attack which made them not only impotent to resist, but also destroyed any hope of future resistance."[4] Strategic bombing had proven to certain members of the Japanese cabinet that the war must be brought to an end. The report went on to explain that by late July 1945 the Potsdam terms for surrender had equally divided the cabinet between those who wanted to accept the terms and those who wanted to continue the war: "Suzuki, Togo and Yonai felt that the declaration must be accepted as the final terms of peace at once, whether they liked it or not. The War Minister [Anami] and the two chiefs of staff [Toyoda and

3. United States Strategic Bombing Survey (hereafter cited as USSBS), Chairman's Office, *Japan's Struggle to End the War* (Washington, D.C.: U.S. Government Printing Office, 1946), 13; USSBS, Chairman's Office, *Summary Report (Pacific War)* (Washington, D.C.: U.S. Government Printing Office, 1946), 26.
4. USSBS, Chairman's Office, *Japan's Struggle to End the War*, 10.

Umezu] on the other hand felt that the terms were too dishonor-able."[5]

According to the survey, aerial bombardment had created the ur-gency for Suzuki, Togo, and Yonai to pursue peace aggressively at any cost, but conventional bombing had not convinced the cabinet's militarist faction to accept the Potsdam terms for surrender, even up to the time when the United States dropped the first atomic bomb on Hiroshima on August 6, 1945. The report argued that the atomic bomb and the subsequent Soviet declaration of war on August 8, 1945, only "provided further urgency and lubrication" for the Japa-nese to accept unconditional surrender"[6]; the decisive factor was the conventional bombing of the Japanese home islands. This analysis led the survey authors to their counterfactual speculation that, even without the bomb and Soviet war declaration, Japan would "in all probability" have surrendered before November 1, 1945, and defi-nitely before December 31, 1945.[7]

If, however, one disregards the survey's speculative concluding remarks, the report's narrative suggests another interpretation: that the atom bomb and Soviet war declaration might have been more critical in forcing Japan to surrender. The narrative indicates that the conventional bombing of the home islands had put some Japanese leaders in a frame of mind to seek a termination of the war. But, as the narrative points out, there was a deadlock stretching into early August over the acceptance of the Potsdam terms.

Contrary to the survey's counterfactual, the war could have con-tinued beyond November 1, and perhaps even after December 31, 1945, without the atom bomb and Soviet declaration of war. Tes-timony by key Japanese leaders during USSBS postwar interroga-tions supports this *possibility*. The survey authors, however, chose not to use this testimony; evidence that challenged their conclusions stayed in their unpublished files.[8]

---

5. Ibid., 8.
6. Ibid., 12.
7. Ibid., 13.
8. Robert P. Newman, "Ending the War with Japan: Paul Nitze's 'Early Surrender' Counterfactual," *Pacific Historical Review* 64 (May 1995): 175–76, 181–84, 189. New-man convincingly shows how survey authors, especially Paul Nitze, failed to ac-knowledge key testimony that brought into question their proposed counterfactual dates for Japan's surrender. See also Barton J. Bernstein, "Compelling Japan's Sur-render without the A-bomb, Soviet Entry, or Invasion: Reconsidering the U.S. Bomb-

Whether or not Japan would have surrendered without the use of the atom bomb and the Soviet war declaration, or would have done so in the face of only one of these events, remains unclear. Because there is a dearth of contemporaneous documentary evidence for the Japanese cabinet during the days leading to the surrender, it is difficult to arrive at a satisfactory conclusion on this issue. Postwar survey interrogations are helpful but, like many memoirs and postevent recollections, tend to let the present cloud the realities of the past. Supreme War Council member Admiral Koshiro Oikawa summed up this problem best. While "looking back upon it now," he shrewdly told his survey interrogators, "I might be able to say that, as a result of the damage from bombing[,] we should give up the fight at a certain time, [but] I could not have said that or even hazarded a guess at the time I was in office."[9]

Probably the best explanation yet is offered by Robert Butow in his 1954 *Japan's Decision to Surrender*. Butow argues persuasively that the atom bomb and the Soviet entrance created an "unusual atmosphere" that allowed the emperor to enter into the equation and to play a decisive role in terminating the war.[10] Butow sees the atom bomb and the Soviet Union as having a more decisive impact on Japan's capitulation than does the survey.

Why did survey authors discount the importance of the bomb and the Soviet Union? Probably early Cold War tensions with the Soviets had some effect on their conclusions. By the spring and summer of 1946, when the authors were completing many of their reports, increasing Cold War tensions might have created an atmosphere that would have made it imprudent for them to give any credit to the Soviet Union for ending the war with Japan. Regarding the atom bomb, Paul Nitze also had strong pre-Hiroshima beliefs that it was unnec-

---

ing Survey's Early-Surrender Conclusion," *Journal of Strategic Studies* 18 (June 1995): 101–48. For memoir accounts of the decisive impact of the atom bomb and the Soviet Union, see Shigenori Togo, *The Cause of Japan*, trans. and ed. Togo Fumihiko and B. B. Blakeney (Westport, Conn.: Greenwood Press, 1977), 315; Toshikazu Kase, *Journey to the Missouri*, ed. David Nelson Rowe (New Haven: Yale University Press, 1950), 169, 212.

9. Interrogation of Admiral Koshiro Oikawa, December 10, 1945, no. 494, USSBS Military Analysis Division, Records of the United States Strategic Bombing Survey (hereafter cited as USSBS Records), microfilm group M1654, National Archives and Records Administration, Washington, D.C.

10. Robert J. C. Butow, *Japan's Decision to Surrender* (Stanford: Stanford University Press, 1954), 231.

essary. In July 1945, about three months before departing for the Pacific to conduct that portion of the survey, Nitze was in Washington, D.C., writing an alternative plan for the air campaign against Japan based on the survey's findings in Europe. In July, weeks before Hiroshima, Nitze concluded that "even without the atomic bomb, Japan was likely to surrender in a matter of months. . . . Japan would capitulate by November 1945."[11] Nitze's pre-Hiroshima predictions were brought to fruition in the pages of the final reports of the Pacific Survey when they were published in July 1946.

At the same time that Paul Nitze was writing his alternative plan for bombing Japan, John Kenneth Galbraith, director of the European Survey's Economic Division, was reaching troubling conclusions about strategic bombing.[12] Parts of his economic report were condensed in two others published under the auspices of the chairman's office and titled *Summary Report (European War)* and *Overall Report (European War)*. The *Overall* and *Summary* reports also included information on the history of air power doctrine, the air war against the German air force, and the effects of strategic bombing on German morale. These two reports and Galbraith's full report share important conclusions about the German war economy and strategic bombing. First, the German economy was not efficiently run; it never achieved its full war potential, mostly because of poor strategic planning and inept economic management by Adolf Hitler and his staff.[13] Second, attacks on urban areas, conducted predominantly by the Royal Air Force (RAF), were not effective in reducing or

11. Paul Nitze, *From Hiroshima to Glasnost: At the Center of Decision* (New York: G. Weidenfeld, 1989), 37. For a good, but undocumented, analysis of Nitze and his influence on defense policy, see Strobe Talbott, *Master of the Game: Paul Nitze and the Nuclear Peace* (New York: Knopf, 1988). An insightful analysis of the ideological underpinnings of the Tokyo war trials is Elizabeth S. Kopelman's "Ideology and International Law: The Dissent of the Indian Justice at the Tokyo War Crimes Trial," *New York University Journal of International Law and Politics* 23 (1991): 373–444.

12. John Kenneth Galbraith, *A Life in Our Times: Memoirs* (Boston: Houghton Mifflin, 1981), 202. For an anecdotal account of the European Survey without much analysis of the survey's findings, see George W. Ball, *The Past Has Another Pattern: Memoirs* (New York: Norton, 1982), 42–53.

13. USSBS, Chairman's Office, *The Effects of Strategic Bombing on the German War Economy*, 7–8; USSBS, Chairman's Office, *Overall Report (European War)*, 31; USSBS, Chairman's Office, *Summary Report (European War)*, 2. For a postsurvey analysis on the inefficiency of Germany's war economy, see John K. Galbraith "Germany Was Badly Run," *Fortune* 32 (December 1945): 200; Burton H. Klein, *Germany's Economic Preparation for War* (Cambridge: Harvard University Press, 1959), 235–41.

breaking German war production.[14] Finally, the AAF achieved its most decisive results by attacking German transportation centers and railroads.[15]

A common theme that runs throughout the *Summary* and *Overall* reports is the decisiveness of air power in the war against Germany. While these two reports acknowledge that "hindsight inevitably suggests that [air power] might have been employed better in some respects," they both contend that air power was decisive:

> In the air, its victory was complete. At sea, its contribution, combined with naval power, brought an end to the enemy's greatest threat—the U-boat; on land, it helped turn the tide overwhelmingly in favor of Allied ground forces. Its power and superiority made possible the success of the invasion. It brought the economy which sustained the enemy's armed forces to virtual collapse. . . . It brought home to the German people the full impact of modern war with all its horror and suffering. Its impact on the German nation will be lasting.[16]

These two reports, however, do not try to conceal the failures of the AAF's strategic air campaign against Germany. Ball bearing plants proved to be extremely resilient and could quickly regain production levels despite heavy pounding from AAF attacks. The AAF's campaign against German airframe factories did not prevent a steady increase in production that peaked in September 1944 during heavy Allied bombardment.[17] Both reports also acknowledge the increase in production levels, in the face of serial attacks, of certain armament industries.[18] Despite these shortcomings in the AAF's campaign, the tone of both reports is still positive. The reports place much emphasis on the AAF's highly successful attacks on oil industries and transportation. According to survey reports, bombing these two targets, in conjunction with the defeat of the German air force,

14. USSBS, *The Effects of Strategic Bombing on the German War Economy*, 13; USSBS, Chairman's Office, *Overall Report (European War)*, 37; USSBS, Chairman's Office, *Summary Report (European War)*, 3, 16.

15. USSBS, *The Effects of Strategic Bombing on the German War Economy*, 12–14, 63, 127; USSBS, Chairman's Office, *Overall Report (European War)*, 61, 64, 108; USSBS, Chairman's Office, *Summary Report (European War)*, 12, 16.

16. USSBS, Chairman's Office, *Summary Report (European War)*, 16; USSBS, Chairman's Office, *Overall Report (European War)*, 107.

17. USSBS, Chairman's Office, *Summary Report (European War)*, 6.

18. Ibid., 12; USSBS, Chairman's Office, *Overall Report (European War)*, 37.

contributed significantly to the collapse of the German economy in April 1945.

Colonel Guido Perera, the onetime head of the Committee of Operations Analysis and later member of the survey chairman's staff, was responsible for editing and writing portions of the *Overall Report*.[19] In his memoirs, he firmly agrees with the conclusion in the *Overall* and *Summary* reports that air power was decisive in the war against Germany. But he is disturbed by some of the conclusions in Galbraith's separate report, *The Effects of Strategic Bombing on the German War Economy,* that tend (more than those in the *Overall* and *Summary* reports) to emphasize the failure of strategic bombing to defeat Germany. Perera devotes ten pages of his memoirs to a vehement refutation of Galbraith's report and of the economist's later writings on World War II strategic bombing. Perera argues that the failures and successes of strategic bombing should be interpreted in light of the AAF's objective in the European theater: to prepare the way for a ground invasion of the continent, and not the destruction of German industry.[20] Perera is partly correct about the AAF's strategic objectives. Up to September 1944, the AAF generally directed its attacks toward supporting the ground invasion. Once the ground operation was under way, however, the AAF committed itself to a full-scale assault on the German war economy. It is in this context of shifting AAF purposes, which Perera fails to acknowledge, that Galbraith and his Economic Division conducted their analysis.

Galbraith's *The Effects of Strategic Bombing on the German War Economy* intentionally has a different tone and emphasis than the *Overall* and *Summary* reports. Galbraith states in his memoirs that in September 1945 he and most of his team had returned to Washington, D.C., and discovered that a secretariat from the chairman's office had written a glowing summary of the strategic air war against Germany. Nowhere in the secretariat's summary was what Galbraith termed in his 1981 memoirs "the disastrous failure of strategic bombing," the assessment that he implied was in his own final survey report.[21] Although Galbraith's survey report does emphasize the failures of certain strategic bombing targets and policies, it never comes close to stating what his later memoirs termed a "disastrous failure."

19. Perera, *Leaves from My Book of Life,* 188.
20. Ibid., 184.
21. Galbraith, *A Life in Our Times,* 227.

Still, Galbraith's analysis for the Economic Division focuses on the inability of the AAF, especially before the fall of 1944, to substantially affect Germany's war production. Not until late in the war, according to the Economic Division's report, when the AAF began to concentrate heavily on oil and transportation, did Germany begin to feel the full weight of the air attack. By this time, however, as the report points out, the ground offensive had also become a powerful factor in crippling Germany's fighting strength; both air and ground efforts were inextricably mixed in the assault on the German war economy.[22]

The most disturbing conclusion brought out in the Economic Division's report was that strategic bombing, during 1943 and into early 1944, might have helped streamline, rather than injure, the German economy. When discussing the measures that Albert Speer, Germany's wartime minister for economics, took to increase output, the report argued that

> [Speer's] effort was also helped by the air attacks. The stress of the air raids permitted him to mobilize the energies of the population just as the growing seriousness of the war permitted him to break the inertia of Germany's governmental and industrial bureaucracy and to induce it to accept procedures which hitherto were sternly rejected. In other words if the debacle at Stalingrad was a decisive stimulus for Speer's drive, the air raids of 1943–1944 . . . may have kept the tension of national danger, and created the requisite atmosphere for sacrifice.[23]

This passage does not claim that strategic bombing assisted Germany after the full weight of the air campaign began in the months leading to D-day. Nor does it suggest that bombing improved the morale of the German civilian population. But, certainly, the notion that the AAF's limited bombing campaign indirectly helped, rather than weakened, the Germany economy was a difficult conclusion for

---

22. USSBS, *The Effects of Strategic Bombing on the German War Economy*, 13–14; Klein, *Germany's Economic Preparation for War*, 234. Klein, who was Galbraith's assistant director, takes this one step further in his 1948 book by arguing that strategic bombing was only decisive in its reduction of Germany's military ability to resist the Allied ground offensive. P. M. S. Blackett argues along the same lines in *Military and Political Consequences of Atomic Energy* (London: Turnstile Press, 1948), which is discussed in a later section of this essay.

23. USSBS, *The Effects of Strategic Bombing on the German War Economy*, 26.

AAF officers to accept. Galbraith's report, by deflating AAF claims that strategic bombing alone could decisively defeat an enemy's economy, threatened the AAF's hopes for an independent air arm. Colonel Perera's strong critique of the Economic Division's report reflected these feelings.

The Pacific Survey's reports contain even more diversity and disagreements than those from its European counterpart: the chairman's *Summary Report (Pacific War)*, though acknowledging that the war against Japanese shipping was an important factor in destroying Japan's war economy, argued that the decisive factor in persuading Japanese leaders to surrender was the conventional strategic bombing of the home islands. But two reports—the Economic Division's *The Effects of Strategic Bombing on Japan's War Economy* and the Transportation Division's *The War against Japanese Transportation*—subtly differed from the *Summary Report*'s argument. In the view of these two division studies, the antishipping campaign had virtually destroyed Japan's economy before the main weight of the AAF's bombing campaign, and therefore these two publications, unlike the *Summary Report*, stress the decisive role of air attacks on shipping in Japan's ultimate defeat.

During World War II, Japan was almost totally dependent upon ocean shipping to support her wartime economy. Shipping provided the basic raw materials for industry and imported many of the staple foods and civilian supplies needed to feed and clothe the Japanese population.[24] Thus, in *The War against Japanese Transportation*, the attack on Japan's merchant shipping, conducted predominantly by submarines and carrier-based aircraft, was the critical factor in the eventual collapse of Japan's economy. In contrast, the chairman's *Summary Report*, while recognizing the powerful impact of the antishipping campaign on imported raw materials for the Japanese economy, falls short of viewing this campaign as decisive. It states only "that by August 1945, even without direct air attack on her cities and industries, the over-all level of Japanese war production would have declined below the peak levels of 1944 by 40 to 50 percent solely as a result of the interdiction of overseas imports."[25] This passage does admit that the depletion of Japanese merchant shipping great-

24. USSBS, Transportation Division, *The War against Japanese Transportation*, 3.
25. USSBS, Chairman's Office, *Summary Report (Pacific War)*, 15.

ly reduced Japan's war production, but it neither uses the term decisive nor explicitly connects the decline in war production with surrender. These later terms only come into play when the report concludes that conventional air power was decisive in forcing the Japanese leadership to accept "unconditional" surrender:

> There is little point in attempting precisely to impute Japan's unconditional surrender to any one of the numerous causes which jointly and cumulatively were responsible for Japan's disaster. . . . It seems clear that, even without the atomic bombing attacks, air supremacy over Japan would have exerted sufficient pressure to bring about unconditional surrender and obviate the need for invasion.[26]

The Economic and Transportation divisions do not disagree with the *Summary Report* about the decisiveness of air power in defeating Japan. What the division reports do bring out more clearly, however, is that the war against merchant shipping had already destroyed a major portion of Japan's war economy before the AAF's attacks on urban areas began in March 1945. The Economic Division's report concludes, "The Japanese economy was in effect drying up at the roots from six months to a year before the period of intensive air attack and ultimate collapse."[27] Considering the importance of raw materials in Japan's economic structure, this was no small accomplishment. The Transportation Division report argues along the same lines: "As 1945 began, the thin remaining life line of the Japanese Empire was a trickle of ships moving from Formosa along the South China coast to Indo-China and on to Malaya and the Indies. . . . Within six months the remaining sea transport was reduced to chaos."[28]

The fact that Japan's economy was for the most part destroyed before the AAF's heavy bombing attacks led the authors of the Economic Division and Transportation Division reports to conclusions that were different in degree from those of the *Summary Report*. The difference rests on the relative importance of conventional bombing

26. Ibid., 26.
27. USSBS, Overall Economic Effects Division, *The Effects of Strategic Bombing on Japan's War Economy*, 32. For other USSBS reports arguing the same point, see Urban Areas Division, *The Effects of Air Attack on Japanese Urban Economy*, v; Urban Areas Division, *The Effects of Air Attack on the City of Nagoya*, 4.
28. USSBS, Transportation Division, *The War against Japanese Transportation*, 3.

of the Japanese home islands and the antishipping campaign in Japan's decision to surrender. These two applications of military power were equally important in the Economic Division's judgment: "While the outcome of the war was decided in the waters of the Pacific[,] . . . well in advance of the strategic bomber offensive against Japan's home islands, the air offensive against Japan proper was the major factor determining the timing of Japan's surrender."[29] In this conclusion, the naval war against Japanese merchant shipping and the resulting loss of raw material was not merely one of the cumulative causes that defeated Japan but actually "decided" the outcome of the war in the Pacific.

The Transportation Division's conclusion goes even further in proclaiming the decisive effects of the antishipping campaign: "The war against [Japanese] shipping was perhaps the most decisive single factor in the collapse of the Japanese economy and the logistic support of Japanese military and naval power."[30] This passage cleverly evades the issue of how the antishipping campaign factored into Japan's surrender decision. The implicit argument throughout the report, however, is that the ruining of Japan's economy by destroying shipping, and thereby depriving its fighting forces of vital supplies, made Japan's complete military and political collapse inevitable. Strategic bombing only accelerated the destruction already accomplished by the antishipping campaign.

Jerome Cohen, a member of the Economic Division who wrote a portion of the final report, used this "antishipping" theme throughout his 1949 book, *Japan's Economy in War and Reconstruction.* Cohen's thesis is concise and to the point: "[The] American blockade of Japan, by shutting off essential supplies of industrial raw materials, brought Japanese war production to a virtual standstill before the main weight of the strategic air attack was delivered, and thereby made it impossible for Japan to continue the war."[31] Cohen's work with the survey—he studied the effects of strategic bombing on Japan's war economy—had much influence on the writing of his

29. USSBS, Overall Economic Effects Division, *The Effects of Strategic Bombing on Japan's War Economy*, 59. Galbraith, in *A Life in Our Times*, 231, also gives equal importance to strategic bombing and naval blockade in critically reducing Japan's war production.

30. USSBS, Transportation Division, *The War against Japanese Transportation*, 6.

31. Jerome B. Cohen, *Japan's Economy in War and Reconstruction* (Minneapolis: University of Minnesota Press, 1949), xi.

book.[32] But his book is clearer than the survey's Economic Division or Transportation Division reports in linking the antishipping campaign to Japan's inability "to continue the war." For Cohen, perhaps in part because of his training as an economist, the disruption of the supplies of the essential raw materials, via the antishipping campaign, rather than conventional air power, proved to the Japanese leadership that its only logical choice was surrender.

Cohen's book—and, to a lesser degree, the reports from the Economic and Transportation divisions—raises an important question about the role of conventional air power in Japan's surrender. If the antishipping campaign was the decisive factor in destroying Japan's economy and leading to its defeat, then was it necessary to bomb conventionally the Japanese home islands? Cohen's book is evasive on this question. On the one hand, he attributes some importance to strategic bombing in accelerating the Japanese leadership to accept "unconditional" surrender. On the other hand, he discounts the effectiveness of conventional bombing in destroying the Japanese economy, arguing that the antishipping campaign and the loss of raw materials had already accomplished that goal.[33]

If conventional bombing did not *substantially* reduce Japan's war production, then what was (or were) the decisive factor(s) leading to Japan's surrender? Was it the attack on shipping, or the impact of urban attacks on morale, or the atom bomb, or the Soviet war declaration, or some combination of these considerations? The ambiguous way in which the survey confronted these troubling questions is the subject of the following pages.

The connection between destroying an enemy nation's will to resist and forcing the capitulation of that enemy's government has always been a murky one. Michael Sherry points out, in *The Rise of American Air Power,* that during the interwar years few AAF leaders ever speculated about how and when an enemy's will would collapse under strategic bombing and how a discouraged populace would force the political leadership to accept surrender.[34] The same

32. Ibid.

33. Ibid., 131, 270. For an argument similar to Cohen's that emphasizes the decisive nature of the antishipping campaign, see Laurence J. Legere, "Unification of the Armed Forces" (Ph.D. diss., Harvard University, 1951), reprinted in Frank Friedel and Ernest May, eds., *Harvard Dissertations in American History and Political Science* (New York: Garland, 1988), 421–42.

34. Michael Sherry, *The Rise of American Air Power: The Creation of Armageddon*

ambiguity that plagued AAF officers in the interwar and war years can also be found in certain survey reports. While the European reports are consistent in their handling of the effectiveness of attacks on cities and lowered morale on Germany's defeat, the Pacific reports on these issues are muddled and confused.

Both the European and Pacific surveys include reports on the impact of urban attacks on the German and Japanese war economies, respectively. An urban attack can be defined as one directed primarily against the population of an enemy city. Its principal objective was to lower enemy morale and will to resist by killing people and destroying homes and workplaces. A precision attack or bombing, conversely, had as its objective a specific industrial or military target that would directly weaken the enemy's ability to support its fighting forces. The *Area Studies Division Report*, which analyzed the impact of urban attacks in the European theater, came to a straightforward conclusion on this matter:

> The major cities of Germany present a spectacle of destruction so appalling as to suggest a complete breakdown of all aspects of urban activity. On first impression it would appear that the area attacks which laid waste these cities must have substantially eliminated the industrial capacity of Germany. Yet this was not the case. The attacks did not so reduce German war production as to have a decisive effect on the outcome of the war.[35]

Perhaps one reason for such a bold statement was that in the European theater the RAF, not the AAF, carried out the preponderance of attacks against the civilian population.[36] Since the AAF relied mainly on precision bombing, survey authors probably felt little external pressure to assess favorably the effectiveness of urban attacks.[37] For instance, workers in a city targeted for bombing would

---

(New Haven: Yale University Press, 1987), 55. Also see Ronald Schaffer, *Wings of Judgment: American Bombing in World War II* (New York: Oxford University Press, 1985), 119.

35. USSBS, Area Studies Division, *Area Studies Division Report*, 1.

36. Conrad Crane, *Bombs, Cities, and Civilians: American Air Power Strategy in World War II* (Lawrence: University Press of Kansas, 1993), 10. For an alternative interpretation that argues that the AAF, by 1944, had switched from precision to area attacks as its primary bombing method, see Schaffer, *Wings of Judgment*, 103.

37. Although the authors of the European morale and area reports probably felt little external pressure, other survey authors most likely did. Galbraith, in *A Life in Our Times*, 226–27, hints at pressure from certain AAF officers to rewrite portions of

be moved to other cities and employed there. Hence, there might be a drop in production in one area but improved production in another. German cities also showed resilience in their ability to rebound quickly after an attack and, in some cases, to return to approximately 80 percent of the preraid production level in a matter of months.[38]

The Pacific Survey's analysis of urban attacks had to wrestle with the fact that, unlike the European theater, the AAF directed the preponderance of its campaign against the civilian population instead of precision-bombing industrial targets.[39] *The Effects of Air Attack on Japanese Urban Economy* credits the AAF with causing great damage to the urban work force and social structure. According to the report, absenteeism of workers, directly caused by air raids, turned an already critical situation into one of complete desperation. The air raids also brought widespread destruction and deprivation not only in the cities but also throughout the Japanese homeland: "Few inhabitants escaped the terror of the raids."[40] But when it comes to assessing the effectiveness of these attacks on Japanese war production, the report becomes less favorable. Indeed, the report's recurring theme is that the Japanese economy had already been destroyed before the AAF began its air campaign. Due to the lack of raw materials, especially steel, stated the report, much of Japan's urban industry was at such a low level from its 1944 peak that the raids in many cases had only a minor effect: "As in Germany, the air attacks against Japanese cities were not the cause of the enemy's defeat. The defeat of Japan was assured *before* the urban attacks were

---

his own report. Former survey members also attempted to block Galbraith's appointment to Harvard in 1949 because of his less than favorable European Economic division report. See James G. Hershberg, *James B. Conant: Harvard to Hiroshima and the Making of the Nuclear Age* (New York: Knopf, 1993), 612–15. Galbraith, in "Albert Speer Was the Man to See," *New York Review of Books*, January 10, 1971, 2, is more blunt in accusing the AAF of externally influencing the writing of certain reports. For this type of AAF influence on Pacific Survey authors, see the testimony of Admiral R. A. Ofstie in House Committee on Expenditures in the Executive Department, *Hearings on National Security Act of 1947*, 80 Cong., 1st sess., June 30, 1947, 629–35. In a forthcoming issue of *Air Power History*, see my "A-bombs, Budgets, and Morality: The Use of the United States Strategic Bombing Survey in the Postwar Armed Services Unification and Strategy Hearings, 1945–1949."

38. USSBS, Area Studies Division, *Area Studies Division Report*, 8, 15.

39. USSBS, Chairman's Office, *Summary Report (Pacific War)*, 17.

40. USSBS, Urban Areas Division, *Effects of Air Attack on Japanese Urban Economy*, vi, 24.

launched. . . . The insufficiency of Japan's war economy was the underlying cause of her defeat."[41] This conclusion, which downplays the effectiveness of urban raids on Japan's war production, is often followed, strangely, by statements giving much weight to the raids in lowering Japan's morale and will to resist:

> The raids brought home to the people the realization that there was no defense against the Allied aircraft; that nothing could prevent the wholesale destruction of every inhabited area in Japan and that further resistance was futile. Popular awareness of these facts, which had been known by the political leaders as early as March 1945, exerted further pressure on those leaders to end the war.[42]

The implicit argument here is that urban attacks had a more decisive impact on morale and its influence on the Japanese leadership to accept surrender than on the destruction of Japan's war economy.

But neither the European nor Pacific Survey reports argue that lowered morale, resulting from conventional strategic bombing, was a decisive factor in forcing the political leadership to accept surrender. Such bombing did reduce the civilian population's morale, but neither survey connects lowered morale and the political recognition of defeat. The European Survey concluded,

> Bombing seriously depressed the morale of German civilians. Its main psychological effects were defeatism, fear, hopelessness, fatalism and apathy. . . . Bombing did not stiffen morale. The hate and anger it aroused tended to be directed against the Nazi regime which was blamed for beginning air warfare and for being unable to ward off Allied air attacks.[43]

Regardless of their demoralization, the German people continued to fight and support the war effort:

> Under ruthless Nazi control they showed surprising resistance to the terror and hardships of repeated air attack. . . . Their morale, their belief in ultimate victory or satisfactory compromise, and their confidence in their leaders declined, but they continued to work efficient-

41. Ibid., v (emphasis added).
42. Ibid., vi.
43. USSBS, Morale Division, *Effects of Strategic Bombing on German Morale*, 1, 12.

ly as long as the physical means of production remained. The power
of a police state over its people cannot be underestimated.[44]

In short, according to the European Survey, strategic bombing had a
debilitating affect on Germany's morale and its will to resist, but not
enough to force capitulation upon its totalitarian regime.

The Pacific Survey's equivalent report, *The Effects of Strategic Bombing on Japanese Morale,* also argued that the attacks against Japanese
cities greatly affected the people's morale. As in Germany, but on a
greater level, defeatism, apathy, and a feeling of inability to continue the war permeated Japanese society.[45] Low morale and apathy toward continuing the war were not, however, decisive factors in the
defeat of Japan: "Throughout the small nation the effects of Allied
bombings were general more than specific and were not confined to
the target areas. The drop in morale which took place throughout the
country was not the factor which defeated Japan."[46] Regardless of
low morale, declared the report, the Japanese would have continued
fighting and working to support the war effort had the emperor so
desired.[47] Their dedication to the Tenno system prevented them
from engaging in subversive activity that would bring an early end
to the war.

Interrogations of Japanese leaders and civilians supported this
conclusion. In a summary appraisal of those interrogations, Nobushige Nishizawa of the survey's Police Affairs Bureau concluded
that even though morale was extremely low there was never any
sign of revolt or panic to end the war.[48] Naoki Hoshino, who had
been head of Japan's Economic Planning Board during the late war
years, told his questioners that the severe drop in Japanese morale
following urban bombings had not created in the people "any direct
or positive tendency toward trying to end the war by force—the big
concern . . . was in trying to keep body and soul together."[49] The
civilian population, the survey concluded, would have persevered

44. USSBS, Chairman's Office, *Summary Report (European War),* 16.
45. USSBS, Morale Division, *The Effects of Strategic Bombing on Japanese Morale,* 1–2.
46. Ibid., 6.
47. Ibid., 23–25.
48. Interrogation of Nobushige Nishizawa, November 17, 1945, unnumbered,
USSBS Morale Division, USSBS Records, microfilm group M1654.
49. Interrogation of Naoki Hoshino, November 28, 1945, no. 505, USSBS Economic Division, USSBS Records, microfilm group M1654.

despite the fire raids and other hardships if the emperor had told it to do so.

The survey acknowledged that the Japanese people's morale influenced, to varying degrees, the political leadership's thinking about whether to continue fighting or terminate the war. Especially affected was the "peace faction"—in particular, Konoye, Suzuki, and Kido—but only to the extent that morale might affect the maintenance of the ruling class. The peace advocates were not concerned about the people's morale for humanitarian reasons, but, rather, because they feared that depressed morale might lead to a communist revolution and destruction of the existing social structure. The ruling class, stated the report on Japanese morale, "wanted a particular kind of surrender. . . . The minimum condition was that the 'national polity[,]' that is, the Emperor system, should remain, with implied hope that most of the structure and privileges [for the ruling class] would remain with it."[50]

Other members of the ruling elite, especially the militarists, while concerned about public morale, were convinced that the people would comply with the decisions of the political and military leadership. "The people's mind was made up to continue to the very last," declared Admiral Kichisaburo Nomura, a member of the emperor's Privy Council, in a statement echoed by others. "Although the people may have sensed the true situation, they were loyal to the government. The Japanese people obey government orders."[51]

Despite such testimony that urban bombing had not brought the Japanese to the brink of surrender, the Pacific Survey's *Summary Report*, written substantially by Paul Nitze,[52] concluded that conventional strategic bombing was decisive in forcing the Japanese to surrender "unconditionally."[53] This is the dilemma that emerges from the pages of the Pacific Survey's reports: how to claim the decisiveness of conventional air power in the face of evidence that a large part of the AAF's campaign, while important, was not crucial in Japan's defeat. The devastating effects of the campaign against shipping and the bombing of cities certainly forced the Japanese leader-

50. USSBS, Morale Division, *Effects of Strategic Bombing on Japanese Morale*, 143–44.
51. Interrogation of Admiral Kichisaburo Nomura, November 8, 1945, no. 429, USSBS Naval Analysis Division, USSBS Records, microfilm group M1654.
52. Nitze, *From Hiroshima to Glasnost*, 45.
53. USSBS, Chairman's Office, *Summary Report (Pacific War)*, 26.

ship to realize that defeat was inevitable. But there is a difference between the realization of defeat and the political acceptance of surrender. Here is where the atomic bomb and the Soviet declaration of war come into play.

If read as a whole, the Pacific Survey reports implicitly suggest that the atom bomb and Soviet declaration transformed the realization of defeat into surrender. The reports also contain an explicit statement to this effect. Tucked away in an often-ignored appendix of *The Effects of Air Attack on Japanese Urban Economy* is a postwar analysis of strategic bombing produced by scholars at Japan's Imperial University. Their findings agree with the survey's main themes, except for this striking remark about the conventional air attack, the atom bomb, and the end of the war: "Though there were many different views [over whether to continue the war], the majority of leaders entirely lost heart to continue hostilities. Particularly, the debut of the atomic bombs in the Pacific War theater was decisive."[54]

It is unclear how this statement made its way into the final report. Paul Nitze himself was one of four survey directors whose approval was necessary before any reports could be released for publication.[55] The official historian for the survey, Major James Beveridge, noted that much of the evidence was "considerably controversial" and required certain reports to be "revised or rewritten."[56] Somehow those responsible for revising or rewriting "controversial" material overlooked the Japanese scholars' findings a well as the other evidence challenging the survey's interpretation of Japan's decision to surrender.

There is no question that Japan was a defeated nation by early August 1945. But would Japan have surrendered "certainly prior to 31 December 1945 and in all probability prior to 1 November 1945" without the atomic bomb or Soviet war declaration? President Tru-

54. USSBS, Urban Areas Division, *Effects of Air Attack on Japanese Urban Economy*, 48.

55. James Beveridge, "History of the United States Strategic Bombing Survey" (unpublished four-volume typescript, Washington, D.C., 1946; available on microfilm at the Hoover Institution, Stanford, Calif.), 2:221.

56. Ibid., 2:135. Paul Nitze himself acknowledged the competing conclusions of various Pacific Survey divisions and the need for an "impartial resolution of the issues" (Nitze to G. L. McMurrin, January 21, 1947, box 166, Library of Congress [courtesy of Professor Barton Bernstein]).

man did not think so. "We have used [the bomb]," he told the American people shortly after the atomic bombing of Hiroshima, "in order to shorten the agony of war; in order to save the lives of thousands and thousands of young Americans." The survey concluded otherwise regarding ending the war speedily with Japan, but in accompanying that judgment with arguments and evidence that both support and undermine it, the survey's authors contributed mightily to a scholarly and public debate that has gone on for nearly fifty years.[57] Among the first to use the survey's findings to defend Truman's decision to drop the bomb was former secretary of war Henry L. Stimson. In a widely read 1947 article in *Harper's Magazine,* Stimson cited the survey and concluded, "All the evidence I have seen indicates that the controlling factor in the final Japanese decision to accept our terms of surrender was the atomic bomb."[58] To Stimson, the Japanese cabinet was deadlocked over whether to accept the Potsdam terms, and the atomic bomb persuaded it to do so, Stimson did not explicitly rebut the survey's opposite conclusion, for he wished to avoid controversy.[59] Still, his implicit critique suggested that the survey's authors had incorrectly interpreted their own evidence. So, too, did a less well-known participant in the debate, War Department historian Rudolph A. Winnacker, who had aided Stimson in writing his essay.[60] In a 1947 article, Winnacker directly challenged the survey for arriving at a conclusion not supported by its evidence.[61]

Fourteen years later Herbert Feis published the first book-length justification of Truman's decision. In his *Japan Subdued: The Atomic Bomb and the End of the War in the Pacific,* Feis argued that the bomb

57. For an analysis of the debate, see Barton J. Bernstein, "The Atomic Bomb and American Foreign Policy, 1941–1945: An Historiographical Controversy," in *Peace and Change* (Spring 1974): 1–16; J. Samuel Walker, "The Decision to Use the Bomb: A Historiographical Update," *Diplomatic History* 14 (1990): 97–115.

58. Henry L. Stimson "The Decision to Use the Bomb," *Harper's Magazine* 194 (February 1947), reprinted in Barton J. Bernstein, ed., *The Atomic Bomb: The Critical Issues* (Boston: Little, Brown, 1976), 15. Stimson cites as his authority USSBS, Chairman's Office, *Japan's Struggle to End the War.*

59. Barton J. Bernstein, "Seizing the Contested Terrain of Early Nuclear History: Stimson, Conant, and Their Allies Explain the Decision to Use the Atomic Bomb," *Diplomatic History* 17 (1993): 43, 49.

60. Ibid., 46.

61. Rudolph A. Winnacker, "The Debate about Hiroshima," *Military Affairs* 11 (Spring 1947): 27.

hastened the end of the war and saved American lives, but he also held—in a nuanced difference from Stimson and Winnacker—that Japan would have eventually surrendered without use of the atomic and as a result of conventional bombing.[62] For Feis, shortening the war by a few months, or even weeks, justified use of the bomb because it halted the devastation of Japanese cities by conventional attacks and saved lives on both sides.[63]

The first major scholarly attack on Feis and Stimson came in 1965 from Gar Alperovitz. In *Atomic Diplomacy: Hiroshima and Potsdam*, Alperovitz agreed with the survey's conclusion that Japan would have certainly surrendered by December 31, 1945, and very probably by November 1, and he argued that Truman and his advisors believed this as well. Nonetheless, Truman ordered the bombs to be dropped, stated Alperovitz, citing no evidence from the survey, primarily to influence Soviet actions in Eastern Europe.[64]

A forerunner of Alperovitz and one of the first Cold War revisionists was P. M. S. Blackett, a Nobel Prize-winning physicist and member of Britain's Advisory Committee on Atomic Energy. Blackett's 1948 book, *Military and Political Consequences of Atomic Energy*, critiqued postwar American perceptions about the absolute nature of atomic weapons. According to Blackett, the American people had incorrectly concluded that the atomic bombings of Hiroshima and Nagasaki had militarily defeated Japan. This led Americans to the erroneous belief that a future war with the Soviet Union could be decided quickly and decisively with atomic weapons.[65] To demystify the absolute nature of atomic weapons and assign them a proper military role, Blackett relied heavily on the report prepared by the survey's European Economic Division: *The Effects of Strategic Bombing on the German War Economy*. That report persuaded him, declared Blackett, that "Germany's defeat in the second world war, as in the first, was brought about primarily by her huge loss in manpower

62. Herbert Feis, *The Atomic Bomb and the End of World War II* (Princeton: Princeton University Press, 1966), 191. This is a revised and updated version of his 1961 publication, *Japan Subdued*. The central argument, for the most part, remained unchanged.

63. Ibid., 192–93; Bernstein, "The Atomic Bomb and American Foreign Policy," 8.

64. Gar Alperovitz, *Atomic Diplomacy: Hiroshima and Potsdam, The Use of the Atomic Bomb and the American Confrontation with Soviet Power* (1965; New York: Penguin, 1985), 286.

65. Blackett, *Military and Political Consequences of Atomic Energy*, 129.

and material incurred in the land battles. . . . Air power played, of course, a decisively important role in all the great land battles."[66] In other words, strategic bombing had produced decisive results only in conjunction with "great land battles." Military strategy based solely on the purported decisiveness of atomic weapons ignored this "lesson" of history.

Blackett also argued that the atomic bomb, because of its destructive capabilities, could only be used against large cities. The relative inaccuracy of contemporary delivery systems and the bomb's overwhelming destructive power made atomic weapons inappropriate for destroying smaller "precision" targets, such as industrial factories or transportation centers. The most efficient use of atomic weapons, concluded Blackett, would be against large, highly populated cities.[67] The United States, consequently, would have to target large urban areas in a major war with the Soviet Union. Then, relying on the survey's conclusion that urban attacks did not substantially reduce Germany's war production in World War II, Blackett contended that nuclear attacks on large Soviet urban areas would also be ineffectual.[68]

Significantly, when analyzing the effectiveness of conventional bombing of Japan during World War II, Blackett, like the Pacific Survey, fell into troubling ambiguity. On the one hand, he maintained that the campaign against shipping had decisively defeated Japan before the bombing of the home islands. Then, however, he went on to argue elsewhere that the bombing of Japanese cities had also been successful. He seemed to be trying to have it both ways. Was bombing successful against shipping and cities by destroying Japan's economy twice over? Blackett does not say. He does, however, on the basis of Pacific Survey reports, contend that in a future war with the Soviet Union atomic bombs would not lower morale to the point where the Soviet political leadership would surrender. "[T]here is not much to choose between the experience of heavy ordinary bombing and atomic bombing," he stated. "Selected survivors of Hamburg, Dresden or Tokyo could have provided equally poignant material for the pen of a John Hersey as the survivors of Hiroshima."[69]

Blackett may have been directing this argument at thirty-five-

66. Ibid., 26–27.
67. Ibid., 45.
68. Ibid., 24, 55–56.
69. Ibid., 56.

year-old Bernard Brodie, a political scientist who was already help-
ing to shape postwar nuclear strategy. Brodie was the antithesis of
P. M. S. Blackett when it came to defining and applying the lessons
of World War II strategic bombing. In *The Absolute Weapon,* Brodie argued that atomic bombs had revolutionized warfare.[70] He agreed
that the fire bombings of German and Japanese cities did not lower
morale to the point that leaders felt compelled to surrender, but he
disagreed that the use of atomic bombs in a future war would prove
equally ineffective. Indeed, based on his reading of the European
Survey reports, Brodie concluded in *Strategy in the Missile Age,* that
even conventional strategic bombing, if carried out in a particular
way, could force a surrender. His example was the attack on Hamburg in late July 1943 that produced a terrible shock not only to the
people of Hamburg but to the entire German state. If attacks of comparable magnitude had been carried out against a substantial number of other German cities at the same time, declared Brodie, the
compounded shock effect would have had a profound impact on the
German population. He likened such attacks to the effect of an atomic bomb: "Under atomic weapons, even ignoring the effects of fallout, the proportion of persons exposed to risk in the cities would be
much greater, the incidence of casualties and of lost homes would
be multiplied, and the disorganizing effects upon the surrounding
countryside would be immeasurably more immediate and direct."[71]
Thus Brodie took a survey conclusion about the limited effects of
bombing on morale in German cities and extrapolated to the effects
of an atomic war on a nation's population.

On a broader level, the survey's numerous reports on the successes and failures of bombing in World War II emphasized to Brodie

70. Bernard Brodie, ed., *The Absolute Weapon: Atomic Power and World Order* (New
York: Harcourt, Brace, 1946), 23–27, 71, 83. For an analysis that traces Brodie's think-
ing on strategy from his earliest writings to his death, see Barry H. Steiner, *Bernard
Brodie and the Foundations of American Nuclear Strategy* (Lawrence: University Press of
Kansas, 1991).

71. Brodie, *Strategy in the Missile Age* (Princeton: Princeton University Press, 1959),
137. For analyses of the impact of atomic weapons on a nation's morale during atomic war by some of Brodie's RAND contemporaries, see Fred Ikle, *The Social Impact of
Bomb Destruction* (Norman: University of Oklahoma Press, 1958); Irving Janis, *Air
War and Emotional Stress: Psychological Studies of Bombing and Civilian Defense* (New
York: McGraw-Hill, 1951). A good analysis of the influence of RAND on defense policy can be found in Fred Kaplan's *The Wizards of Armageddon* (Stanford: Stanford University Press, 1991).

the crucial importance of selecting the right targets before an atomic war began with the Soviet Union. This line of thinking was not apparent when he published *The Absolute Weapon* in 1946, but became more pronounced in the late 1940s and early 1950s when, as Fred Kaplan puts it, Brodie "was beginning to think through the problems of the bomb, not just in peace but also in war, not just how to live with the bomb but how to use it."[72]

The main lesson Brodie drew from strategic bombing in World War II was that proper target selection depended on the enemy's political economy and social structure. In 1952, while serving as a special air force advisor, Brodie critiqued the Air Targets Division for basing postwar target selection in the Soviet Union on a survey conclusion that German electrical facilities were vulnerable to bombing and, if attacked, would have had a crippling effect on the economy.[73] While German power facilities might have been the proper targets during World War II, they were not necessarily the correct targets in a nuclear war today with the Soviets. Brodie believed that war planning had to reflect contemporary technological capabilities and the shifting priority of targets in a particular enemy nation.

The first and, so far, only book-length study of the survey, David MacIsaac's *Strategic Bombing in World War II: The Story of the United States Strategic Bombing Survey*, did not appear until 1976. The author, a career air force officer, included an especially revealing section on the interservice wrangling between survey representations of the AAF and U.S. Navy over two reports: the navy's *Campaigns of the Pacific War* and the AAF's *Air Campaigns of the Pacific War*. General Orvil Anderson of the AAF and Admiral R. A. Ofstie of the navy were determined to publish survey reports demonstrating the decisive role that each officer's own service played in winning the Second World War. Neither Anderson nor Ofstie, according to MacIsaac, had "covered himself with glory, but men rarely do when they are evenly matched, when the stakes are so high; and when the battle must be fought out in the degrading mire of bureaucracy."[74]

72. Kaplan, *Wizards of Armageddon*, 38.
73. Steiner, *Bernard Brodie*, 94–98. For a more current use of the survey's findings on electrical systems as targets for strategic bombing, see Thomas E. Griffith Jr., "Strategic Attack of National Electrical Systems" (Thesis, School of Advanced Airpower Studies, Maxwell Air Force Base, Alabama, 1994).
74. MacIsaac, *Strategic Bombing in World War II*, 133.

Their respective reports, however, were not equal in their parochialism. The navy's report was a calm, methodical narrative of the major naval battles of the Pacific War. There were no grandiose claims about the decisiveness of the navy's antishipping campaign or of its carrier-based aircraft. The most sweeping conclusion, if one can call it that, was the following:

> By January 1945, Japan was in fact a defeated nation. . . . All hope of future resistance had depended upon oil and now the tankers were sunk and the oil cut off. . . . At home the bad news began to be known and mutterings of negotiated conditional peace arose even in the armed forces. Japan was defeated: it remained only necessary to persuade her of the fact.[75]

This statement does not differ from observations found in other Pacific Survey reports: Japan's economy had been broken before the main AAF attacks; the antishipping campaign had been decisive in Japan's defeat; and conventional strategic bombing had persuaded the political leadership to realize defeat and accept "unconditional surrender."

In stark contrast to the navy's study was that of the AAF as crafted primarily by General Anderson:

- Airpower dominated its own element.
- Airpower dominated naval warfare.
- Airpower dominated ground warfare.
- Airpower possessed powerful and independent logistical capabilities.
- Airpower established effective area interdiction by occupation of the air space over an objective area.
- Airpower was capable of forcing the capitulation of an enemy without surface invasion.

If our Nation is to survive in this atomic age, logic demands that our national defense agencies be oriented toward airpower, and, further, that the future development of airpower not be restricted, as in pre-World War II years, by the inertia of established organizations or personalities.[76]

---

75. USSBS, Naval Analysis Division, *Campaigns of the Pacific War*, 290.
76. USSBS, Military Analysis Division, *Air Campaigns of the Pacific War*, 69. The re-

Strident in tone, the report bluntly demanded a larger air force budget and creation of an independent air force. No other survey reports on the European or Pacific theaters contained such sweeping and self-serving proclamations. The AAF's language clearly indicates both the insecurity and future hopes of the air force, but both reports, even the less bombastic naval study, are contradictory in their assessments of the role played by the two services. In this respect, they reflect the competing interpretations found throughout the USSBS.

The survey's contradictions and ambiguities have made it a very malleable source. In part, this is the result of the complex and controversial subject being analyzed: strategic bombing in World War II. The survey also reflects the predisposition of its authors to interpret the evidence in ways that served their divergent interests. Brigadier General Haywood S. Hansell, who commanded the Twenty-first Bomber Command in the Pacific, told an interviewer that the survey "was much like the Bible in one respect. If you reach deeply enough you can find substantiation for almost any preconceived notion or prejudice."[77] George Ball, among the directors of the European Survey, acknowledged that there were "wide differences of view as to the interpretation of the data" and that the survey "settled nothing; the central arguments are likely to continue for years."[78]

Although the central arguments may well continue, it is clear that the USSBS should not be represented as an unimpeachable authority, as has frequently been done, but as a collection of interpretations, subject to close reading, rigorous scrutiny, and thoughtful challenge. As an effort at history, the survey provides useful data and points of view about U.S. bombing during World War II. The challenge to scholars is to use them critically, not slavishly, in their attempts to better understand a crucial period of the past.

---

port also recommends a preventive war and implicitly indicates that it would be with the Soviet Union (68).

77. Haywood S. Hansell to David MacIsaac, July 27, 1970, addendum 1, box 3, folder 5, Haywood Hansell Papers, U.S. Air Force Academy Library (courtesy of Professor Barton Bernstein).

78. Ball, *Past Has Another Pattern*, 61.

Hiroshima and the Trashing
of Henry Stimson

ITH THE CEREMONIES AND controversies surrounding its
fiftieth anniversary, World War II has regained prominence
in our national discussions. Those of us who fought that war
have, in the main, a unitary point of view. Few of us regarded it as a
crusade, but all of us believed it was necessary: necessary to eradi-
cate an oppressive fascism, to restore independence to friendly peo-
ples in Europe and preserve Britain's independence, and necessary
to lift the boot heel of Togo's soldiers from the necks of the Chinese,
Filipinos, and other Asians who, we now know, suffered twenty million dead from the Japanese onslaught.[1]

There are, however, no "good" wars. Many accounts of strategic
bombing—beginning with the Axis in Spain and with Japan in
Shanghai and culminating with the Allied destruction of Dresden,
Tokyo, Hiroshima, and Nagasaki—have revealed the extent to
which total war dissolves inhibitions solemnly embodied in the
Hague treaties. At the outset, both Winston Churchill and Franklin
Roosevelt disdained bombing cities and endorsed the principle of
noncombatant immunity; by the end, that principle was honored
primarily in the breach, most dramatically when America unleashed
its atomic power on Japan.[2] Harry Truman, who assumed the presi-

1. The necessity for conclusive victory in Europe is rarely challenged; the ratio-
nale for exacting unconditional surrender from the Japanese empire is more controversial. On the Pacific War, see Toshio Iritani, *Group Psychology of the Japanese in
Wartime* (London: Kegan Paul, 1991); and Pacific War Research Society, *The Day Man
Lost* (Tokyo: Kodansha International, 1972); and Iokibe Makoto, "American Role toward Japan's Unconditional Surrender," *Japanese Journal of American Studies* 1 (1981):
29.

2. On the inhumanity of the Pacific War, the best source is John Dower's *War without Mercy: Race and Power in the Pacific War* (New York: Pantheon, 1986). On the rejection of the principle of noncombatant immunity, see Ronald Schaffer, *Wings of
Judgment: American Bombing in World War II* (New York: Oxford University Press,

dency just as the Manhattan Project—the nation's Herculean effort to outpace Germany's expected development of atomic explosives—came to fruition, was blamed for this most spectacular destruction.[3]

The chief defender of the bomb decision was Henry Stimson, the secretary of war under Roosevelt and Truman and the author of "The Decision to Use the Atomic Bomb," which appeared in *Harper's Magazine* in February 1947. Purporting to be a personal account, drawn from his diaries, his memory, and his office files, Stimson's article addressed the concerns of those (mostly churchmen and conservatives) who in 1946 began to gain an audience for their dissenting view about how the war with Japan had been concluded. Dubbed the official narrative about the decision to drop the bomb, Stimson's article only temporarily silenced the critics; in time it drew their redoubled ire.[4]

During the Vietnam War, as large numbers of Americans began to question their government, particularly its bellicose policies, the decision to use the atomic bomb in World War II was revisited. Reinterpreted as an action principally intended to intimidate the Soviet Union, the drop on Nagasaki and Hiroshima was seen as the kickoff to the superpowers' nuclear-overkill arms race.[5] Stimson, as author of the 1947 article explaining the process of reaching that decision, was seen as Truman's apologist and considered even more blameworthy than the embattled president by writers such as Gar Alperovitz, Robert J. Lifton, Greg Mitchell, Philip Nobile, Murray Sayle, and others. Stimson's reputation took a nosedive in the 1980s and 1990s.[6]

1985), and Michael Sherry, *The Rise of American Air Power: The Creation of Armageddon* (New Haven: Yale University Press, 1987).

3. There is no landmark history of the Manhattan Project. Richard Rhodes's *The Making of the Atomic Bomb* (New York: Simon and Schuster, 1986) probably leads the field but has flaws. See Barton J. Bernstein, "An Analysis of Two Cultures: Writing about the Making and the Using of the Atomic Bomb," *Public Historian* 12 (Spring 1990): 83–107.

4. Henry L. Stimson, "The Decision to Use the Atomic Bomb," *Harper's Magazine* 194 (February 1947): 97–107.

5. The first Vietnam-inspired work was Gar Alperovitz's *Atomic Diplomacy: Hiroshima and Potsdam, The Use of the Atomic Bomb and the American Confrontation with Soviet Power* (New York: Simon and Schuster, 1965). It was followed by Martin J. Sherwin's *A World Destroyed: The Atomic Bomb and the Grand Alliance* (New York: Knopf, 1975).

6. See Gar Alperovitz, *The Decision to Use the Atomic Bomb and the Architecture of an American Myth* (New York: Alfred A. Knopf, 1995); Robert Jay Lifton and Greg

It's time for a reassessment. Insofar as Stimson's opponents have misunderstood him—and, to be fair, insofar as Stimson himself failed to frame the process he recounted in its proper terms—the national debate on this crucial event has been skewed. We would do well to take another look at the article and at the man.

The *Harper's* article that has, for so long, dominated our understanding about the atomic bomb was not Henry Stimson's idea. James B. Conant, the president of Harvard and one of the prominent scientists involved in the Manhattan Project, prevailed upon Stimson to write his account.[7] Conant, who believed that an impressive U.S. atomic arsenal could induce the Soviet Union to join an international atomic control structure felt that attacks on the World War II atomic bomb decision deflected attention from that pressing agenda.

The first serious challenge was posed by the Federal Council of Churches, as reported by the *New York Times* of March 6, 1946. A committee charged with considering the atomic bombings of Japan concluded that because no specific advance warning had been given, the attacks were illegitimate: "morally indefensible" and sinful. Reinhold Niebuhr, a "realist" theologian whom Conant knew and admired, was among the signers. Conant wrote Niebuhr to protest. The theologian backed down a bit: of course the main objective had been to win the war, but responsible citizens could not ignore how that goal had been accomplished. There were other attacks on the use of the bomb from journalists, some of whom Conant knew personally.[8]

Conant's pique intensified in July 1946 when the United States Strategic Bombing Survey (USSBS) issued its conclusions, from Vice Chairman Paul Nitze's office, about Japan's readiness to surrender. Japan would have surrendered, read the survey report, "certainly prior to 31 December 1945, and in all probability prior to 1 November 1945 . . . even if the atomic bombs had not been dropped, even if Russia had not entered the war, and even if no invasion had been

---

Mitchell, *Hiroshima in America: Fifty Years of Denial* (New York: Putnam's Sons, 1995); Philip Nobile, ed., *Judgment at the Smithsonian* (New York: Marlowe, 1995); and Murray Sayle, "Did the Bomb End the War?" *New Yorker*, 31 July 1995, 41–64.

7. The genesis of the *Harper's* article is best described in James G. Hershberg's *James B. Conant* (New York: Knopf, 1993), chap. 16.

8. Ibid., 283–85.

planned or contemplated." This startling conclusion carried the authority of a fact-finding commission originally appointed by President Roosevelt and headed by civilians; it was bolstered by the preemptive claim that it was "based on a detailed investigation of all the facts, and supported by the testimony of the surviving Japanese leaders involved."[9]

Opponents of the atom bombing were ecstatic, supporters almost apoplectic. General Leslie Groves, who had superintended construction of the bombs, could only sputter disagreement. Conant was appalled but confined his disparagement to the rather bland charge of "Monday morning quarterbacking." Nitze's claim to have examined "all the facts" about a complex Japanese situation was made with such finality that no one even thought to demand access to the survey files.[10]

And, of course, no one could demand access to the MAGIC decryptions, the translations of Japanese diplomatic cable traffic; American code-breaking capabilities were kept under the tightest wraps. Had the decryptions been available to Conant and friends, the USSBS report would have been readily discredited, for MAGIC showed the Japanese elite desperately trying to persuade Russia to act as mediator in the Pacific War, to secure for Japan an armistice with easy terms. The elite peace-seekers were clearly not in control, not able to agree among themselves on what terms they would accept; but they never spoke of surrender, only of negotiating an armistice.[11]

Japanese military cables tell the same story. Allied cryptography deciphered them too (the ULTRA operation). From these messages

9. United States Strategic Bombing Survey (USSBS), Chairman's Office, *Japan's Struggle to End the War* (Washington, D.C.: U.S. Government Printing Office, 1946), 13. Scholars, journalists, and curators continue to the present day to demonstrate their gullibility about this "official" government report. Martin Harwit, director of the National Air and Space Museum during the preparation of the *Enola Gay* exhibit, emphatically rejected the possibility that a survey commissioned by President Roosevelt and delivered to President Truman could have been corrupt, a stand that demonstrates a touching faith in government that is now rare. See Harwit's *An Exhibit Denied: Lobbying the History of the Enola Gay* (New York: Springer-Verlag, 1996), 340.

10. Hershberg, *Conant*, 292.

11. On Japanese efforts to avoid surrender but to negotiate a favorable armistice, see Herbert P. Bix, "Japan's Delayed Surrender: A Reinterpretation," in *Hiroshima in History and Memory*, ed. Michael J. Hogan (Cambridge: Cambridge University Press, 1996), 101–9.

it was clear that despite strenuous efforts by American air and naval forces, Japan was building up her homeland defenses at an amazing rate. American bombing and blockade were simply not effective. Edward Drea, the foremost student of ULTRA intelligence, puts it this way: "Japanese reinforcements seemed to blossom with the warm May weather in Kyushu." But none of this evidence was available to Conant and to others who disbelieved the USSBS report.[12]

Most of all, however, Conant and his allies never had another essential piece of information: that Nitze, who wrote the crucial parts of the USSBS report, was firmly committed to the ambition of the army air force to establish, after the war, a large, independent air arm. The atomic bomb was a threat to that goal. If one plane carrying one bomb could wipe out a whole city, what need could there be for thousands of planes? Only if the ultimate necessity of the atomic bombing of Hiroshima and Nagasaki were denied would the nation's faith in the war-winning capabilities of conventional air power be restored.[13]

For this reason and perhaps for others we will never be able to fathom, Nitze wholly misrepresented the testimony of the "surviving Japanese leaders." With a single exception, the USSBS informants stated that Japan would have fought through at least the first wave of an American invasion.[14] The plan was to inflict so many casualties that, to halt the slaughter of its troops, America would be persuaded to offer an armistice on favorable terms.

These "surviving Japanese leaders" had ample reason to prevaricate. If they feigned that their nation had seriously considered sur-

12. Edward J. Drea, *MacArthur's ULTRA: Codebreaking and the War against Japan* (Lawrence: University Press of Kansas, 1992), 207.

13. The airmen's ambitions were the subject of much gossip. David MacIsaac noted that "On the very day that the first of the Survey reports was released to the public, John O'Donnell's column in the *Washington Times Herald* mentioned the Survey and how its report might have been important in future debates over air strategy: 'What might have become a good old-fashioned row now becomes an academic discussion thanks to the atom bomb. Come the next war, there will be fleets of bombers pouring down death on civilian populations. Just one little atom bomb will do the work of a thousand blockbusters'" (*Strategic Bombing in World War Two* [New York: Garland, 1976], 165). James A. Field Jr., who worked on the USSBS, told me in November 1993 that survey members believed that Nitze was aiming for the secretaryship of a postwar independent air force.

14. Records of the United States Strategic Bombing Survey (hereafter cited as USSBS Records), microfilm groups M1654 and M1655, National Archives and Records Administration, Washington, D.C. (hereafter cited as NARA-DC).

rendering before the bomb was dropped, they could shift international opinion against the U.S. The Japanese government's official position was that atomic power was an unconscionable weapon. If, however, the United States could prove that the atomic bombs were the decisive factor in ending the war, then it could claim that the bombings were legitimate, for continuing the war would have perpetuated terrible casualties on both sides and brought the firebombing of additional Japanese cities. Individual Japanese leaders also had a compelling personal motivation to lie for they would surely face stiffer sentences in upcoming war crimes trials if they proclaimed that they had been prepared to keep on fighting.

And yet, favoring honor over expediency, Japanese leaders testified that, had the atomic bombs not been dropped, Japan would have fought on. Several, entirely unrepentant, even bragged about how they would have destroyed the first invasion forces.

Admiral and former ambassador to the United States Nomura Kichisaburo told Nitze and his interrogators that "it was the destiny of our country to continue this very unwise war to the very end." Prince Konoye Fumimaro, three times premier, said that absent the bomb, the war would have lasted beyond November 1: "The army had dug themselves caves in the mountains and their idea of fighting on was fighting from every little hole or rock in the mountains."[15]

Admiral Toyoda Soemu, the chief of the Naval General Staff, believed that the bomb and Soviet entry on the China front had enabled Japan to surrender without "too great chaos"; before that, the navy would not have accepted an imperial rescript ending the war. Lieutenant General Endo Saburo delighted in celebrating the Japanese fighting spirit to his American interrogators. Winning didn't matter, he had told his soldiers; they should be willing to die gladly if they must. Field Marshal Hata Shunroku, the commanding general of the Second General Army (Hiroshima), stated he had believed that "Japan would win the final decisive battle of the homeland"; after the Hiroshima bomb, however, he thought "we might as well give up."[16]

15. Nomura's statement is in USSBS Records, microfilm group M1654, roll 1; Konoye's is in M1654, roll 5. Details about the interrogations can be found to my "Ending the War with Japan: Paul Nitze's 'Early Surrender' Counterfactual," *Pacific Historical Review* 64 (May 1995): 167–94.

16. Toyoda's and Endo's statements are in USSBS Records, microfilm group M1654, roll 1; Hata's is in M1655, roll 208A.

Baron Hiranuma Kiichiro, the president of the Privy Council, conceded that the "biggest factor" prompting the Japanese surrender was the atomic bomb. Lieutenant General Kawabe Torashiro, the director of Kamikaze operations in the Okinawa battle, proclaimed, "we intended to continue to fight into the very end." Fleet Admiral Nagano Osami, the supreme naval adviser to the emperor, said, "Speaking very frankly, I think we would have been able to extend the war for a considerable time at considerable sacrifice on your part." Premier Suzuki Kantaro was equally blunt: "The Supreme War Council . . . had proceeded with the plan of fighting a decisive battle at the landing point . . . until the Atomic Bomb was dropped."[17]

The whole interrogation series, lasting over two months, offered a uniform view, except for the testimony of the privy seal, Baron Kido Koichi. At first, Kido insisted that the atomic bomb had persuaded many "fence sitters" to favor surrender. But the American interrogators badgered him for about fifteen minutes, mostly with leading questions, and Kido finally relented. "I personally think the war would have ended prior to November 1," he said. This was not, however, Kido's considered opinion. Two years later, speaking to an interrogator for the Tokyo War Crimes Trial, who lacked USSBS biases, Kido declared that the bomb and Soviet entry had ended the war, and without them, he maintained, there would have been twenty million Japanese and tens of thousands of American casualties.[18] Nitze's sole bit of testimonial evidence thus evaporated, and the consensus of those who knew best was that Japan clearly was not ready to surrender in the fall of 1945.

Conant knew none of this in 1946; Nitze's fabrication stood unchallenged.

On August 31, 1946, shortly after Nitze's report was issued, a skillful narrative about six survivors of the bombing of Hiroshima, written by John Hersey, appeared in the *New Yorker*. The issue sold out immediately. Subsequently published as a book, *Hiroshima* became a runaway best seller. Thereafter, in Spencer Weart's words, that one bombing "inspired more debate than the rest of the war's destruc-

17. Hiranuma's, Kawabe's, and Nagano's statements are in USSBS Records, microfilm group M1654, roll 1; Suzuki's is in microfilm group M1655, roll 208A.
18. Kido's statement is in USSBS Records, microfilm group M1654, roll 5; his later testimony is in *The Tokyo War Crimes Trial*, ed. R. John Pritchard and Sonia M. Zaide (27 vols., New York: Garland, 1981), 13:31, 205.

tion put together. It was as if all the other recent massacres could be set aside and the entire moral problem of modern war could be concentrated in this one question."[19]

Hersey did what no one else had done: he converted the Japanese enemy, previously thought by most Americans to be an "undifferentiated subhuman mass," into recognizable human beings. Modeled on Thornton Wilder's *Bridge of San Luis Rey*, the narrative betrayed little emotion; it simply described what had happened to the town and six fictional survivors. Technical details were few; those that were included were drawn from the USSBS findings. Like the bombing survey's report, *Hiroshima* passed itself off as an unbiased account.[20]

Hersey was an unlikely author for a sympathetic treatment of the Japanese. During the war, he had been as appalled over Japanese actions as any of his fellow correspondents. His account of the battle on Guadalcanal, *Into the Valley*, accepts the nonracist explanation for why American soldiers despised the Japanese: they were treacherous on the battlefield. They used "white surrender flags to suck us into traps." His article "Kamikaze," in the July 30, 1945, issue of *Life*, is openly contemptuous. Tokyo radio had exhorted the entire Japanese empire of 100 million men, women, and children "to become a great suicide unit," and Premier Suzuki promised "victory" even if "no Japanese still is alive to enjoy it." Such absurdity was a symptom of societal degeneracy. Hersey acknowledged that individual acts of self-sacrifice have their place in wars, but "The Japanese have done something no other nation in the world would be capable of doing. They have systematized suicide; they have nationalized a morbid, sickly act."[21]

It is interesting to muse about the course of the "blame game" had Hersey devoted his talents to telling an equally elaborate and sympathetic story of six victims of Japan's Rape of Manila in 1944, or of

19. Hersey's *Hiroshima* was republished (by Knopf) in 1985 with a new chapter noting that non-Communist anti-nuclear groups in Japan favored banning all nuclear weapons, but the very substantial Communist group excepted the Soviets (194). See also Spencer Weart, *Nuclear Fear* (Cambridge: Harvard University Press, 1988), 107.

20. Michael J. Yavenditti, "John Hersey and the American Conscience: The Reception of 'Hiroshima,'" *Pacific Historical Review* 43 (February 1974): 33.

21. John Hersey, *Into the Valley* (New York: Knopf, 1943), 20, and "Kamikaze," *Life*, July 30, 1945, 75.

her lethal treatment of slave laborers who built the Burma-Siam railway, or of Unit 731's biological warfare against the Chinese. Even the story of six innocent American sailors maimed at Pearl Harbor would have cast the question about culpability in a different light.[22]

The atomic bomb victims probably drew Hersey's attention because their incineration was the most spectacular event of that deadly war, but Japanese depredations killed far more people, most in horrible ways. United Nations figures indicate ten million Chinese dead at Japanese hands, four million Dutch East Indians, a million and a half Bengalis, a million Vietnamese, etc., but in no case, of course, was there such a single, instantaneous apocalypse. And, thus, there was no comparable explosion in international consciousness. Postwar American eagerness to rehabilitate Japan as the Pacific bastion of our pathological anti-Soviet policy encouraged amnesia about the Japanese empire's twenty million victims. Hersey's book simply put the imprimatur on Hiroshima as *the* atrocity of the war.[23]

Norman Cousins, an editor of the *Saturday Review of Literature*, read Nitze's USSBS report and Hersey's novel and had a conversion experience. During the war, Cousins had been a cheerleader for the "bomb the hell out of them" approach. In an April 8, 1944, editorial, he explained, "Once the enemy starts it, it becomes no longer a matter of argument but a matter of action. The weapons have been dictated by the enemy." Two years later, he reversed himself. An editorial in *Saturday Review* on September 14, 1946, entitled "the Literacy of Survival" sounded all the objections to strategic bombing that Cousins had previously rejected. He bluntly called the bombing of Hiroshima and Nagasaki a crime. USSBS conclusions were reiterated. Japan had been ready to surrender. The United States should have issued a warning before using this new weapon, and so forth.[24]

22. On Manila, see Ronald H. Spector, *Eagle against the Sun* (New York: Free Press, 1985), chap. 22. On the infamous railway, see *The Burma-Thailand Railway,* ed. Gavan McCormack and Hank Nelson (New York: Allen and Unwin, 1993). On Unit 731, see Sheldon H. Harris, *Factories of Death* (New York: Routledge, 1994).

23. On Pacific War casualties, see United Nations, Economic and Social Council, *Report of the Working Group for Asia and the Far East,* Supplement 10 (New York: United Nations, 1948). Japanese historians are beginning to acknowledge the extent of deaths caused by the Japanese empire. See Toshio Iritani, *Group Psychology of the Japanese in Wartime.*

24. Norman Cousins, "The Non-Obliterators," *Saturday Review,* April 5, 1944, 14, and "The Literacy of Survival," *Saturday Review,* September 14, 1946, 14.

Cousins's turnabout was the last straw for Conant. It propelled him into pro-bomb activism. As Barton Bernstein puts it, Conant thought that he had to seize the "contested terrain of early nuclear history." America had a world-historical mission. There must be no more slipping back into isolationism. And America *had* to maintain a nuclear capability, for only by doing so could the expansionist Soviet Union be forced to accept international control of the atom.[25]

For Conant, there was only one person whose stature and knowledge were equal to the task of defending the first use of the bomb and legitimizing an American nuclear arsenal.

That person was Henry Stimson.

An 1888 graduate of Yale, then of Harvard Law, Henry Stimson was well fitted for success in both private life and public service. Membership in the New York law firm at which Elihu Root was senior partner drew him into diplomatic circles; friendship with Theodore Roosevelt brought him an invitation to serve as U.S. attorney for the Southern District of New York, a post he occupied from 1906 to 1909.[26]

Stimson was never thereafter entirely out of public life. He was secretary of war under President William Howard Taft, served as a colonel of artillery in World War I (and preferred, all his life, to be called "Colonel"), was governor general of the Philippines in 1928, and became President Herbert Hoover's secretary of state the next year. In 1931, the Japanese launched the invasion of Manchuria that rankled the United States and led to Pearl Harbor a decade later. Stimson firmly opposed Japanese aggression; even the mediocre education I received in small-town Missouri taught me that nonrecognition of territory seized by force of arms was known as the Stimson Doctrine. Stimson served Hoover well; American foreign relations were tidier than domestic affairs when Franklin Delano Roosevelt replaced Hoover in 1933.

Although out of office, Stimson did not withdraw from public life.

25. Barton J. Bernstein, "Seizing the Contested Terrain of Early Nuclear History: Stimson, Conant, and Their Allies Explain the Decision to Use the Atomic Bomb," *Diplomatic History* 17 (Winter 1993): 35–72.

26. My account of Stimson's career is taken from Elting E. Morison's *Turmoil and Tradition* (Boston: Houghton Mifflin, 1980); Godfrey Hodgson's *The Colonel: The Life and Wars of Henry Stimson* (New York: Knopf, 1990); and Richard N. Current's *Secretary Stimson: A Study in Statecraft* (New Brunswick: Rutgers University Press, 1954).

For the first seven years of Roosevelt's administration, Stimson often opposed the president, objecting particularly to Roosevelt's plan to pack the Supreme Court. But in the area of foreign affairs, Stimson firmly and vocally endorsed Roosevelt's policies: encouraging free trade; opposing rapidly expanding German, Italian, and Japanese militarism; and strengthening American military forces. When Britain and France caved in to Hitler at Munich and war broke out in Europe, Roosevelt decided that new leadership was needed at the War Department. On June 19, 1940, Roosevelt asked the lifelong conservative Republican, aged seventy-two, to take another tour of duty as secretary of war. Stimson thought it his duty to oblige.

The war having been satisfactorily concluded, Stimson retired to his Long Island estate. During the summer of 1946, the seventy-eight-year-old former statesman was working on his memoirs with the assistance of McGeorge Bundy, the son of Stimson's wartime aide Harvey Bundy. Prodded by Conant, former War Department associates of Stimson's prevailed upon him to undertake a defense of the decision to drop the bombs on Hiroshima and Nagasaki. Bundy did most of the writing, and his drafts were critiqued by Conant, General Groves, and others who had been involved. Conant insisted that the emerging article be "a mere recital of the facts." It should not advocate one view of the matter or another, and it should not position itself against those who had expressed their opinions in print.[27]

When "The Decision to Use the Atomic Bomb" was published in *Harper's*, it carried a note stating that anyone was free to reprint it because of its "exceptional public importance." The *New York Times* quickly approved the historical contribution:

> As Mr. Stimson shows . . . [the reasoning of the War Department] was grim but irrefutable. The Japanese had been gravely weakened, but they were still determined to fight to the death. . . . [T]hough they had sent out peace feelers through Russia, they still counted on posing as victors and keeping much of the areas they had conquered. . . . [I]t would cost at least a million American—and many more Japanese—casualties, and a war lasting to the latter part of 1946, to beat them to their knees.

27. Bernstein, "Seizing the Contested Terrain," 49.

The *Washington Post*'s editors ran the *Harper's* article in full but were less convinced that Stimson had presented the whole story. Referring to the USSBS conclusions that Japan was about to surrender, a *Post* editorial hinted that Stimson might have been mistaken about the Japanese will to fight to the death. Nonetheless, the article was commended as a "powerful apologia."[28]

The aspect of Stimson's article that most perturbed skeptical minds two decades later was its tone of certainty. There were no second thoughts; what had been done was unquestionably right: "At no time, from 1941 to 1945, did I ever hear it suggested by the President, or by any other responsible member of the government, that atomic energy should not be used in the war. . . . The possible atomic weapon was considered to be . . . as legitimate as any other of the deadly explosive weapons of modern war."[29]

Stimson explained that his Interim Advisory Committee had fielded various suggestions for warning Japan about the new weapon, but none had passed muster. Nothing could have been more disastrous for American morale, or as encouraging for Japan's, as the failure of a much-hyped new weapon, and the Manhattan engineers could give no guarantees. One type of bomb had not yet been tested; the other, which was to be detonated with a new kind of fuse, had not yet been dropped from a plane. Moreover, even if a demonstration were carried out successfully, it was not clear that the Japanese people would ever know about it since the Japanese government had total control over the dissemination of news. And, most important, Stimson stressed his responsibility to his own compatriots. Americans were sick of the war and eager to bring their boys back home. If people learned that a weapon that could potentially end the war had not been used, Stimson could not, he declared, have "looked my countrymen in the face."[30]

There was much more in the article, including Stimson's advice to Truman about guaranteeing the retention of the emperor, about issuing Japan an ultimatum, about sharing atomic know-how with the

28. "War and the Bomb," *New York Times*, January 28, 1947; "Why We Used the Atom Bomb," *Washington Post*, January 28, 1947.

29. Stimson "The Decision to Use the Bomb," 98.

30. Ibid., 106. Stimson's Interim Committee to advise him on atomic issues consisted of three scientists (James Conant, Vannevar Bush, and Karl Compton), representatives from the navy and the Department of State, and James F. Byrnes representing President Truman.

Soviets. The conclusion was upbeat: "the bombs dropped on Hiroshima and Nagasaki ended a war. They also made it wholly clear that we must never have another."[31]

Conant, the instigator of this rhetorical tour de force, gloated behind the scenes. Stimson's article was an amazing success. McGeorge Bundy was also triumphant: "I think we deserve some sort of medal for reducing these particular chatterers to silence," he chortled.[32]

The chatterers Bundy had in mind may have been reduced to silence, but in Britain one man remained totally unconvinced. Ignoring Stimson's article and drawing his information from the USSBS report, physicist P. M. S. Blackett, who insisted that destroying Hiroshima and Nagasaki was not a military necessity, redefined the debate. "So we may conclude that the dropping of the atomic bombs was not so much the last military act of the Second World War, as the first major operation of the cold diplomatic war with Russia now in progress."[33] Marxist and pro-Soviet, Blackett was not a neutral investigator, but his credentials were impressive. Previously honored for his contributions to antisubmarine warfare, he was named Nobel laureate in physics in 1948, the same year *Military and Political Consequences of Atomic Energy* appeared.

The book caused a sensation. Lord Cherwell attacked it violently in the *Daily Telegraph*. Government ministers attacked it in Parliament. Soviet foreign minister Andrei Vishinsky quoted it ten times in a speech at the United Nations. In 1949, an American edition was published with the title *Fear, War, and the Bomb*. According to Hanson Baldwin in the *New York Times*, "The American edition of this book, severe though its strictures are, has been considerably softened." It was widely reviewed, mostly with mild praise. A 1951 edition in Japanese became the bible for left-wing groups in the island nation.[34]

Blackett's attack served as the blueprint for Gar Alperovitz's

31. Stimson, "The Decision to Use the Bomb," 107.

32. McGeorge Bundy to Stimson, February 18, 1947, in Henry Lewis Stimson Papers (hereafter cited as Stimson Papers), Yale University Library.

33. P. M. S. Blackett, *Fear, War, and the Bomb* (New York: Whittlesey House, 1949), 139.

34. Lord Cherwell, "Atomic Bombing the Decisive Weapon—And Deterrent," *London Daily Telegraph*, December 9, 1948; Hanson Baldwin, review of *Fear, War, and the Bomb*, *New York Times*, July 3, 1949, 11; Asada Sadao, "Japanese Perceptions of the A-Bomb Decision," in *The American Military and the Far East*, ed. Joe C. Dixon (Col-

Atomic Diplomacy: Hiroshima and Potsdam, published in 1965. Even though he dedicates the book to "A Great American Conservative, Henry L. Stimson," Alperovitz sets out to prove that the diplomatic maneuverings before Potsdam were designed to keep Russia in line, and that the most effective means of doing so was boldly to demonstrate Allied power and will.[35] That motive, however, is nowhere to be found in Stimson's private diary, on deposit at the Yale University library, and no fair-minded reader of it could possibly propose that relations with the Soviets were Stimson's governing concern. Ending the war and securing international control of atomic energy, precisely in that order, were Stimson's priorities. Thus Alperovitz's book, dedicated to Stimson, delivers an anti-Stimson message.

Hostility toward Stimson spread in 1995 along with retrospectives on the Pacific War. In many respects that phenomenon is ironic. Stimson was easily the least bloodthirsty and vengeful of our World War II leaders. Having dealt with the Japanese in the 1930s as secretary of state, Stimson believed that Japan was torn between enlightened aristocrats and reckless militarists. Before Hiroshima, Stimson led a movement to define the terms of surrender so that Japan could retain its emperor; he lost that point to James F. Byrnes and the military experts.

Stimson's diaries and correspondence betray an acute concern for the sufferings of wartime, not just for Allied soldiers engaged in pitched battles but for civilians caught up in their own struggles as well. He often urged that U.S. air forces avoid bombing noncombatants, though the contagion of all-out war rendered his entreaties nothing more than impotent requests. He strongly recommended halting all bombing after the first Japanese offer to surrender was received on August 10, but he was overruled. His demand that Kyoto be removed from the atomic bomb target list because of its cultural and religious significance was, however, honored. He also advocated trusting the Soviets and sharing nuclear information with them

---

orado Springs: U.S. Air Force Academy, 1980), 208; and Hatana Sumio, "The Pacific War," in *Japan and the World, 1853–1952,* ed. Asada Sadao (New York: Columbia University Press, 1989), 373.

35. Gar Alperovitz, *Atomic Diplomacy.*

as the most reliable guarantee for assuring international control of the atom and avoiding an arms race. He lost this battle too.[36]

But Stimson had accepted Conant's challenge to defend the decision to deploy the atomic bomb, and in so doing he had put himself on the front line. Harry Truman receded into the background. Those who took up the standard with Alperovitz were not just attacking the former president for making a bad decision; they were attacking their government for telling (as in Vietnam) a misleading story (Stimson's).

Stimson was accused of misleading the public on two counts. The first involved omission and exaggeration. Stimson implied that the Interim Advisory Committee had carefully considered, first, a non-hostile demonstration of the bomb, and then, that possibility eliminated, a specific warning before dropping the bombs. Interim Committee deliberations were not carefully recorded, however, and surviving minutes do not bear out Stimson's conclusion, likely an overstatement.[37]

Critics like Murray Sayle, who stated emphatically that the decision to use the bomb was made "thoughtlessly, by default," and Gar Alperovitz, who made the same point with special vehemence, have failed to look further.[38] Indeed, history would have been better served had Stimson characterized the Interim Committee deliberations as what they truly were: the capstone of lengthy and continual discussions about the bomb by the secretary, the president, army chief George Marshall, and the War Department staff. Evidence of those conversations is abundant. By my count, between March 5, 1945, and the Hiroshima bombing on August 6, Stimson recorded in his diary face-to-face discussions about the atomic bomb with the following people:

36. See Morison, *Turmoil and Tradition;* Hodgson, *The Colonel;* and Henry L. Stimson and McGeorge Bundy, *On Active Service* (New York: Harper, 1948). Stimson's remarkable opinion that we should trust the Soviets is displayed extensively in Stimson's diaries (microfilm edition, reel 9, frames 1115, 1125, 1126, 1144, 1148, 1149, 1155, 1171, 1176, 1200), Stimson Papers. On Stimson's belief system in general, see John Bennett, "Jekyll and Hyde: Henry L. Stimson, Mentalité, and the Decision to Use the Atomic Bomb on Japan," *War in History* 4 (1997): 174–212.

37. Manhattan Engineer District Records, Harrison-Bundy files, folder 76, NARA-DC.

Harvey Bundy, assistant to the secretary of war, on 32 days
George Harrison, assistant to the secretary of war, on 26 days
President Truman, on 14 days
Army chief Marshall, on 12 days
John McCloy, assistant secretary of war, on 8 days

In addition, there was at least one and as many as four meetings with each of the following officials: Secretary of State James Byrnes, Undersecretary of State Joseph Grew, Field Marshal Sir Henry Wilson, Winston Churchill, Anthony Eden, James Conant, and others, all in addition to three lengthy meetings with the Interim Committee. Clearly, the atomic bomb was rarely off Stimson's agenda during the spring and summer of 1945.

Of course, given world enough and time, the bomb could have been considered more carefully; but the War Department had other things to do. Henry Stimson oversaw a massive military machine and monitored its efficiency to the very end. Even without major land battles, deaths and destruction were accumulating. On July 29 the *Indianapolis* was sunk, and 883 lives were lost. POWs and slave laborers were dying in significant numbers, and at least one hundred thousand British, Dutch, and American POWs were slated for extermination if the Allies attacked Southeast Asia, an event set for September 6. Laurens van der Post, a prisoner in Marshal Terauchi's empire, noted the increasing tempo of death from untreated disease, starvation, and constant beatings in the camps. The Japanese, he believed, would try to "pull down their sprawling military temple, Samson-like, and to destroy the European Philistine along with themselves rather than endure defeat with ignominy."[39] Given such circumstances, drawing out discussions of a potentially war-shortening weapon would have been considered grossly irresponsible. Who would dare call use of this super bomb illegitimate when all agreed that it was quite legitimate to mass 210 B-29s to drop an equivalent explosive force?

More serious than the charge of exaggeration was the accusation

38. Sayle, "Did the Bomb End the War?" 54; Alperovitz, *The Decision to Use the Atomic Bomb,* chap. 12.

39. Laurens van der Post, *The Prisoner and the Bomb* (New York: Morrow, 1971), 122, 22.

that Stimson had misrepresented the options available in August
1945. He seemed to pose the dilemma as a simple choice between using the bomb and invading Kyushu as scheduled on November 1.
Stimson's critics multiplied the alternatives: 1) modifying unconditional surrender to allow for retention of the emperor; 2) waiting for
Soviet entry into the war; or 3) tightening the naval blockade and
continuing conventional and fire bombing until thousands starved
and the rubble bounced. Some critics claim that the Truman administration *knew* that these were all viable choices.

Of course, Stimson himself had recommended guaranteeing the
emperor before the bombs were used in hope that the concession
might help the Japanese peace party triumph over the militarists,
and he so stated in his *Harper's* article. Ultimately, however, he succumbed to the better wisdom of George Marshall and the Joint
Chiefs, who believed that giving in on this crucial point *before* Japan
surrendered would embolden General Anami to boast about the terrible punishment Japanese troops had inflicted on American forces
at Iwo Jima and Okinawa and to argue that the Allies were soften-
ing, recoiling from further ground combat.[40]

The American victory on Okinawa had the perverse effect of encouraging the Japanese military. Ronald Spector's classic account of
the Pacific War notes that Japanese army planners gloated after Okinawa, "less than three divisions, cut off from all supplies and subject to naval gunfire, had nonetheless held out for over a hundred
days against an American force more than twice as strong."[41] In the
aftermath of Okinawa, American war leaders feared that relaxing
the terms of surrender would lend strength to the Japanese bitter-
enders. Stimson could not say they were wrong. Critics of Stimson's
article do not engage this argument.

Alperovitz makes much of Undersecretary of State Joseph Grew's
1947 opinion that "the surrender of Japan could have been hastened"
if the emperor had been guaranteed in May 1945. Grew, however,
was a waffler. In October 1945, he told Admiral J. F. Shafroth, "it was
the atomic bomb that broke the camel's back, even though the Japa-

---

40. Stimson, "The Decision to Use the Bomb," 104; Bix, "Japan's Delayed Surrender"; Asada Sadao, "The Shock of the Atom Bomb and Japan's Decision to Surrender" (Paper, Conference of the Society for Historians of American Foreign Relations,
Washington, D.C., June 23, 1995).
41. Spector, *Eagle against the Sun,* 543.

nese were thoroughly licked even before it was ever used. Without the use of the bomb by us, the Japs might well have fought to the last ditch and might have made our invasion by force exceedingly costly." And to the Reverend Charles Reifsnider, he wrote that same month, "I fully appreciate your support of the position I took about the Emperor. . . . Stimson was splendid through it all—a really great statesman with a thorough understanding of Japanese mentality and great vision."[42]

In 1947 Grew reversed himself. He probably believed the USSBS report. Stimson did not. The work of Japanese scholars studying the question supports the rightness of Stimson's skepticism.[43]

The critics' second point—that a Soviet attack on Japan, which Stalin promised to launch by mid-August, may well have forced a surrender—has little validity, whether viewed contemporaneously or in hindsight. Gar Alperovitz faults Stimson for failing to acknowledge that a cable from Foreign Minister Togo to the Japanese ambassador in Moscow "stated that Japan was prepared to surrender on the basis of the Atlantic Charter," which guaranteed access to raw materials for all nations. There was no such cable. Togo never used the word *surrender;* he was only seeking a negotiated cease fire. Alperovitz compounds his error by referring to a April 30, 1946, report by Colonel R. F. Ennis of the War Department Operations Division. Ennis offers a ludicrous account of Japanese deliberations in August 1945; he misdates Premier Suzuki's concession to surrender, writes of cabinet meetings that did not take place, misidentifies the messengers who took bad news to the emperor, and confuses Suzuki's activities with those of Privy Seal Kido. Ennis then concludes, "The war would almost certainly have terminated when Russia entered the war against Japan." Ennis presents no warrant for this claim.[44]

42. Joseph Grew to J. F. Shafroth, October 18, 1945, and Grew to Charles Reifsnider, October 19, 1945, quoted in Masanori Nakamura, *The Japanese Monarchy* (Armonk, N.Y.: M. E. Sharpe, 1992), 83, 84.

43. Bix, "Japan's Delayed Surrender"; Asada, "The Shock of the Atom Bomb." Stimson did still wonder, in 1947, if guaranteeing the emperor *might* have shortened the war. Bix, Asada, and other modern scholars make it clear that Stimson was right to yield to military opinion in 1945.

44. There is a July 25, 1945, cable from Foreign Minister Togo to Ambassador Sato in Moscow that says, "we have no objection to a peace based on the Atlantic Charter." The context makes it clear that Togo is talking about a negotiated peace with favorable terms for Japan, not about surrender. See *Foreign Relations of the United States:*

Despite the flimsiness of Alperovitz's challenge to Stimson, it cannot be denied that at one point in June Marshall and Truman suggested that Soviet entry into the war might end it, even though they believed that that success also hinged on a coincidental Allied invasion. It must be noted as well that Japanese premier Suzuki is reported to have declared upon learning that the Soviet army was penetrating Manchuria, "Then the game is up."[45] When we turn to the USSBS interrogation records, however, we find not one well-placed Japanese official claiming that a Soviet attack *alone* would have prompted capitulation. Some officials believed that the atomic bomb *and* the Soviet presence had caused Japan to surrender, but many others credited the bomb solely.

The Japanese military had clearly anticipated Soviet involvement early in the summer of 1945. They had intelligence of massive Soviet troop movements to the Eastern Front in June and July, and on May 30 Tokyo ordered its armed forces in China to retreat, fighting all the way, and to make a stand in the mountains along the Manchurian-Korean border, where soldiers were expected to hold out for six months.[46] On August 15, 1945, even after the atomic bombs had been dropped and the Soviets had joined the war against Japan, General Okamura, commander of the Japanese armies in China, saw scant justification for surrendering. "Such a disgrace as the surrender of several million troops without fighting," he said, "is not paralleled in the world's military history, and it is absolutely impossible to submit to unconditional surrender of a million picked troops, in perfectly healthy shape."[47]

We cannot ignore such comments, now available in the declassified Japanese cable traffic. Who can read such statements and with any

---

The Conference of Berlin (The Potsdam Conference), 1945 (Washington, D.C.: U.S. Government Printing Office, 1960), 1:1261. Alperovitz involves the Ennis document nine times in *The Decision to Use the Atomic Bomb*. For a critique of Ennis, see my *Truman and the Hiroshima Cult* (East Lansing: Michigan State University Press, 1995), 22–23; and D. M. Giangreco, "Operation Downfall," *Joint Force Quarterly* (Autumn 1995): 89–90.

45. Lester Brooks, *Behind Japan's Surrender* (New York: McGraw-Hill, 1968), 17.

46. On USSBS interrogations, see my "Ending the War with Japan"; on Japanese knowledge of Soviet intentions, see Edward J. Drea, "Missing Intentions: Japanese Intelligence and the Soviet Invasion of Manchuria, 1945," *Military Affairs* 48 (April 1984): 66–73.

47. Okamura to Minister of War (Anami), August 15, 1945, Records of the National Security Agency, Central Security Service, SRH-090, box 17, RG 457, NARA-DC.

conviction whatsoever assert that Soviet entry into the war alone would have brought Japan to its knees? We do not know now; how could we possibly have known then? Dominating the deliberations of Marshall and the Joint Chiefs was the horrible lesson of Germany, which, even though its cities were devastated and Soviet armies were closing in, staged a death's-door counterattack in the Battle of the Bulge. Germany never surrendered until the country was overrun.

Why should Japan have been different? Japanese determination had been burned into the consciousness of Allied forces. On August 12—after the shocks of the 6th to the 9th, after the emperor's intervention and the first tentative offer of surrender from Tokyo, and after an American overture implying that unconditional surrender did not involve displacing the emperor—the American army G-2 (Intelligence section) told Marshall that "atomic bombs will not have a decisive effect in the next 30 days." Given such reservations so late in the day, Soviet intervention can only have been considered as one factor among others designed to end the war. Barton Bernstein, the most knowledgeable student of the decision to use the bomb, is clear that Soviet entry into the war did not promise prompt surrender.[48]

The final charge leveled at Stimson is that he minimized the option of mounting an invasion against Japan by overestimating its potential for human destruction, which he calculated at "over a million casualties, to American forces alone." Alperovitz calls this Stimson's "most enduring single obfuscation" and asks, "Where did Stimson and Bundy get their 'over a million' estimate? We do not know."[49]

Indeed, we do know. In Stimson's office were several consultants who avoided the limelight. One of them, Edward L. Bowles, ranked sixth on Stimson's preferential list of aides. Bowles headed the team of scientists and engineers who oversaw the development of new military technologies (except atomic) that eventually surpassed Axis expertise. Working under Bowles was future Nobel laureate William Shockley, a scientist credited with the ultimate success of the Allied antisubmarine campaign.

48. Major General Clayton Bissell to Chief of Staff (Marshall), "Estimate of Japanese Situation for Next 30 Days," War Department General and Special Staffs, OPD, file 2, box 12, RG 165, NARA-DC; Barton J. Bernstein, "Understanding the Atomic Bomb and Japanese Surrender: Missed Opportunities, Little Known Near Disasters, and Modern Memory," in Hogan, ed., *Hiroshima in History and Memory*, 57–62.
49. Alperovitz, *The Decision to Use the Atomic Bomb*, 466–67.

When Shockley's antisubmarine work was complete, he was given the task of "gathering and organizing information bearing on the problem of casualties in the Pacific War." On July 21, 1945, while Stimson was in Potsdam, Shockley handed Bowles a lengthy report. In it Shockley complained that the eccentric casualty figures and projections issued by G-1, G-2, army ground forces, and the surgeon general's office were worthless. His investigations to date, he noted, were based on a hypothesis requiring further testing, namely, that if their nation were invaded, the Japanese would recapitulate the behavior their soldiers had demonstrated in recent battles. In that event, he wrote, "the Japanese dead and ineffectives at the time of defeat will exceed the corresponding number for the Germans. In other words, we shall probably have to kill at least 5 to 10 million Japanese. This might cost us between 1.7 and 4 million casualties including 400,000 to 800,000 killed."[50]

Shockley's astounding report resides in the Bowles papers at the Library of Congress. We cannot be certain that Bowles showed it to Stimson. We can assume, however, that Stimson did not draw his figure out of thin air. Bowles reported to Stimson aides George Harrison and Harvey Bundy constantly. Stimson returned to Washington from the Potsdam Conference on July 28. From July 30 through August 3, Stimson saw both Harrison and Bundy at least once and often several times a day. It stands to reason that such an explosive communication as Shockley's would have been passed on to the boss.[51]

It also stands to reason that a secretary of war who had been advised by the military that Germany would surrender in 1944 (which it did not) and that MacArthur would recapture Leyte in forty-five days with four divisions (it took three months and nine divisions) would be skeptical of estimates put forth by casualty-shy generals.[52]

50. W. B. Shockley to Edward L. Bowles, July 21, 1945, "Proposal for Increasing the Scope of Casualty Studies," Edward L. Bowles Papers, box 34, Library of Congress.

51. The Stimson diaries do not refer to Shockley's report; hence revisionists insist that Stimson could not have known about it and thus made up his million-casualty figures out of whole cloth. A fair reading of Stimson's diaries shows that the secretary of war failed to mention all but a minuscule fraction of the thousands of documents that came to him.

52. Even MacArthur, abetted by Marshall, fudged casualty estimates for the start of the Kyushu invasion for fear that Truman would recoil from them and settle for a long, drawn-out war of attrition or for less than decisive victory. See my *Truman and the Hiroshima Cult*, 10–11.

The Shockley figures were not the only information reaching Stimson. D. M. Giangreco, in a thorough analysis of military culture and the functions of casualty estimates, shows that from 1944 on, the operating assumption throughout the War Department was that subduing the Japanese home islands would cost at least five hundred thousand American casualties, possibly as many as two million.[53] Revisionists have fixed on estimates for the beginning of the Kyushu invasion (below one hundred thousand) and failed to consider the larger implications. That the worst was being anticipated, however, is obvious from a number of sources: plans for medical evacuation and hospital beds; a large increase in Selective Service inductions in the spring of 1945; expanded capability for retraining European soldiers for Pacific warfare; and alarming reports from ULTRA monitors that Japanese strength on Kyushu was rapidly increasing even as American bombs were being dropped to inhibit troop movements. The intelligence reports General Charles Willoughby sent MacArthur implied that landing on Kyushu would cause a bloodbath that would outrun Okinawa's by a factor of ten.[54] General Marshall responded on August 6 by demanding a detailed scenario for bypassing Kyushu and landing on northern Honshu. A ninety-six-page plan was in his hands three days later.[55]

Given Japan's apparently unrelenting determination to fight on, the Allies would have been unwise to give much credence to the argument that starvation would lead to surrender. Certainly the Japanese food supply was inadequate, and malnutrition was evident by August 1945. But history urged caution. In 1914, the British had blockaded Germany; not until 1918 did significant numbers of Germans die of starvation. And even then, it is not certain that starvation was a factor in urging Germany to sign a cease-fire agreement.[56] The wisdom of distrusting the starvation incentive is also clear through hindsight. Countless Japanese soldiers on islands con-

---

53. Giangreco, "Operation Downfall."

54. G-2 General HQ U.S. Army Forces, Pacific (Willoughby) to G-3 (same HQ) July 28, 1945, S. J. Chamberlain Papers, U.S. Army Military History Institute, Carlisle Barracks, Pa.

55. Joint War Plans Committee 398/1, "Plan for the Invasion of Northern Honshu," August 9, 1945, box 615, RG 218, NARA-DC.

56. Moralists who argue directly, or imply, that starvation would have been superior to atomic bombs in ending the Pacific War should consult Vera Brittain's *Humiliation with Honor* (New York: Fellowship Publications, 1943) and Weart's *Nuclear Fear*, 93.

quered by the Allies chose to starve to death rather than surrender. Even after their nation had capitulated, many considered suicide preferable to dishonor.

On August 9, Stimson wrote in his diary that he was leaving Washington the next day "for a long rest": "The bomb and the entrance of the Russians into the war will certainly have an effect on hastening the victory. But just how much that effect is or how long and how many men we will have to keep to accomplish that victory, it is impossible yet to determine." Then, on August 10, Stimson noted,

> Today was momentous. We had all packed up and the car was waiting to take us to the airport where we were headed for our vacation when word came from Colonel McCarthy at the Department that the Japanese had made an offer to surrender. Furthermore they had announced it in the clear. That busted our holiday for the present and I raced down to the office, getting there before half past eight.[57]

Not even two atomic bombs *and* Soviet entry into the war in the Pacific could convince Henry Stimson that the Japanese were prepared to surrender any time soon.

If Stimson is thus relieved of these charges of exaggeration, omission, and gross misrepresentation, then can't we conclude that he basically told it like it was? Not quite. The major fault of Stimson's recitation of the facts is that *it framed the issue falsely.* Truman did not confront a *choice* between dropping atomic bombs on Japan and launching a costly invasion. He confronted the necessity of using *every legitimate means available to end a global war*—not one means as opposed to another, not invasion *or* bomb, not waiting for Soviet intervention or blockade/starvation, not continued conventional bombing or atomic bombs. It was simply not an either/or situation.

Backing down from unconditional surrender was not a viable option; intelligence indicated that such a concession would probably have stiffened Japanese resistance. Use of poison gas to neutralize the ubiquitous Japanese cave redoubts was considered, but that was not a legitimate course. The atom was. No well-placed American of-

---

57. Stimson diaries, August 9 and 10, 1945, reel 9, frames 1100 and 1107, Stimson Papers, quotations by permission.

ficial at the time questioned the legitimacy of an atomic weapon, notwithstanding Eisenhower's later (false) claim to the contrary.[58]

Stimson's framing of the issue—the atom versus invasion—created the impression that the American high command knew that either of those alternatives would quickly end the war. They did not. Marshall at one point thought that the atomic bomb coupled with invasion would end the war, but he did not know when. Truman, euphoric after Alamogordo, boasted, "Believe Japs will fold up before Russia comes in. I am sure they will when Manhattan appears over their homeland." ULTRA intercepts, showing a determined Japanese military successfully reinforcing Kyushu, soon quashed his optimism, a condition to which Stimson never succumbed.[59]

Stimson gave us, in the *Harper's* essay, a "calm, dispassionate narrative," according to Robert J. Lifton. "Guided description, not explicit argument," maintains Barton Bernstein, was the "most powerful way to persuade." And, indeed, Stimson's "just the facts" narrative did win a skirmish in the contest to seize control of early nuclear history.[60]

But Stimson lost the war. There is no invulnerable narrative. Opponents can always tell a contrary narrative, and shifting public attitudes can create new audiences sympathetic to it. Until the country became disillusioned with government during the Vietnam War, Stimson's narrative held the field. In the 1960s, "the claim [that] we made the least abhorrent choice" fell into the "credibility gap," pushed by USSBS fictitious conclusions and Hersey's sympathetic treatment of the "Japanese as victims." By 1947, rehabilitating Japan to serve as the anchor for American efforts to contain communism in Asia was a project already well under way. MacArthur had acted to purge Japan of her militarists; the Japanese appeared docile and friendly. And Americans were demonstrating an unbelievable, collective amnesia about Japan's atrocities, well documented in Gavan Daws's *Prisoners of the Japanese*, which also allowed suspicions about Truman's decision to flourish.[61]

---

58. On Eisenhower, see Barton J. Bernstein, "Ike and Hiroshima: Did He Oppose It?" *Journal of Strategic Studies* 10 (September 1987): 377–89.

59. See Drea, *MacArthur's ULTRA*, chap. 8.

60. Lifton and Mitchell, *Hiroshima in America*, 103; Bernstein, "Seizing the Contested Terrain," 71.

61. Gavan Daws, *Prisoners of the Japanese* (New York: Morrow, 1994).

No one reading Stimson's diaries and correspondence with an open mind could possibly accept the revisionists' characterization of him as a self-serving liar, a racist imperialist, a willing perpetrator of unnecessary atrocity. Against that view advanced by the revisionists, we should consider a statement by one of Stimson's contemporaries, a man who himself vividly recalled the tensions of the times. Acknowledging the gift of Stimson's biography, *On Active Service*, largely written by McGeorge Bundy but closely supervised by Stimson, Vannevar Bush wrote,

> It will take me back to strenuous days, when the issue was in doubt, nerves were frayed, and counsels were at times confused; days when we were very grateful that you could be in command, for we knew that there was one rock stable in the current. . . . I also remember the day the first V-bombs landed, and you and I rode up on the Hill to explain further why large amounts of money needed to flow into strange things, and our relief when we realized that the V-bombs carried only conventional warheads. . . . During the war you were to me as a father to a son, and my greatest satisfaction of the whole war experience came from that relationship. I shall cherish it always.[62]

Stimson was never happy with the options he claimed were available to him and his president; their decision was only the "least abhorrent choice." The atom bomb, at that time, was as legitimate a weapon as LeMay's incendiaries or the flamethrowers on Okinawa. Stimson knew it had to be used; he also knew and said that it was a terrible weapon that required international control. He was right on both counts. It is too bad, then, that simply because he framed the argument about bombing Hiroshima and Nagasaki in misleading terms, he left himself vulnerable to the vicissitudes of history.

62. Vannevar Bush to Stimson, April 21, 1948, microfilm edition, reel 119, frame 0696, Stimson Papers, quotation by permission.

Enola Gay at Air and Space
Anonymity, Hypocrisy, Ignorance

MARTIN HARWIT TOOK CHARGE OF THE National Air and Space Museum (NASM) in August 1987, facing a demand from veterans that he do something about the most glaring omission of historic aircraft from the museum's displays: *Enola Gay*, the aircraft that dropped an atomic bomb on Hiroshima and, along with Soviet entry into the Pacific War and a second bomb on Nagasaki, effectively ended the war.[1]

Enola Gay was under Smithsonian control but housed in inadequate facilities of Silver Hill, Maryland. It had been neglected for almost a decade. The veterans wanted the plane completely refurbished and "displayed proudly" in a setting that would commemorate the heroism of those who won the war, as well as recognize the genius of American technology. In the lingo of memorialists, this means that the veterans wanted a narrative of good triumphant over evil.

Leading the agitation about *Enola Gay* were members of the 509th Composite Group, the U.S. Army Air Force's contingent under Paul Tibbets that had been assigned to prepare an attack with atomic bombs against both Germany and Japan. When it appeared that Germany would surrender before the first bomb was ready, the 509th found itself practicing for early August drops on Hiroshima and Nagasaki.

Members of the 509th founded the *Enola Gay* Restoration Association in the summer of 1984. Partly due to their campaign NASM began to restore the aircraft in 1985. When Harwit took over NASM in 1987 a display of *Enola Gay* was already top priority. World War II pi-

---

1. The most useful account of the NASM *Enola Gay* event is Martin Harwit, *An Exhibit Denied: Lobbying the History of the Enola Gay* (New York: Springer-Verlag, 1996).

lots were determined to see the aircraft displayed in pristine condition before they died; if NASM wouldn't do it, they had many suggestions of museums and airfields where it would be welcomed.

The plane had a bittersweet welcome at NASM. The paper trail establishes that Director Harwit and his chief assistants were convinced

1. that scholarly research would show using atomic bombs against Japan had been a mistake;
2. that the Japanese would have surrendered soon without them;
3. that had Truman told the Japanese they could keep their emperor, surrender could have come even before the bombs were dropped;
4. that the huge casualties Truman said he had been told to expect if we invaded Japan as scheduled November 1, 1945, were a postwar creation;
5. that racism, revenge, and intimidating the Soviet Union were important and illegitimate motives for Truman's decision;
6. that the obscene nuclear arms race with the Soviet Union was a legacy of the two atomic bombs we dropped, not caused by Soviet determination to have any weapon its adversaries had;
7. and that the veterans who believed the bombs foreclosed an invasion and thus saved their lives were simply ignorant and mistaken.

This heavy ideological baggage made it difficult for the NASM team to put together an exhibit that would be true to their own beliefs and satisfy the veterans. If all these antibomb claims were warranted, the *Enola Gay* should be on a junk heap somewhere, not displayed prominently in a national museum controlled and financed by the United States government.

But the *Enola Gay* was securely under the control of NASM, and Harwit had to produce. To say that what followed generated trouble is to understate the situation. Ultimately, after much expenditure of time and money, the planned exhibit was canceled. There have been many postmortems; here I argue that the exhibit died of anonymity, hypocrisy, and ignorance. No minds were changed.

Museum exhibits, like other scholarly efforts, require documentation. Of all the debilities a "scholarly" presentation might suffer, surely the most unusual is anonymity of sources. Most critiques of the often erroneous products of the CIA and other intelligence services note that one liability of such bureaucratic operations is their anonymity. They are *secret* organizations, and no one person is responsible for false information. Who told Kennedy that the Cubans were ready for revolt when Brigade 4506 landed at the Bay of Pigs? Who was really responsible for the catastrophic U.S.-backed overthrow of Mossadeq in Iran in 1953? Even if one thinks it necessary for national security reasons to keep such CIA findings secret, what possible reason could Harwit have had for hiding the identities of the scholars on whom NASM relied?

Even in everyday arguments, the common challenge "Says who?" requires an answer. Where, as in the *Enola Gay* case, the whole structure of NASM's narrative depends on the claim of the curators to possess "the best scholarly research," the necessity for identifying *whose* research is inescapable, yet nowhere in the text of the exhibit are we told whose research underwrote the narrative.

Two critics of the NASM objected to this violation of scholarly norms. Richard Kurin, the director of the Center for Folklife Programs and Cultural Studies at the Smithsonian, speaking at a symposium sponsored by the Smithsonian and the University of Michigan at Ann Arbor on April 19, 1995, had harsh words for his colleagues. According to Kurin, their first script on *Enola Gay* had an anonymity that "conveys a sense of disembodied authority we know to be inappropriate." As the editor of the symposium summarized Kurin's presentation, "Kurin thought that a small group of scholars and curators was no longer in sole possession of knowledge; the lived experience of those who flew *Enola Gay* was, he believed, not 'fully and honestly' engaged by the curators."[2]

More sympathetic to the NASM curators, but aware of liabilities in their product, Daniel Seltz, in a monograph of the East Asian studies program at Brown University, December 1996, noted,

> The Smithsonian also confronted the problems of accountability. The exhibit never cited any of the historians whose theories they had integrated into the script by name. This meant that these historians were not involved in a direct way in defending the findings of their research, and it also grouped scholars with varying perspectives un-

2. Richard Kurin, "Presenting History: Museum in a Democratic Society" (Smithsonian Institute, Washington, D.C, April 19, 1995), 30.

der vague and encompassing phrases such as "most historians believe."[3]

We were indeed never told which historians believed what, nor what they based this belief on.

The *Enola Gay* script mentioned a miscellany of people: various U.S. Marines and Army privates who fought in the Pacific; three Japanese kamikaze pilots; Roosevelt, Hitler, Chamberlain, Churchill, Stalin, Truman, Einstein; General Leslie Groves, J. Robert Oppenheimer, Henry Stimson, Joseph Grew; B-29 pilots and their crews; survivors of the firebombing of Tokyo; the *Los Angeles Times;* Admiral William Leahy; and Dwight Eisenhower. None of these were scholars of the bomb decision, of the Japanese decision to surrender, or of the causes of the Cold War nuclear arms race. But over and over the curators wrote that "the consensus of historians" says Truman had other ways to end the war, or "recent scholarly research reveals" that Japan was ready to surrender before Hiroshima, or some such weasel phrase. Of course these were not new conclusions at all; they were simply knee-jerk recitations of what Paul Nitze wrote in 1946.

Thus the NASM curators sought, using what Pamela Walker Laird calls "unattributed presentations, with all the authority of the institution housing them," to gain credibility without specific attribution.[4] But here the institutional authority, that of NASM, was not powerful enough to prevail. And only after the planned exhibit was cancelled did we find out who actually wrote the script.

The limitations of Harwit's peculiar notion of scholarly competence come through clearly in his claims for the quartet who wrote the script. Harwit tells us,

> When the Museum sought in 1990 to hire a lead curator for the exhibition of the *Enola Gay* we followed federal procedures and first approached numerous senior American scholars, but none of them were willing or available to take on this complete task. Finding none, we offered the position to Mike Neufeld, a Canadian citizen who clearly had the required credentials.[5]

3. Daniel Seltz, *The Enola Gay Exhibition and the Challenge to American Memory* (Providence: East Asian Studies, Brown University, 1996), 67.
4. Pamela Walker Laird, "The Public's Historians," *Technology and Culture* 39 (July 1998): 476.
5. Harwit, *An Exhibit Denied,* 51.

These credentials were training as a social historian and writing a book on the German V-2 rocket. Neufeld was the lead curator.

Harwit describes Tom Crouch, the NASM's aeronautics chief, as "a prolific historian of the early years of flight," which enabled him to "exhibit the impact that the technology has had on life in the twentieth century."[6] Crouch had been at the Smithsonian for many years. He was also a prime writer.

The other two involved in writing the script were junior employees of Crouch's aeronautics department: Thomas Dietz, who had trained in the navy as an aviation electronics technician, and Joanne Gernstein, a doctoral candidate in American studies at George Washington University, who came to the Smithsonian from the Science Discovery Center in Ithaca.[7]

This quartet of scriptwriters obviously lacked the status of experts in any of the relevant fields. Two of them were, and the two junior ones might become, genuine scholars—in some field. No doubt given sufficient time, and making great effort, they could digest the relevant scholarly research on (1) the decision of the Truman administration to drop the bombs; (2) the Pacific War; (3) the decision of the Japanese government to surrender; (4) the origins of the nuclear arms race; and (5) the morality of war fighting. There is no evidence that they did so.

Backing them up were other NASM employees, the most prominent of whom was Gregg Herken, the head of NASM's department of space history and author of three books on the relations of scientists to government policy. In one of these books, *The Winning Weapon: The Atomic Bomb in the Cold War, 1945–1950,* Herken viewed the Cold War arms race as a direct outcome of Truman's decision to use the bomb against Japan; Truman's decisions "to proceed with the 'Super' and with NSC-68 were properly the culminating events of the policy on the atomic bomb that had begun with the destruction of Hiroshima."[8] Of all the NASM personnel who appear in Harwit's pages, Herken is the only one who claims distinction in a field that might be relevant to this exhibit. Harwit gives no hint as to why Herken was not in charge of *Enola Gay.* Herken's advice during the

6. Ibid.
7. Ibid., 206.
8. Gregg Herken, *The Winning Weapon: The Atomic Bobm in the Cold War, 1945–1950* (Princeton: Princeton University Press, 1981), 329.

various critiques was generally apropos, and mostly well informed. Herken's judgment on the place of the atomic bombs in the origins of the Cold War is at odds with that of specialists on the Soviet nuclear program, but he did not claim this as a specialty.

Although the names of the scriptwriters eventually became known to the press and hence to some wider publics, the names of the historians whose work they appropriated did not. Why did Harwit do it this way? The archives give a clue. The curators believed that Gar Alperovitz, the anti-Truman writer whose 1965 polemic against the bomb decision was the most-read document of Nitzean derivation, could not be acknowledged as a source. His conclusions outran his data, he was strident, and most other writers on the subject disagreed with him; NASM would not identify him as a source.

Despite this public distancing from the most prominent exponent of the Nitze-Blackett narrative, NASM files tell us that Alperovitz's beliefs were very much present. On December 8, 1993, Herken wrote the two lead curators about their preliminary draft. In regard to page 39, he advised,

> I would avoid "revisionist," in or out of quotes, and just go with "some historians . . ." Revisionism is still a fighting term. Also, I wouldn't mention Alperovitz by name; Blackett was first to make the argument [that Truman's main motive was to intimidate the Soviet Union] in 1948. If I were writing this label, I would just say that most historians argue the military motive was primary and sufficient, but that the political motive was reinforcing in the decision.[9]

So Alperovitz never appeared in print.

The archives, however, tell us that on April 21, 1994, when Neufeld was pressed by a group of military historians who had seen the script to provide "some evidence" for its claims, he wrote the following to them:

> In response to comments and criticism made at our recent meeting or in the written comments from Air Force History, I am enclosing three photocopies of secondary sources which provide evidence, I think, for three points: (1) that the Soviet Factor was of some influence in the

9. Gregg Herken to Tom Crouch and Michael Neufeld, December 8, 1993, Smithsonian Institution Archives (henceforth SIA), *Enola Gay* Exhibition Records (henceforth EGER), Accession 96–140, box 4.

thinking of Stimson, Byrnes and Truman before and during the Potsdam Conference; (2) that this position is now the consensus among
historians, although there is wide disagreement over how significant
a factor it was; and (3) that Bernstein and the historians of the "consensus" position on the "decision to drop the bomb" form a separate,
middling group from the Alperovitz "revisionists."[10]

Finding this document in the files of the U.S. Naval Historical Center, but without the three photocopies of what Neufeld believed to
be evidence, I wrote Neufeld on September 25, 1999, asking if he
could recall what the photocopies were. He responded that he was
sure one of them was from J. Samuel Walker's 1990 article on the historiography of the bomb decision; the others were probably from articles by Martin Sherwin and Barton Bernstein. Neufeld also explained that "the 'consensus' historians on the center and the left had
split away from Alperovitz and did not support many of his positions while remaining somewhat skeptical of the atomic bomb decision."[11]

The military historians were not convinced that Alperovitz had
been banned from the *Enola Gay* script. Wayne Dzwonchyk, the historian in the Office of the Chairman, Joint Chiefs of Staff, wrote
Neufeld on April 28, 1994. Dzwonchyk believed that the exhibit
script contradicted Neufeld's letter. Dzwonchyk observed,

It cannot be demonstrated that the U.S. conducted any atomic diplomacy at Potsdam. In fact, the interesting thing about the conference is
the demanding and aggressive stance taken by the Soviets. To flatten
all nuance and state, as the script did, that Truman delayed the conference in order to have the bomb in hand for tough negotiations with
the Soviets is pure Alperovitz strategy of a delayed showdown which
in its bald form is rejected by Sherwin and Bernstein . . . To reiterate a
point I tried to make at our recent meeting, perhaps without sufficient
clarity, the script's repeated reference to the Soviet factor and to US
desire to "intimidate the Soviet Union," inflated it out of proportion
to its actual importance. The bomb would have been dropped on Japan, as Bernstein says, even if the Soviet Union had not existed.[12]

10. Neufeld to Edward Drea et al., April 21, 1994, *Enola Gay* Records, U.S. Naval
Historical Center, Washington Navy Yard, D.C.
11. Neufeld to author, September 25, 1999.
12. Dzwonchyk to Neufeld, April 28, 1994, SIA-EGER, Accession 96–140, box 9.

Neufeld responded on May 12, 1994:

> Part of the problem with that section stems from the fact that the script
> tries to represent the *range* of the debate, and not merely my view of
> these matters—that is especially the case in the "Historical Contro-
> versies" labels, at least as they were in recent drafts of the script. Those
> labels often use the Alperovitz thesis as a place to start, but end up
> saying that most scholars reject his one-sided formulations. . . . Even
> if I think Alperovitz is wrong and tendentious, I refuse to write him
> out of the historiography since he has played and continues to play
> an essential role in stimulating debate and research.[13]

In June 1994, Tom Crouch was more positive than Neufeld. M. K.
Stone of Philadelphia wrote Crouch protesting the absence of Alperovitz's doctrines from the script as he understood it. Crouch answered with a form letter about the exhibition, which did not engage
Stone's complaint. Stone protested in another letter: "I would appreciate receiving a letter that deals with the particular points I mentioned." Crouch tried again, on June 28: "My apologies. It was a form
letter. I can assure you that a clear statement of the Alperovitz thesis
and the arguments in its favor are included in the exhibit."[14]

The military historians were also clear about this. Mark Jacobsen,
a U.S. Marine Corps Command and Staff College historian on the review board for the second version of the script, was censorious primarily about the curators' concealing the Alperovitz doctrine. As he
wrote his superior on July 18, 1994,

> The Air and Space Museum is right to discuss the Alperovitz thesis
> and right to assign it to a controversy sidebar. But like a "bad penny,"
> it keeps coming back. By force of repetition in one form or another, the
> Smithsonian pounds it into its readers' heads that the US dropped
> the bomb to influence the Soviet Union. Although the authors of the
> Smithsonian script deny their intellectual debt to the oeuvre of Gar
> Alperovitz, the central contention of his 1964 *Atomic Diplomacy* in-
> formed the previous script and survives in several places in this lat-
> est version.[15]

    13. Neufeld to Wayne Dzwonchyk, May 12, 1994, SIA-EGER, Accession 96–140,
box 9.
    14. M. K. Stone to Smithsonian Institution, May 22, 1994; Crouch to Stone, June 17,
1994; Stone to Crouch, June 23, 1994; Crouch to Stone, June 28, 1994, all in SIA-EGER,
Accession 96–140, box 4.
    15. Mark Jacobson to Alfred Goldberg, July 18, 1994, *Enola Gay* Records, U.S.
Naval Historical Center, Washington Navy Yard, D.C.

So Alperovitz was in, but he was not in. Clearly the curators felt that to acknowledge the reputed leader of American anti-Hiroshima discourse would bring them grief. But why did they not acknowledge Sherwin, Walker, and Bernstein in the exhibit text?

Perhaps had the NASM been open about their dependence on the small group of anti-Hiroshima writers who had made their reputations as scholars of the bomb decision, the museum would have gotten away with it. Their feeling that Alperovitz's ideas had to be camouflaged is understandable. But the judgment that complete anonymity of their sources would enable the institutional authority to prevail miscarried. When the hostility of the veterans was reinforced by the rightward shift of Congress, their anonymity did not save them.

One of Harwit's first approaches to an *Enola Gay* exhibit came in a November 1, 1988, letter to Ruth Adams of the international security program at the MacArthur Foundation. His projected exhibit was to be entitled "From Guernica to Hiroshima: Strategic Bombing in World War II." The title would change many times, but the concept lasted. He wanted to

> hold a colloquium series on strategic bombing, which would culminate in a retrospective symposium with members [of] the 1946 Strategic Bombing survey. We plan to videotape the proceedings (and a number of ancillary interviews) in order to document vividly for future generations the ways in which participants such as John Kenneth Galbraith, Paul Nitze, and George Ball came to understand the role and legacy of strategic bombing after more than 40 years of reflection.[16]

Would MacArthur like to sponsor this series?

Apparently Adams's division of the MacArthur Foundation would not, as the subsequent correspondence is with Denise McIntosh of MacArthur's program on peace and international cooperation, which did approve. The proposed series, promised Harwit, would result in published proceedings. There would be open programs at which audience members could ask questions, and there would be closed programs at which outside experts would hold

16. Harwit to Ruth Adams, November 1, 1988, SIA, Record Unit 355, Office of Cooperative Programs, box 2.

workshop sessions with NASM staff who would produce the resulting exhibit. There would be eight parts to the series, beginning as soon as possible, following the history of strategic bombing chronologically. The preliminary draft outline for this series was six pages single-spaced.[17]

On page four of this prospectus, Harwit anticipated a new thrust for Air and Space. He noted that the museum had been criticized as "largely a giant advertisement for air and space technologies," and that the omission of *Enola Gay* from NASM exhibits in the face of pressure to display her "can be seen as the first crisis of the new museum." Harwit appealed to the peace-minded at the MacArthur Foundation with this departure from NASM's past: "The proposed exhibition on Strategic Bombing will deal honestly and forthrightly with what might be called 'the dark side of aviation.' Its centerpiece will be the fully restored *Enola Gay*."

This candid statement of where Harwit intended to take the museum apparently never came to the attention of the Air Force Association and other enemies of the exhibit. "The dark side of aviation" would have made a beautiful sound bite for a vigorous press campaign. And there was more. Appealing no doubt to the MacArthur people, but certainly heretical for the director of a national air and space museum dependent on the largesse of the U.S. government:

> Strategic Bombing presents a classic case of what can happen when military planners place excessive reliance on the supposed infallibility of technology and on doctrines evolved in the absence of empirical evidence. The subject of the efficiency of strategic bombing is a highly controversial one; we may be able to treat this aspect by presenting the most cogent available statements of the opposing positions by the major participants. We should aim at presenting the facts as objectively as possible, drawing no conclusions, but providing enough information for viewers of the exhibition to draw their own.[18]

The mood of the exhibition would be "somber." Text captions would be "understated, letting photographs, artifacts, and participants speak for themselves." Joseph Heller's *Catch 22* and Kurt Vonnegut's *Slaughterhouse 5* (these are somber?) could be used to reveal "the existential absurdity of life in a bomber crew [and] the surreal

17. Attachment to document listed in note 18.
18. Ibid.

quality of mass destruction by fire storm." And the capstone evaluation of the success or failure of World War II strategic bombing
would be videotaped interviews with those stalwarts of the United
States Strategic Bombing Survey, Nitze, Galbraith, and Ball.

A final hint to the MacArthur people that this exhibit would be a
real departure from past NASM practice came when Harwit noted
that "the *Enola Gay* cannot be exhibited in the present Museum
building." Not only was the plane too large to fit there, but "the appropriate mood to be evoked by the strategic bombing exhibit surrounding this airplane would clash with the predominately soaring
spirit of aviation which dominates" the other galleries. *Enola Gay*
would go to a new museum extension then being planned.[19] The
tone of this whole proposal was evangelistic; Harwit was remaking
the chauvinistic NASM.

MacArthur made a generous grant, the symposia were duly held.
Harwit brags in his 1990 book, *An Exhibit Denied,* "Fifty prominent
people were invited. Incredibly, forty-nine responded. I do not remember who declined."[20] Note well his designation of the participants: "prominent" people, not scholars, not Pacific War experts, nor
Truman biographers, nor specialists in Japan's decision to surrender,
nor moralists on war fighting, nor experts on the Soviet decision to
build nuclear weapons as fast as possible.

The need for political backing became clear as veterans pressured
NASM to speed the restoration and display of *Enola Gay.* As NASM
increasingly had to respond to veterans' groups, Harwit began to see
that presenting the dark side of aviation as it related to this particular airplane would be inflammatory to thousands of Americans.

On the other hand, Japanese sensitivities to a display of *Enola Gay*
had to be taken into account. Harwit notes a warning he received
from Morihisa Takagi, the president of Nippon Television, in November 1988: "The Hiroshima and Nagasaki bombings remain firmly imprinted in the Japanese consciousness, much as the Holocaust
does with the Jewish people." Harwit was sensitive to the danger of
"precipitating a potentially serious international incident between
the United States and Japan."[21] And he wanted to borrow artifacts

19. Ibid.
20. Harwit, *An Exhibit Denied,* 59.
21. Ibid., 56.

from the Hiroshima and Nagasaki museums; Japanese goodwill was absolutely essential for this purpose.

The only viable stance for NASM was therefore complete neutrality on the question of whether the bomb's use against Japan was justified. There were two sides to this question, and NASM would support neither one—in principle. The exhibit would simply lay out the facts, and let the viewer judge. The artifacts and the accompanying test had to be "balanced." The contentious years at NASM between 1990 and 1991 were one long struggle between the political necessity to develop an exhibit that would not bias viewers' opinions, that would be nonjudgmental, and the gut instinct of Harwit and his crew to display the dark side of aviation, thus inducing Americans to regret the use of two atomic bombs against Japan.

It is perhaps unnecessary to present the many repetitions of NASM's "we take no sides, we only let the visitors choose" mantra, but some of the rhetoric is surprising. One of the persons Harwit strained to convince of the curators' neutrality was Robert Adams, secretary of the Smithsonian until shortly before the exhibit was to open, and hence Harwit's boss. On April 16, 1993, reporting on a trip to Japan, Harwit wrote Adams,

> We had an opportunity in Hiroshima, last Monday, to talk at length with mayor Takashi Hiraoka, who very clearly voiced the strong sentiments of his city that all atomic weapons must be eliminated, and who wanted to assure himself that our exhibition would not convey a message contrary to that spirit. . . . I told the mayor that the museum was not in a position to make political statements, so that advocacy of the abolition of all nuclear weapons was not a message we would be presenting. The intent of the exhibition was, rather, to make visitors think and come to their own conclusions.[22]

By contrast, when dealing with Japanese whose goodwill he solicited, Harwit had a different story. This in a letter of May 18, 1993, to Akihiro Takahashi, a bomb sufferer then working for the Hiroshima Museum:

> I can well understand the depth of feeling that the exhibition proposed by our museum must evoke in you. . . . I would like to assure

22. Harwit to Bob Adams, April 16, 1993, SIA-EGER, Accession 96–140, box 2.

you, therefore, that we do not plan to simply dwell on the Manhattan Project or the technical aspects of the bombing.... For most of us in America, the *Enola Gay* is an uncomfortable symbol. It represents a destructive act, which many of us feel to be incompatible with our perceived national character. The *Enola Gay* is a symbol that does not agree with that national characterization.[23]

In early 1994, when he got negative comments on the bias or lack of balance of the script, Harwit sought a second opinion from six NASM employees, most with a military background, and wrote them on April 26, 1994,

> Whatever the origin of these differences, the Museum must be certain that the exhibition we mount is indeed balanced. I am therefore asking you to serve on an independent Tiger Team, once more, specifically to look for any signs of imbalance, and to report back to me by Friday, May 13. I regret the short deadline, but the exhibition schedule is tight and corrective action if needed will have to be taken at once.[24]

The Tiger Team did report, on May 24, 1994. Their report was devastating.

This was no group of enemies out to get the curators: Brigadier General William M. Constantine, USAF (Ret.), volunteer NASM docent and team chairman; Colonel Thomas Alison, USAF (Ret.), NASM curator for military aviation; Dr. Gregg Herken, chairman, NASM Department of Space History; Colonel Donald Lopez, USAF (Ret.), former NASM deputy director and senior advisor emeritus; Kenneth Robert, NASM volunteer docent; and Dr. Steven Soter, special assistant to the director of Air and Space. These critics produced more than one hundred pages, nineteen of which included negative comments agreed to by the whole group.[25] Although this Tiger Team did not say, "The script is unbalanced and tendentious because its authors are crusaders against Truman's decision," one can read this between the lines.

23. Harwit to Akihiro Takahashi, May 18, 1993, SIA-EGER, Accession 96–140, box 2.

24. Harwit to Bill Constantine et al., April 26, 1994, SIA-EGER, Accession 96–140, box 1.

25. Report of the National Air and Space Review Team, May 25, 1994, *Enola Gay* records, box 3, U.S. Naval Historical Center, Washington Navy Yard, D.C.

Later criticism by the Air Force Association may have been more prickly, but the Tigers were equally clear: this script would not do. Lopez's comments were typical:

> the script reflects the viewpoint of the writer rather than an impartial historical view. The labels are written for the peers of the authors and not for the average museum visitor . . . the imbalance is almost palpable. A visitor, expecting something honoring 50th anniversary of WWII, either a veteran, or with some connection to a veteran, will be appalled. . . . I would leave the exhibit with the strong feeling that Americans are bloodthirsty, racist killers who after beer parties and softball go out and kill as many women and children as possible.[26]

Michael Neufeld attended the first meeting of this Tiger Team at Constantine's request. He was troubled by what he heard and wrote to Harwit and the Tiger Team about it on April 25, 1994.[27] Harwit says Neufeld's was a "thoughtful" response; I read it as defensive and evasive of the Tiger Team's critique. Neufeld refers to the "thirty years of research" that went into the script, which shows that "the decision is debatable on its political and military merits." He then reiterates the anti-Truman litany, determined to change even the Tiger Team's responses. At this stage, it should have been abundantly clear to Harwit that his curators could *talk* about being nonjudgmental, but they were not going to produce a script that achieved this.

Harwit and the curators were constantly responding to hundreds (perhaps thousands—the archives are full of them) of letters inquiring about the exhibit. They usually answered with a form letter. One such went from Tom Crouch to David Blasco of Fort Lauderdale, Florida, on August 17, 1994:

> Thank you for your letter regarding our exhibition, "The Last Act: The Atomic Bomb and the End of World War II." I can assure you that the exhibition, which is scheduled to open in the spring of 1995, will most certainly honor the brave Americans who fought and suffered for their nation during World War II. Moreover, it will identify Japan as the aggressor nation in the Pacific War, and outline the nature of the atrocities committed by the Japanese. At the same time, it will present

26. Ibid.
27. Neufeld to Tiger Team, April 25, 1994, cited in *An Exhibit Denied*, 281.

the reality of the atomic bomb as experienced by the people of Hiroshima and Nagasaki. In short, the presentation will be an honest, balanced treatment that encourages our visitors to think about a critical turning point in the history of the 20th century.[28]

But it was all in vain. The script was conceived, written, and revised by true believers in the Nitze-Blackett narrative of the bombings. When the big, glaring phrases were removed from the text under prodding from inside and outside NASM, the small, subtle bias remained, through hundreds of hours of conferences with critics. The fifth and final script was perceived, even by some of the initially hostile military historians, as acceptable, but it was too late. The Air Force Association and other groups had gone to Congress, newly under the control of Newt Gingrich and conservative Republicans, who readily believed that *these* curators were basically un-American and could never get it right. The un-American charge was of course false. It was no more un-American to oppose the use of atomic bombs on Japan than it was to oppose the American intervention in Vietnam. But the politics were different. Thousands of survivors of World War II approved of the bomb for ending the war as soon as possible and no adequate warrant for changing their minds came out of NASM. In contrast, almost the whole country regretted Vietnam.

Harwit, the unlucky leader of this attempt to change the collective mind about *Enola Gay*, went through agony. Periodically he had to admit that the effort to be neutral, to create an exhibit that presented balanced facts and let visitors make up their own minds, had failed. The cognitive dissonance must have been tremendous. It shows in his 1996 book. Through the long, detailed narrative, he reinforces his claims to want a balanced, nonjudgmental exhibit, only to be foiled by wayward curators. Thus, on July 2, 1993, in a memo to Tom Crouch about Neufeld's latest draft, he explodes in a memorable chewing out:

> I am absolutely convinced Mike's new draft, as written, will be rejected out of hand, by the Secretary. . . . The consistent problem with Mike's headings, subheadings, and introductory paragraphs, is that they do not do what the Museum always claims it intends to do: To

28. Crouch to David Blasco, August 17, 1994, SIA-EGER, Accession 96–140, box 4.

let visitors judge. Mike appears at each stage to prejudge. . . . His headings consistently emphasize only the most dramatic. A central image in the opening section will show "a small boy taken immediately after the bombing of Nagasaki." Does one have to add "streaks of blood are visible on his cheek"? Why not let the visitor see for himself what the boy looks like? The opening paragraph again reverts to the form Mike has had all along. The context of Europe and Japan in World War II has been eliminated, after I had painstakingly inserted it at the Secretary's suggestion. The broader picture has been erased. . . . Where is it that the visitor ever has a chance to formulate an independent opinion? Where does a visitor have a chance to see for himself whether the war in the Far East differed from that in Europe, or for that matter from other wars throughout history?[29]

When he wrote his book, Harwit included much of this memo. When he had finished his text and began to wrestle with a preface, however, he appears to have forgotten his earlier pique with his subordinates. In the preface he attacks the new Smithsonian secretary, I. Michael Heyman, who cancelled Harwit's elaborate plans. Harwit says Heyman implies "that a true history of the mission of the *Enola Gay* could not adequately honor the nation's veterans; and that it was more important for America to accept a largely fictitious, comforting story in this commemorative year than to recall a pivotally important twentieth century event as revealed in trustworthy documents now at hand in the nation's archives."[30] The fancy language did not conceal what Harwit thought of the veterans: "You've got nothing to commemorate. You don't know what went on in the decision centers." But if Harwit really believed this, how could he have castigated Neufeld for saying practically the same thing?

Most of the veterans continued to find that the exhibit demonstrated NASM's evangelical mission to upset their beliefs. Richard Hallion, an air force historian, complained to Tom Crouch on August 9, 1994, about Crouch's statement that

veterans are only concerned with one exhibit unit (the Ground Zero portion of the exhibit) out of five, as if all five sections were equal. But they aren't all equal; the real core of your exhibit is Ground Zero. That's the section about which you stated—in our very first meeting

29. Harwit to Crouch, July 2, 1993, SIA-EGER, Accession 96–140, box 1.
30. Harwit, *An Exhibit Denied*, viii.

with Martin, Mike, and Herman—"That will rip the visitor's heart out." You may recall that I said at the time, "I hope their hearts will also be ripped out when they see what was happening in the Pacific War on the road to Japan." You are too experienced in museum affairs not to recognize the powerful influence of artifacts, photographs and graphics. They overwhelm words. They cannot be balanced by some minimal text on Japanese aggression.[31]

And Preble Stolz, a prominent law professor at the University of California who was furnished a copy of the text when Michael Heyman took over as Smithsonian secretary, found almost nothing but bias: "I think there is a problem. I am not sure I would describe it as a problem of 'balance' or 'fairness.' Rather, what I come away with is a distinct sense that I am being preached at, and that, I think, is wrong." Stolz went on for eleven pages with illustrations of preachiness, which he did not believe was "the business of the Smithsonian."[32]

Lance Morrow, in *Time* magazine, was close to the mark. He had been in Hiroshima, watching school children come out of the Peace Memorial Museum:

Now it is common for Japanese children to practice their English on the *gaijin,* and . . . a little boy danced up, peered into my face and said brightly, "Murderer! Hello!" I thought of that Japanese schoolboy in recent months as Washington's Smithsonian Institution shuffled through one script after another, trying to figure out how to deal with Hiroshima in a 50th-anniversary exhibition about the end of the war. . . . The first script for the exhibition, which will display a part of the reassembled *Enola Gay,* was way left of the mark. It interpreted Hiroshima and Nagasaki in a way that managed to transport a righteous '60s moral stance on Vietnam ("Baby killers!") back in time to portray the Japanese as more or less innocent victims of American beastliness and lust for revenge. As if the Japanese had been conquering Asia by Marquis of Queensbury rules. The curators said to the American public, "Murderer! Hello!"[33]

31. Richard Hallion to Crouch, August 9, 1994, SIA-EGER, Accession 96–140, box 4.

32. Preble Stolz to I. Michael Heyman, September 2, 1994, SIA-EGER, Accession 96–140, box 1.

33. Lance Morrow, "Hiroshima and the Time Machine," *Time* 144 (19 September 1994): 94.

Tom Crouch saw part of the problem clearly in a memo to Harwit of July 21, 1993. "Do you want to do an exhibition intended to make veterans feel good, or do you want an exhibition that will lead our visitors to think about the consequences of the atomic bombing of Japan? Frankly, I don't think we can do both."[34] Given his assumption that the consequences were all bad, he was right.

Crouch was woefully wrong about one thing. The curators were ill informed about the consequences of the atomic bombing.

Attempting to change American minds about bombing Hiroshima while you are pretending to be nonjudgmental is—there is no kinder word for it—hypocrisy. It was a replay of Genesis 27:22: "And Jacob went near unto Isaac his father; and he felt him, and said, The voice is Jacob's voice, but the hands are the hands of Esau." In the final edition of the *Enola Gay* script, perhaps some of the words were words of neutrality, but the tone was the tone of judgment.

The curators were, however, sensitive enough to the rhetorical bind they were in to realize that, even though *they* believed that the Nitze-Blackett narrative was the correct one, the exhibit text could not straightforwardly offer evidential support for much of that narrative. They therefore adopted the technique of indirect, suggestive phrasing common in the discourse of advocates operating in a hostile environment. This technique is exposed famously in Charles S. Maier's *The Unmasterable Past: History, Holocaust, and German National Identity.* Maier shows that

> disguised theses, proposed in a pseudo-interrogative mode . . . travel under false passports. This seems to be the case of Nolte's argumentation [that Hitler was only anticipating Soviet destruction of Germany when he attacked] . . . Nolte, Fest, and Hillgruber argue that, the historian who objects is substituting taste for truth, and aesthetic zing a political argument. But there is a test. A genuine historical question will not influence opinion unless it is actually answered. A spurious one is designed to sway opinion by virtue of its just being asked.[35]

Asking spurious questions is what the curators did on many of the pressure points of *Enola Gay* argument. A series of "Historical Controversies" in the text are phrased as pseudo questions, which the

34. Crouch to Harwit, July 21, 1993, SIA-EGER, Accession 96–140, box 4.
35. Charles S. Maier, *The Unmasterable Past: History, Holocaust, and German National Identity* (Cambridge: Harvard University Press, 1988), 83.

curators dare not answer according to their foundational documents since this would expose their bias. So they ask, "Would the bomb have been dropped on the Germans?" "Did the United States ignore the Japanese Peace Offensive?" (Note in this instance they avoid calling it an offer to surrender, since nowhere in the Togo-Sato decrypts did Togo use the word *surrender*.) "Would the war have ended sooner if the United States had guaranteed the emperor's position?" "How important was the Soviet factor in the decision to drop the bomb?" "Was a warning or demonstration possible?" (Here they load the question heavily; of course it was possible. The real question was, would it have been effective?) "Was the decision to drop the bomb justified?" On all of these questions the text waffled. On all of them, the massive scholarly research on Japan's decision to surrender would have weighed strongly against the Nitze-Blackett narrative, but the curators systematically excluded all discourse that did not come from their preferred sources.

Various journalists realized that asking these questions was not legitimate framing of the issues, but they lacked Maier's sophisticated analysis to show why.

Racing the Enemy
A Critical Look

TSUYOSHI HASEGAWA'S *Racing the Enemy: Stalin, Truman, and the Surrender of Japan* (Harvard University Press, 2005) has received a great deal of favorable press since its publication. Reviewers in leading newspapers have called it "brilliant and definitive," "a landmark book," and "the definitive analysis" of the American decision to use the atomic bomb against Japan. Hasegawa's extensive use of Japanese and Russian sources has added to the book's luster. His multilingual source base is what presumably gives his book the vital "international context" allegedly missing from earlier volumes on the American use of atomic weapons against Hiroshima and Nagasaki and the Japanese surrender that finally put an end to World War II.

Racing the Enemy is an opportune arrival for the increasingly beleaguered critics of America's use of atomic weapons against Japan, who, in the historians' debate over the bomb, usually have been classified as "revisionists" (as opposed to "orthodox" or "traditional" historians who have evaluated the atomic bomb decision as necessary to end the war). As made by Gar Alperovitz more than forty years ago, the original revisionist argument maintained that the atomic bomb was used primarily to intimidate the Soviet Union in order to gain the upper hand in Eastern Europe and to keep Moscow out of the war in the Far East. While the whole cloth of this "atomic diplomacy" thesis was too extreme for most revisionists, they wove bits and pieces of it into their own critiques of the bombing of Hiroshima.

Revisionism's heyday lasted until the 1990s. Then the historiographical ground began to shift. A new body of scholarly work emerged, often based on hitherto unavailable documents, which countered revisionist arguments that the atomic bomb was primarily a diplomatic weapon in 1945, that Japan would have surrendered before the planned U.S. invasion had the bomb not been used, and that projected casualty figures for the anticipated invasion of Japan were far lower than those cited by supporters of the decision to use the bomb. The scholars producing these books and articles provided powerful support for Truman's decision to use the atomic bomb against Japan. Thus Edward Drea's *MacArthur's ULTRA: Codebreaking and the War against Japan* (1992) chronicled how Allied intelligence tracked the Japanese military buildup on the southernmost home island of Kyushu in the months before Hiroshima, a buildup that demonstrated Tokyo's intent to fight to the bitter end and rendered all "low" casualty estimates dating from the spring and early summer of 1945—the estimates relied upon by revisionist historians—obsolete and irrelevant months before American soldiers were scheduled to land in Japan. In 1995 Robert P. Newman's *Truman and the Hiroshima Cult* demolished the credibility of the United States Strategic Bombing Survey's claim that Japan would have surrendered in the fall of 1945 absent both the atomic bombs and the Soviet entry into the war, while Robert James Maddox's *Weapons for Victory: The Hiroshima Decision* effectively dismantled what was left of the "atomic diplomacy" thesis. Two years later, in "Casualty Projections for the U.S. Invasion of Japan, 1945–1946: Planning and Policy Implications" (*The Journal of Military History*, July 1997), D. M. Giangreco conclusively documented the existence of enormous casualty projections, some of which undeniably reached Truman and his top advisers. The next year, in "The Shock of the Atomic Bomb and Japan's Decision to Surrender—A Reconsideration" (*Pacific Historical Review*, November 1998), Sadao Asada, relying on a thorough review of Japanese language sources, exposed as untenable the contention that Japan was prepared to surrender before Hiroshima or that a modification of the Potsdam Declaration guaranteeing the status of the emperor would have produced a Japanese surrender.

These and other works culminated in Richard B. Frank's *Downfall: The End of the Imperial Japanese Empire*, published in 1999. Frank brought together the evidence already mentioned and a great deal more, including crucial Japanese-language sources, leaving virtually every aspect of the revisionist case in tatters. It was not long before *Downfall* gained widespread recognition as the definitive work on the subject. Against this background, the cancellation of the

Smithsonian Institution's proposed exhibit to mark the fiftieth anniversary of the bombing of Hiroshima, which relied almost exclusively on revisionist scholarship, was only the most publicized setback suffered by proponents of the revisionist case during the 1990s.

Hasegawa's *Racing the Enemy* runs counter to this scholarly current. *Racing the Enemy,* however, is not all good news for revisionists. Hasegawa rejects some parts of the revisionist case, including the critically important thesis that Japan could have been induced to surrender before the events of August 6–9, when atomic bombs were dropped on Hiroshima (August 6) and Nagasaki (August 9) and the Soviet Union declared war on Japan (August 8). Instead, Hasegawa attempts to resuscitate the revisionist critique of Truman by arguing that the United States wanted to use the atomic bomb against Japan before the Soviet entry into the war in order to thwart Moscow's ambitions in the Far East. This in turn created a race to use the bomb and to get Tokyo to surrender before the Soviets declared war on the beleaguered empire. That race, of course, was lost, for although Hiroshima preceded the Soviet entry into the Pacific War, the Japanese surrender did not. Beyond that, Hasegawa argues, Japan surrendered not because of what happened at Hiroshima and Nagasaki but because of the Soviet declaration of war that took place between those two dreadful nuclear explosions.

Despite Hasegawa's sources in three languages, his evidence does not back up his claims. Furthermore, at times his methodology is faulty. In particular, Hasegawa at key points in his narrative takes excessive liberty in interpreting his sources.

It certainly is true, as Hasegawa points out, that Truman and his advisers wanted to get the bomb ready and to use it against Japan as soon as possible. After all, as leaders of a democratic and war-weary county, they were in a great hurry to end the war. Both General George Marshall and Secretary of War Henry Stimson were deeply worried about the state of public and military morale. Hasegawa transforms that well-documented concern into a race to keep the Soviet Union out of the Pacific War, with the key planning in that race being done at Potsdam. But the American (and Anglo-American) discussions at Potsdam regarding their difficult communist ally were not about keeping the Soviets out of the Pacific War. They were about the postwar price the U.S. would have to pay to get the Soviets *into* the war, and the problem was that Stalin's price was turning out to be too high. That is why after he received the report from General Leslie Groves about the successful atomic bomb test, Truman had Stimson ask Marshall if the American military could do without the Soviets. (Marshall's response was that the Soviets were in a position to take what they wanted in the Far East, with or without a declaration of war.) The president wanted Soviet military help, but he did not want to pay Stalin's rising price. For example, as Maddox points out in *Weapons for Victory*, Truman's intent to have the Soviets enter the Pacific War is demonstrated by what he wrote to his wife on July 18: "I've gotten what I came for—Stalin goes to war August 15 with no strings on it."

At times, Hasegawa attempts to create his American race against the Soviet entry into the war by implying that something is in a document (or documents) when in fact it isn't. On page 141, for example, he focuses on the Truman-Churchill discussion of July 18 regarding if and when to tell Stalin about the successful A-bomb test. Hasegawa contends, "The danger was that if they told Stalin about the bomb, it might trigger immediate Soviet entry into the war." Yet none of the sources Hasegawa cites even remotely suggests such a concern. In making his point, Hasegawa correctly quotes Churchill: "It is quite clear that the United States does not at the present time desire Russian participation in the war against Japan." This statement comes from page 639 of *Triumph and Tragedy*, where Churchill quotes what he wrote in a "Minute" dated July 23, 1945. A review of the actual "Minute" to Anthony Eden (which Hasegawa does not cite and therefore presumably did not consult) reveals something interesting and crucial. The basis of Churchill's judgment was Secretary of State James Byrnes, who had told Churchill he hoped that Chinese foreign minister T. V. Soong would not "give way on any point to the Russians." Yet, as Maddox points out in *Weapons for Victory*, Byrnes's "musings" during the course of a few days in July about keeping Russia out of the war "were not translated into policy." Instead, on July 28 Truman pointedly instructed Byrnes to tell the Chinese that discussions with the Soviets should resume as soon as possible "in the hope of reaching agreement."

The same problem arises on page 150, where Hasegawa maintains that Truman was "delighted to know that the atomic bomb would be available for use before the Soviets joined the war." The relevant footnote cites three contemporary sources: a cable from George L.

Harrison (Stimson's assistant) to Stimson, July 21, 1945; Stimson's July 22 diary entry; and a notation in volume 2, page 1373 of *Foreign Relations of the United States (The Potsdam Conference), 1945.* None of them refers to dropping the atomic bomb before the Soviets enter the war. Stimson does say that Truman was "intensely pleased with the accelerated timetable," but that was to be expected, given the long-established American objective of ending the war as soon as possible.

The spuriousness of the "Truman did not want the Soviets to enter the war" thesis emerges even more clearly when one considers Truman's reaction to Stalin's demand (through Foreign Minister Molotov on July 29) that the Soviets receive a formal request to enter the Pacific War. Lisle Rose's *Dubious Victory* provides an excellent analysis of this incident. As Rose correctly points out, "Here, in fact, was the perfect opportunity for the Americans to tell the Russians that they were no longer needed or wanted." Of course, the Americans did no such thing; rather, on July 31, Truman, in a draft letter prepared for Stalin, insisted that Moscow already had pledged to enter the war and that the time had come to honor the pledge. This does not sound like a president trying to delay the Soviet entry into the war.

What is strange about all of this is that Hasegawa explicitly debunks revisionist historians who argue that the U.S. pressured the Chinese "to hang tough in order to prevent the Soviets from entering the war" (174). How Hasegawa can write this and still say we were racing the Russians in our use of the bomb is a mystery. It appears the right hand does not know what the left one is doing. More evidence on this point comes from Maddox, who wrote that on August 9 Truman told aides he went to Potsdam to get the Soviets into the war. The president then added that the Hiroshima bombing had pushed the Soviets to get into the war earlier and, as Maddox put it, Truman then "gave no indication this move displeased him."

Indeed, it did not displease him, as is incontrovertibly clear when one looks closely at Truman's brief press conference that day, where he announced the Soviet entry into the Pacific War. According to Hasegawa, Truman began the press conference "with a smile on his face" but "quickly assumed a solemn expression." He then spoke four sentences and added, "That's all." Hasegawa comments, "This terse statement reveals the profound disappointment Truman must have felt over the news" (193). But does it? Hasegawa's sources include the *New York Times* and *Washington Post*. Here is how Felix Belair Jr. of the *New York Times* reported it. The president, who was holding his first news conference in more than a month, was seated at his desk "with one leg carelessly over the arm of his chair." He gave no hint of the "importance of the information he was about to impart." Truman then stood up and made his announcement:

> His concluding words, "That is all," were all but drowned out by the scramble of news and radio reporters for the nearest exit to rush to their telephones. Mr. Truman and White House officials present rocked with laughter at the sensation his "simple announcement" had precipitated.

All of this is extremely unlikely behavior for a president who was suffering "profound disappointment." The same can be said for the aides, who would be most unlikely to "rock with laughter," in public no less, if their president were upset about what he just had announced.

To be sure, Edward T. Folliard of the *Washington Post* reported that Truman, who had previously been smiling, "assumed a solemn expression" when he stood up to make his announcement. Is that surprising? How would it look for a president to be smiling when he announces that a country, any country, is going to war? But what is most interesting about Folliard's coverage is that he included a detailed description—fully three paragraphs, with direct quotations—of the draft letter (Folliard calls it a memorandum) Truman handed to Stalin on July 31 at Potsdam that in effect told the Soviets the time had come for them to enter the Pacific War. Hasegawa does not mention that part of Folliard's article.

Nor are these the only contemporary accounts regarding Truman's attitude toward the Soviet entry into the Pacific War. Ernest Vaccaro, a *New York Times* reporter who accompanied Truman back and forth across the Atlantic aboard the cruiser *Augusta* when the president went to the Potsdam Conference, reported on August 9 that Truman had "repeatedly told newsmen" en route to Europe that his main concern was to end the Pacific War with the minimum cost in American lives. According to the president's reasoning, a Soviet declaration of war might save "hundreds of thousands of Americans from injury or death." And what did the president think *after* Potsdam? According to Vaccaro, "The results were evident in his demeanor. . . . He could not confide in reporters but his pleasure was evident." That pleasure, Vaccato suggested in his article, may have been the reason "Mr. Truman personally announced the war declaration at a news conference today."

Meanwhile, upon hearing about the Soviet entry into the war, General Marshall on August 8 sent a personal message to Averell Harriman, the American ambassador to the Soviet Union, which reads as follows: "My congratulations and thanks to you for your great part in bringing about the events of the day." It is inconceivable that General Marshall would have sent this message had the "events of the day" not been in accord with the president's wishes.

In the end the whole "racing Moscow" thesis rests on the assumption that Truman and his advisers were sure, or at least very confident, that one or two bombs would do the trick. Otherwise, from Hasegawa's perspective, there was no point in being in such a hurry to bomb Hiroshima and Nagasaki. But the assumption that there was any certainty about one or two bombs ending the war immediately defies the available evidence. There might have been some *hopes* that one or two bombs would do it, but a huge pile of evidence makes it crystal clear that even with the atomic bombs *nothing* was certain to Truman and his advisers.

Hasegawa is even less convincing when he turns to Byrnes's memoirs to suggest that Byrnes's first priority, like Truman's, was to use the atomic bomb rather than to end the war. Hasegawa builds his case by asking why Byrnes, who was "not as ideologically committed" to removing the emperor as some State Department hardliners, nonetheless insisted on unconditional surrender. The "clue to this puzzle" comes from Byrnes's memoirs, where he argues that "had the Japanese government surrendered unconditionally, it would not have been necessary to drop the atomic bomb." Hasegawa can't make much use of this, so he suggests that "perhaps this statement can best be read in reverse: 'if we insisted on unconditional surrender, we could justify using the atomic bomb'" (135). If Hasegawa is going to read Byrnes's memoirs "in reverse," which is a highly dubious analytical technique at best, he certainly must provide solid supporting documentation from the summer of 1945. This he does not do.

Many of the same problems of evidence arise when one considers

Hasegawa's discussion of the atom bomb versus the Russian entry into the war as the primary cause of Japan's surrender. To give the Soviet entry primacy, Hasegawa must ignore everything covered by Asada's "The Shock of the Atomic Bomb and Japan's Decision to Surrender," Newman's *Truman and the Hiroshima Cult,* and Frank's *Downfall* about testimony given by Japanese officials from Prime Minister Kantaro Suzuki on down. Beyond that is a matter of methodology that emerges in what may be called the document count on pages 197–98. Hasegawa counts contemporary Japanese sources on the surrender decision, some of which mention the atomic bomb, some of which mention the Soviet declaration of war, and some of which mention both. He reports the score as atomic bomb 2, Soviet entry 3, and both 7. Therefore, Frank is wrong to stress the bomb as the most important factor, since the Soviet entry won three to two. In this mechanical calculation Suzuki's offhand comment to his doctor (which comes from *Japan's Longest Day,* a volume based primarily on postwar interviews conducted by the historians of the Pacific War Research Society) is historically equal in value to the August 14 Imperial Rescript, the most important statement of Hirohito's life and the one he personally read to tens of millions of his subjects, who at noon of August 15 were glued to their radios to hear their emperor's voice for the first time. This "all documents are equal" approach obscures rather than clarifies. Whatever the problems with the Imperial Rescript in terms of veracity on a number of key points, it certainly has more probative value than an offhand comment Suzuki made to a navy doctor. But simply adding up the documents on each side without evaluating their significance does not constitute a credible argument. In any event, as Asada has demonstrated, there is compelling testimony from Japanese leaders to suggest the primacy of the Hiroshima bomb in producing Japan's surrender.

Hasegawa fails to sustain his main arguments with the necessary evidence. At best, he leaves the revisionist case as he found it, in ruins. Indeed, he makes the rubble bounce by convincingly demonstrating that the Soviet Union very much was racing to get into the Pacific War in order to facilitate its expansionist policies in the Far East. Those who seek the definitive analysis on the end of the Pacific War will have to look elsewhere. A good place to begin is Frank's *Downfall.*

Sadao Asada graduated from Carleton College and received a Ph.D. in American history from Yale University. He taught diplomatic history at Doshisha University, Kyoto, from 1963 until his retirement in 2006. His *Japanese-American Relations between the Wars* (in Japanese) won the prestigious Yoshino Sakuzo Prize in 1994. He has edited *Japan and the World, 1853–1952: A Bibliographic Guide* (1989). He is the author of *From Mahan to Pearl Harbor: The Imperial Japanese Navy and the United States* (2006). For his articles he has been awarded the Edward Miller History Prize from the president of the U.S. Naval War College and the Louis Knott Koontz Memorial Award from the American Historical Association (PCB). He has contributed to a wide variety of journals, including the *American Historical Review, Journal of American History, Pacific Historical Review, Diplomatic History, Naval War College Review, Journal of Strategic Studies,* and *Journal of American-East Asian Relations.* He lives in Kyoto.

Edward J. Drea is a graduate of Canisius College in Buffalo, New York. After military service in Japan and Vietnam, he received his MA in international relations from Sophia University in Tokyo, Japan, and his Ph.D. in modern Japanese history from the University of Kansas. He has taught at the Army Command and Staff College and the U.S. Army War College, and he was Chief of the Research and Analysis Division at the U.S. Army Center of Military History. In 2003 he received the Society for Military History's prestigious Samuel Eliot Morison Prize for lifetime achievement. He is the author of *MacArthur's ULTRA: Codebreaking and the War against Japan, 1942–1945* (1992) and *In the Service of the Emperor: Essays on the Imperial Japanese Army* (1998), and many articles.

Gian P. Gentile is a lieutenant colonel in the U.S. Army and is currently in command of an Armored Reconnaissance Squadron in Baghdad, Iraq. He received his BA in history from the University of California, Berkeley, and his Ph.D. in history from Stanford University where he studied under Barton Bernstein. He has published articles in the *Journal of Military History, Pacific Historical Review,* and the *Washington Post,* among others. His book, *How Effective Is Strategic Bombing? Lessons Learned from World War II to Kosovo,* was published by the New York University Press in 2000. Lieutenant Colonel Gentile has taught American and military history at the United States Military Academy at West Point.

D. M. Giangreco has lectured widely on national security matters and served for twenty years as an editor for the U.S. Army's professional journal *Military Review,* published by the Command and General Staff College at Fort Leavenworth, Kansas. He is an award-winning author of nine books on military and historical subjects. Several of his works have been translated into French, German, Russian, and Spanish. Giangreco was awarded the Society for Military History's Moncado Prize for his article "Casualty Projections for the U.S. Invasion of Japan: Planning and Policy Implications."

Michael Kort is Professor of Social Science at Boston University. He is the author of *The Soviet Colossus: History and Aftermath* (1985; 6th ed., 2006), *The Columbia Guide to the Cold War* (1998), and *The Columbia Guide to Hiroshima and the Bomb* (2007), and coauthor of *Modernization and Revolution in China* (1991; 3rd ed., 2004). He has also written more than a dozen books for young adult readers.

Robert James Maddox is Professor Emeritus of History at the Pennsylvania State University. He has published six books, including *Weapons For Victory: The Hiroshima Decision Fifty Years Later* (1995; reissued in paper, 2004). He also edited *American History* (2006).

Kathryn Moore is the coauthor of *Dear Harry . . . Truman's Mailroom, 1945–1953: The Truman Administration through Correspondence with "Everyday Americans"* and *Eyewitness D-Day: Firsthand Accounts from the Landing at Normandy to the Liberation of Paris.* She has written articles for *American Heritage, American History,* and numerous daily newspapers such as the *Washington Times, Kansas City Star,* and *Milwaukee Journal Sentinel.* Moore was formerly a historical interpreter at Colonial Williamsburg and teaches history at Lee's Summit, Missouri. Her *Encyclopedia of United States Presidents* will be published in

2007, and she is currently working on *First Lady of Monticello,* a biography of Thomas Jefferson's wife, Martha.

Robert P. Newman received his Ph.D. from the University of Connecticut. He taught for more than thirty years at the University of Pittsburgh and has also taught at the University of Connecticut, the University of Iowa, and the University of North Carolina. Newman has published more than seventy articles in communication, history, and general periodicals. He has won numerous awards for his articles and books. His *The Cold War Romance of Lillian Hellman and John Melby* won the Gustavus Myers Center's Outstanding Book on Human Rights Award; his *Owen Lattimore and the Loss of China* won the Winans-Wicheins Award for Distinguished Scholarship; and his *Truman and the Hiroshima Cult* won the National Communication Association's Diamond Anniversary Book Award.

Acknowledgments and Permissions

Sadao Asada, "The Shock of the Atomic Bomb and Japan's Decision to Surrender: A Reconsideration," *Pacific Historical Review* 67, no. 4: 477–512. © 1998, The Pacific Coast Branch, American Historical Association. Used by permission. All rights reserved.

Edward J. Drea's essay is reprinted with permission from *MHQ: The Quarterly Journal of Military History* 7, no. 3 (Spring 1995): 74–81.

D. M. Giangreco, "'A Score of Bloody Okinawas and Iwo Jimas': President Truman and Casualty Estimates for the Invasion of Japan," *Pacific Historical Review* 72, no. 1: 93–132. © 2003, The Pacific Coast Branch, American Historical Association. Used by permission. All rights reserved.

D. M. Giangreco and Kathryn Moore's essay first appeared in *American Heritage* 51 (December 2000): 81–83.

Gian Peri Gentile, "Advocacy or Assessment? The United States Strategic Bombing Survey of Germany and Japan," *Pacific Historical Review* 66, no. 1: 53–79. © 1997, The Pacific Coast Branch, American Historical Association. Used by permission. All rights reserved.

Robert P. Newman's essay on Henry Stimson is from *The New England Quarterly* 71, no. 1 (March 1998): 5–32. It is reproduced by permission of the publisher and the author. Newman's piece on the *Enola Gay* is from his *"Enola Gay" and the Court of History* (New York: Peter Lang Publishing, 2004). It is reprinted by permission of the publisher.

Michael Kort's review appeared in *Historically Speaking: The Bulletin of the Historical Society* 7, no. 3 (January/February 2006): 22–24.

About the Editor

Robert James Maddox is Professor Emeritus of History at Pennsylvania State University. His other books include *Weapons for Victory: The Hiroshima Decision* and *The United States and World War II.* He lives in State College, Pennsylvania.